Servants of All

Servants of All

A History of the Permanent Diaconate
in the Archdiocese of Toronto
1972–2007

Michael Power

NOVALIS

© 2010 Novalis Publishing Inc.

Cover design: Blaine Herrmann

Cover image: **The Menil Collection**
Saint Stephen Protomartyr, ca. 1330–1350
Tempera and gold over gesso and cloth on wood panel
26.7 x 22.8 x2.5 cm
Access #85-057-03 DJ
Photographer: Hickey-Robertson, Houston
This photograph may not be used for reproduction without specific written permission
from The Menil Collection, 1511 Branard St, Houston, TX 77006

Layout: Audrey Wells

Interior photos: p. 1: Photographer unknown, courtesy ARCAT.
Permission to reproduce and publish is granted by ARCAT; pp. 2–8: © Bill Wittman.

Published by Novalis

Publishing Office
10 Lower Spadina Avenue, Suite 400
Toronto, Ontario, Canada
M5V 2Z2

Head Office
4475 Frontenac Street
Montréal, Québec, Canada
H2H 2S2
www.novalis.ca

Library and Archives Canada Cataloguing in Publication

Power, Michael, 1953–
     Servants of all : a history of the Permannent Diaconate in the
Archdiocese of Toronto, 1972–2007 / Michael Power.

Includes bibliographical references and index.

ISBN 978-2-89646-218-6

     1. Deacons--Ontario--Toronto--History. 2. Catholic Church.
Archdiocese of Toronto--History. 3. Deacons--Catholic Church.
I. Title.

BX1912.P68 2010   262'.142713541   C2010-901675-0

Printed in Canada.

We acknowledge the financial support of the Government of Canada through the
Book Publishing Industry Development Program (BPIDP) for our publishing activities.

5   4   3   2   1   14   13   12   11   10

CONTENTS

ACKNOWLEDGMENTS

My thanks go to the following people, without whom I could not have written this book:

His Eminence Cardinal Aloysius Ambrozic, generous benefactor and friend of Church history, for suggesting the subject of this book

His Grace Archbishop Thomas Collins, for giving his blessing to this project

His Excellency Bishop John A. Boissonneau, for taking care of the practical details

His Excellency Bishop John A. O'Mara, for giving an interview, answering my questions and writing the Preface

His Excellency Bishop Remi De Roo, for sharing his memories of the Second Vatican Council and the work of the Canadian Conference of Catholic Bishops on the diaconate

Dr. Mark McGowan, friend and colleague, for suggesting my name to Cardinal Ambrozic

Marc Lerman and the staff of the Archives of the Archdiocese of Toronto, for their timely and professional assistance and for giving me access to their superbly organized archives

Deacon Tab Charbonneau, Deacon Dan Murphy and Deacon George Newman, for taking the time to answer my many questions of clarification

Deacon John Grieve, for supplying valuable material from St. Augustine's Seminary

Father Charles Amico, for sharing his knowledge and understanding of the early years of the diaconate program

Father Tibor Horvath, SJ, for giving me a personal tutorial on his theology of the diaconate

Deacon Bert Cambre, for his infectious enthusiasm for the project and for finding a publisher in record time

Joe Sinasac of Novalis Press, for publishing the book

Anne Mastrovita of the diaconate office, for supplying me with information and important lists

Brigitte Pollock, head of archive services for the Canadian Conference of Catholic Bishops, for digging out important material on the CCCB's work on the diaconate

Dr. Stephen Miletic of Franciscan University in Steubenville, Ohio, for reading and commenting on the manuscript

Kenneth Whitehead, diplomat and scholar of the Second Vatican Council, for his generous comments on Chapter Two

John Burtniak, retired librarian/archivist at Brock University, for copyediting the manuscript in his usual ruthless fashion and saving me from many a blunder

Theresa Power, my daughter, for her constant encouragement

Kathleen Power, my wife, for copyediting the manuscript and dispensing wise advice.

PREFACE

At the installation of the Most Reverend Thomas Collins as the Archbishop of Toronto, his predecessor, Cardinal Aloysius Ambrozic, thanked the Catholic community for their generous support during his tenure of office. He made specific mention of the ministry of the permanent deacons, saying that the Archdiocese could not have provided the same broad level of ministerial service to the community without their competent participation. He further recommended that a history of the permanent diaconate program be written to document the origins and success of this ministry. This narrative is the fruit of his request. It provides background on the theology of the diaconate and sketches the history and development of the archdiocesan program.

Since its inception, the Toronto permanent diaconate program has been a program of St. Augustine's Seminary. It was developed with the assistance and concurrence of the seminary faculty who continue to monitor its progress. When I was appointed the Rector/President of St. Augustine's in the summer of 1969, the priestly formation program was in a state of transition. The seminary was committed to becoming a founding member of the Toronto School of Theology. This occasioned a major transformation in the priestly formation program since the students would henceforth attend their classes at the theological sister-colleges on the downtown campus of the University of Toronto. St. Augustine's Seminary faculty met each Wednesday of term to review the spiritual, academic, and pastoral programs as well as the progress of the individual students.

Archbishop Philip Pocock asked the seminary faculty to consider the advisability of creating a permanent diaconate program in the archdiocese. We saw this to be within our mandate since we understood our responsibilities to include the education and preparation of candidates for ministry. To begin, we reviewed the current literature on the diaconate, the documents of the Second Vatican Council, and the letters of Pope Paul VI on the subject. We had two preliminary meetings with a group of interested laity and clergy, and Father Paul Giroux and I attended a meeting in Chicago that brought together representatives of eleven programs in the United States.

Subsequently, the seminary faculty recommended that the program be established and Archbishop Pocock gave us the mandate to proceed with its organization and development. Individual members of the faculty assumed different tasks: Father John Moss looked to the spiritual formation, Father Charles Amico to the academic and Father Paul Giroux agreed to be the director of the diaconate program, which was considered to be mainly pastoral.

In developing the program, we monitored closely those already established in the United States and, in particular, the one in the Archdiocese of Chicago. These two-year programs comprised ten weekend meetings each year plus an annual retreat; this was the pattern we followed.

Since the program was pastorally oriented, the academic requirements for admission were minimal. Father Giroux interviewed each candidate in a home visit, where the implications of the program for the candidate and for his wife and family could be explored in the unique context of family life. He was seeking mature candidates who had some experience of ministry in the Church, good listening skills, and the ability to read seriously, to assimilate information and then to present it to others. The curriculum provided a basic overview of the teachings of the Church and included Christology, ecclesiology, introduction to the Old and New Testaments, moral decision making, and the liturgy with special emphasis on the Eucharist. Community building and spiritual formation were given particular attention at each of the monthly weekend sessions. One of the candidates in the first group, Dr. Colin Chase, a professor at the University of Toronto and a former director of Cursillo, was particularly helpful in monitoring the progress of the program.

The program was launched at a very interesting and exciting time in the Church of the twentieth century. I was fortunate to share in its development. Earlier, I had attended the Second Vatican Council as *peritus*/secretary to Cardinal James McGuigan. In that capacity I was present for the discussion of the diaconate during the second and third sessions of the Council.

Archbishop Pocock initiated the program and continued to monitor each stage of its development; Cardinal Gerald Emmett Carter and Cardinal Aloysius Ambrozic supported its growth and maturity during the ensuing years. Now thirty-five years have passed since the ordination of the first permanent deacons, and if there is a measure of the success of the program, it is in the zealous and competent ministry of the more than 135 permanent deacons serving in the Archdiocese of Toronto.

In his overview of the permanent diaconate in the Archdiocese of Toronto, Michael Power has given us a timely and inspiring illustration of how grace became a reality through the collaborative efforts of the priests and candidates who launched the permanent diaconate program and who continue to develop and support it as an important ministry in the Church.

+ John A. O'Mara
Bishop Emeritus of St. Catharines
Past President/Rector of St. Augustine's Seminary
and Founding Member of the Board
of the Toronto School of Theology

INTRODUCTION

"Such is the case with the Son of Man, who has come, not to be served by others, but to serve, to give his own life as a ransom for the many." (Matt. 20:28)

From 1974 to 2008, the Archdiocese of Toronto has ordained 242 candidates to the permanent diaconate. In 2010, it will ordain another sixteen. This is a wonderful achievement and should be a source of pride for everyone in the diaconal community, for each ordination is a witness of the essential character of the servant Church and a testimonial of the Church's love and recognition of the spiritual worth of the poor. Also, seven other Canadian dioceses have adopted Toronto's well-honed diaconal program. They are Kingston, Hamilton, London and St. Catharines, in Ontario, and Calgary, St. Paul and Edmonton, in Alberta. All this is very inspiring. The diaconate works. It is still with us. How did this come to pass?

Servants of All: A History of the Permanent Diaconate in the Archdiocese of Toronto, 1972–2007 answers this question. It is the first substantial history of a North American diocesan diaconate program. It begins in an unlikely setting, the Dachau concentration camp. Dachau proved to be a fertile ground for the diaconate. The suffering and persecution experienced by the Catholic priests and religious incarcerated in the camp produced so much clear and prophetic thinking about the Church's future, including a diaconate of married men for the benefit of the Catholic faithful who, many believed, had become too distant from the clergy. The story moves to "diaconate circles" in postwar Germany and France. They were hotbeds of theological thinking and agitation on behalf of the restoration, producing in the process reams of published material on the diaconate in the Early Church and its rightful place in the hierarchy and the liturgical and charitable life of the present-day Church. From Germany and France, the narrative makes it way to Rome and the Second Vatican Council (with a sidebar on the Council of Trent). Next is the Canadian Conference of Catholic Bishops in Ottawa, which treated its mandate from Paul VI seriously, and, after considerable reflection and theological writing, decided to give its imprimatur to the permanent diaconate.

Finally our story lands on home territory, the Archdiocese of Toronto – a universe removed from Dachau but, in our history, intimately connected to it. The archdiocese restored the permanent diaconate in 1972 and ordained its first (and to this date largest) class of candidates in 1974. It was an Abrahamic leap of faith that said, unconditionally, "Yes!" to the promptings of the Holy Spirit and to the wisdom and foresight of the Council at a time when the post-Conciliar Church was experiencing a period of transition and turmoil. Time, however, has amply justified that leap of faith.

When His Eminence Cardinal Aloysius Ambrozic kindly offered me the opportunity to write this history, in April 2007, I realized to my discomfort that, aside from having occasionally seen a permanent deacon in the sanctuary of the cathedral in St. Catharines, I knew nothing about the permanent diaconate. In my ignorance, I was not alone. I dare say that most Catholics still do not know what a permanent deacon is, often muddle the meaning of his call to Holy Orders with his functions at Mass, and are amazed to be informed that most permanent deacons have a wife and family. Of real astonishment for many is the fact that deacons receive no remuneration for their work. I knew that the scriptural, theological and historical learning curve would be a steep one.

No matter. Cardinal Ambrozic did not let me leave his office empty-handed. He had compiled a list of books and articles to read and names of people to interview. The list ran for a page and a half and was subsequently revised and lengthened. As I ordered copies of the more recent books and hunted down the articles, I quickly discovered that the modern permanent diaconate, while still very much in its infancy, had already produced a sizeable library of secondary literature, most of it American in origin. While poring through the literature, I began to interview deacons from the classes of 1974 and 1975. Pioneers in the Toronto diaconate, they and their wives were most helpful and gracious. And in between interviews, I embarked on a search for primary material, in the course of which I happily learned that the Toronto diaconate had generated a small mountain of paper that was readily accessible in a number of Toronto-area archives. The motherlode was housed in the Archives of the Roman Catholic Archdiocese of Toronto. Then there were the open stacks at the Kelly Library of the University of St. Michael's College. They revealed a treasure trove of books and articles on the mid-twentieth-century investigations of the diaconate and on the procedures, debates and writings of the Council of Trent, which briefly considered the diaconate, and the Second Vatican Council, which finished what Trent had begun.

How fortuitous for the diaconate in the Archdiocese of Toronto to have been blessed from the very outset of its corporate existence with the active encouragement and presence of Archbishop Philip Pocock, a Council Father. Once he made up his mind, on the advice and recommendation of the Senate of Priests, that the Council wanted a permanent diaconate and that the archdiocese needed it, he did everything to facilitate its inception and initial growth. This kind of episcopal encouragement continued with Cardinal G. Emmett Carter, another Council Father, and Cardinal Ambrozic, who enjoyed a very long and fruitful relationship with the diaconate program, and continues to this day with Archbishop Thomas Collins. Also fortuitous was the work of Bishop Robert B. Clune, the second and longest-serving vicar of deacons. He exerted a positive and steady influence on the diaconal community during its formative years, shepherding it through reviews and self-studies and during times of crisis and painful growth.

The different rectors and staff members of St. Augustine's Seminary should also receive their due. They did the teaching and provided the spiritual direction on the training program side, and they made the seminary a home away from home for the deacons and their families. It was not easy for them to take on this new ministry. Then there is the first generation of deacons. It is truly remarkable that the archdiocese attracted so many splendid and dedicated candidates to the diaconate, along with their supportive wives and families, right at the start of the program. No wonder then that, despite the program's occasional stumbles to live up to its own ideals of service and spirituality, the diaconate was bound not only to survive with its model of service intact and flourishing but also to succeed in ways unimaginable for those early deacons.

The commencement of any new project, when there is little more than the writer and blank notepaper, is always the loneliest and yet the most hopeful time for an historian, as he embarks on yet another adventure of digging up the past – and in this case the recent past – and making sense of it. I wanted to be fair to the facts, as well as to the people involved in the diaconate's history, in a rational and objective manner, and to leave enough room to celebrate the many wonderful accomplishments of the diaconate community in the Archdiocese of Toronto, without recourse to adulation.

The deacons have been my inspiration. Their personal testimonies – on their call, their work, and their hopes for the diaconate – which I received on request early in my writing *Servants of All*, have sustained me during these past two years and given me an entirely fresh perspective on the power and glory of the Gospel. They indeed have come not to be served but to serve.

To all the deacons, past, present and future, I dedicate this history.

Michael Power
Welland, Ontario
Feast of St. Nicholas 2009

Note on permanent deacon and deacon. A deacon is a deacon, and thus the diaconate should not be described as if there were two kinds of diaconate in the Church: permanent or final for those not proceeding to the priesthood and transitional for those who are. There is one diaconate, as Cardinal Carter was fond of reminding everyone during discussions on the diaconate. However, the use of the phrase "permanent diaconate," although theologically imprecise and at times misleading, is a practical necessity for the historian. The phrase has appeared so often in the literature on the history of the diaconate, especially in relation to its restoration by the Second Vatican Council, that it has acquired a widespread legitimacy. Meaning is use. In this book, I use both "permanent diaconate" and "diaconate" interchangeably, with "diaconate" gaining the upper hand by Chapter Five. In either case, I want to maintain the Church's understanding of the one Sacrament of Order, bishop, priest and deacon.

1

FROM DACHAU TO ROME

Introduction

In the Catholic Church, every movement that flourished and successfully adapted to changing circumstances began as an idea – an insight – concerning the betterment and strengthening of the spiritual and material welfare of the Catholic faithful. The twentieth-century European movement to re-establish the permanent diaconate for married and single men in the Latin Rite Church rested on the idea, long dormant but never dead, that the diaconate deserved to be restored to its proper place in the one Sacrament of Order – bishop, priest and deacon – and that its true nature should not be limited to a transitional phase along the path to priesthood. It was separate and distinct from the priesthood. The diaconate, moreover, was understood not only as a matter of right because of its proven historical place in the Apostolic and post-Apostolic Church, but also as a matter of urgent necessity in the modern era, for both the Church and the world it was called by Christ to serve. The primary issue was the meaning of ministry or service.

By the 1950s, there had grown a small but influential body of Catholic opinion that claimed that the Church, if it were to fulfill its mandate as servant to all, needed permanent deacons, and that those who felt called to ordination to the diaconate needed to take their place once again in the Church hierarchy of office. During this period, the most notable promoters of the restoration of the diaconate were from Europe, in particular Germany and Austria, or were European-born prelates in mission territories. Among them were the following three priests and two laymen whose opinions on the restoration will form the substance of this chapter. They were Father Otto Pies, SJ (1901–1960); Father Wilhelm Schamoni (1905–1991); Josef Hornef (1896–1971); Father Karl Rahner, SJ (1904–1984); and Hannes Kramer (b.1929). Their publications, although differing in scope and influence, will be treated as generally representative of the many diverse voices that promoted the diaconate during the fifteen or so years leading up to the opening of the Second Vatican Council, on 11 October 1962.[1]

Father Otto Pies, SJ

Father Otto Pies, SJ, a former novice master, was one of 2,579 Catholic priests, brothers and seminarians interned at the Dachau concentration camp, northwest of Munich, starting in 1933. They came from 133 dioceses located in thirty-eight countries, and included members from twenty-nine religious orders and congregations.[2] The wholesale Nazi persecution of the Church in effect turned Dachau into the largest Catholic community of priests and religious in Europe, a powerhouse of Christian prayer, conversion and hope. At one point, there were so many Catholic clergy incarcerated at Dachau, busily ministering to the general population, that their Nazi guards decided to put them together in Cell Block 26, known as *der Priesterblock*. The daily regime consisted of hard labour, little food and indescribably filthy living conditions. Little wonder that more than 1,000 of Dachau's priests and religious perished before the liberation of the camp by American soldiers in April 1945.

Despite having to work long hours on a starvation diet, the priests used what energy they had left at the close of nearly every day to engage in frank and fruitful discussions about the Church of the recent past and to share their ideas for its postwar future. They were appalled by the violence of Christians against each other. What had gone wrong? Spiritual awakenings and insights can occur in the oddest of places and under the most appalling of circumstances. The concentration camp at Dachau was one such place. Many priests there felt that the Holy Spirit was calling forth a new era in pastoral ministries in the Church, such as the ministry of the permanent diaconate. Such talk must have sounded rather theoretical at times in the grim and death-filled confines of Dachau, all the more so when it came to the topic of the diaconate. Pre-war literature and talk on the subject were relatively rare and not widely known. Yet for Father Pies and many of his fellow priests, one of the few things that made any sense in the face of their own and others' suffering was their hope for a Church that would exercise the fullness of its Christ-centred *diakonia* or service for the greater good of all society, in every part of the world. A reborn diaconate, apostolic in its origins and spirit, tailored to meet contemporary social and spiritual needs and open to married men, would be a cornerstone to a hoped-for revivification of the Church's essential missionary nature.

Father Pies survived Dachau but lived the rest of his life in ill health. He had enough strength and determination, however, to author two significant works on two very different subjects: a 1947 article that included a call for the restoration of the permanent diaconate; and a 1957 biography of Father Karl Leisner, who was ordained a priest in Dachau and died of tuberculosis at the age of thirty. He was named a martyr for the faith and later beatified by Pope John Paul II on 23 June 1996. Father Pies' biography of Father Leisner, called *The Victory of Father Karl*, solidified Father Pies' reputation in the world of German Catholicism, but it was his eighteen-page article, "Cell Block 26: Experiences of Priestly Life in Dachau," that has assured him a place of high honour in the historiography of the modern diaconate. What he wrote was so confident and so compelling in its portrayal of "a diaconate of married, employed and proven men"[3] that it could not help but attract and influence like-minded men in the Church. By going straight to the heart of the matter, in unvarnished but forceful prose, Father Pies held up for all to see the essence of the idea of the diaconate for the twentieth century and beyond. Its ability to inspire others in the early days of the movement cannot be underestimated, for they would take the torch from Father Pies and carry it all the way to Rome.

Father Wilhelm Schamoni

One such person was Father Wilhelm Schamoni. A diocesan priest and theologian, he spent the entire war in Dachau. A close collaborator of Father Pies, he was an active participant in the discussions on the state of the Church, in Cell Block 26. By the end of 1944, he had written a series of notes outlining his preliminary impressions and conclusions about the diaconate. The single most compelling reason for the restoration of the diaconate, according to him, was the shortage of priests in established parishes throughout much of Europe and in the mission territories. Any prolonged absence of ordained leadership at the level of the parish would have a disastrous impact upon the integrity of the sacramental life of the Catholic faithful and would diminish the effectiveness of the Church as a servant community of believers in a world of unbelief. At stake was the viability of the parish church, the traditional centre of Catholic faith and experience, at a time that also featured a burgeoning liturgical renewal and the rise of the catechetical movement.

(We must keep in mind that the pre-eminence of diocesan ministry, one of the defining components in the work of deacons today, had yet to emerge in the dialogue on diaconal ministry during Father Schamoni's time, because that same dialogue, although quite orthodox on the theology of ordination, had yet to explore in any meaningful degree the theology of diaconal service not explicitly tied to the priest, the altar and the parish. Such a theology, now the staple of numerous books on the diaconate, would not begin to develop until after the Council had restored the permanent diaconate and diaconate programs were already underway. Today we do not look upon the deacon as the priest's helper – rather, he is the *bishop's* helper – or promote the diaconate as an answer to what has become a severe shortage of priests in the West, but that was not how Father Schamoni saw matters. He was hardly alone. Other writers on the diaconate in the 1950s and early 1960s, and even a good many of the Church Fathers at the Second Vatican Council, understood the diaconate the way that Father Schamoni did.)

The diaconate, according to Father Schamoni, was a special and sacred ecclesiastical office by virtue of the ordination of those called to it. The grace and authority of diaconal ordination would enable the deacon to be an auxiliary at the altar to the priest's liturgical-sacramental ministry and also allow him to provide liturgical-sacramental leadership, proper to his calling, in parishes and missions in lieu of a parish priest.[4] The deacon would assist overtaxed parish priests, especially in the area of catechesis, lead parishes where there was no priest in charge, win back the de-Christianized population camped outside the Church, and take the Church away from the bureaucrats and return it to the people. As married men with families and careers, deacons would be able to preach in a down-to-earth manner, and their exemplary family life might even increase vocations to the Catholic priesthood. Moreover, the married diaconate would open the door to Protestant ministers who had converted to Catholicism and desired to remain in ministry in some official capacity, and it would act as a bridge to the Eastern Churches, which since time immemorial had a venerable tradition of married deacons.[5]

Encouraged by Father Pies, Father Schamoni turned his unpublished notes into the twentieth century's first book on the Catholic diaconate. It was published in Germany in 1953 under the title *Familienväter als geweihte Diakone*, and it was translated into English and published in London in 1955 as *Married Men as Ordained Deacons*. A more revealing and correct translation would have been *Family Fathers as Ordained Deacons*. Next, it appeared in a French-language edition in 1961 under the title *Ordonner Diacres des Pères de Famille*.[6]

Married Men as Ordained Deacons is scriptural, historical, theological and practical in its plea on behalf of the restoration of the permanent diaconate. Especially noteworthy, and very relevant today, is Father Schamoni's concept of the intimate and dynamic interrelation between the parish community as a spiritual dynamo and the phenomena of life outside its doors, with the married and working deacon acting as a vital conduit between the two.[7] Central to Father Schamoni's views on the necessity and justification of the diaconate, in addition to what he perceived to be a crisis in the number of priests, were five Scripture passages and two significant events from the history of the Church, each one of which pointed to the practical and functional nature of the work of the diaconate as it related to the work of the priest in parishes and missions.

The first three passages were Acts 6:1-7 (the seven men chosen to wait on table), 6:10 (Stephen) and 8:40 (Philip). They shed light on the importance of ordination – the laying on of hands – in the election of members of the community for a particular hierarchical office,[8] and as a result they distinguish deacons from lay people in the administration and transmission of spiritual and corporal duties connected to the liturgical and charitable life of the Church.[9] Then there were Philippians 1:1 and 1 Timothy 3:1-13, which demonstrate that deacons were officeholders. In Father Schamoni's view, the fact that deacons were ordained office-holders in the Apostolic Church was reason enough for the twentieth-century Church to renew the diaconate. In addition, with the crisis of a lack of priests to minister to every Catholic congregation, there was no question that the diaconate deserved a new beginning.

Alongside Scripture, there was history. Father Schamoni looked to the past to buttress his argument in *Married Men as Ordained Deacons*. He paid special attention to two historical events. The first was the twenty-third session of the Council of Trent (1545–63), which addressed the Sacrament of Order, as a follow-up to the previous session's teaching on the Sacrifice of the Mass. "The evidence indicates," writes William Ditewig, "that it was the understanding of Trent that the diaconate was indeed part of the Sacrament of Order because of its scriptural roots and because of the diaconate's ancient and long-standing association with the Eucharist."[10] On 6 July 1563, there was presented to the Council a schema that delineated the original tasks and services of the deacon. It seems that some of the Council Fathers wanted a discussion on the diaconate for the very practical reason that the large number of priests that had deserted the Church to join the Reformers had left countless Catholics in many parts of Europe without the benefit of the sacraments and clerical leadership at the local level of the parish. Although this schema was never promulgated in a decree, Father Schamoni quoted a large portion of it.[11] To him, it was too foundational to ignore. Sustained by the enduring witness of Sacred Scripture, the modern diaconate could be built and developed upon the wisdom of Trent.

The second item was a curious and intriguing chapter in the history of the Church in Hungary, from near the end of the sixteenth century to the middle of the eighteenth. During that time, Turkish rule severely limited the presence of priests among the Catholic population, forcing the bishops to create a class of lay ministers called Licentiates. They were given an episcopal licence to baptize, perform marriages, conduct burials, lead the congregation in prayer, give catechism lessons and read or deliver sermons. They wore a black gown with surplice when performing their liturgical functions, were paid a stipend and were not required to be celibate. These Licentiates preserved the Catholic faith in the hope of better times to come, saving many parishes from needless extinction. They were deacons in practically everything, but lacked the grace and authority that comes with sacramental ordination.[12]

Father Schamoni's *Married Men as Ordained Deacons* helped to move the discussion about the diaconate onto the broader European stage, and, since it was translated into English, it introduced the topic at least to Catholics in the United Kingdom (the extent to which the English translation of his book made any headway in North America remains uncertain). It set the standard for later and more elaborate works on the history and theology of the diaconate that have become standard fare in the canon of literature devoted to the subject.

Josef Hornef

By far, the most significant work to immediately follow Schamoni's was *The New Vocation* by Josef Hornef. It was published in Germany in 1958 and translated into English in 1963. Hornef was a devoted and learned Catholic. He was educated at three universities – Freiburg-im-Breisgau (the future home of the diaconate movement in Germany), Bonn and Giessen – earning doctorates in Civil Law and Canon Law. Soon after the end of the Second World War, he was appointed chief provincial court judge in Fulda. An ardent anti-Nazi, Hornef was forced into internal exile for thirteen years.

It was not the concentration camp, but it was still a punishment to be endured by him and his family. Internal exile may have stifled his opposition to the regime, but it gave him plenty of time to share his thoughts with others about the future of the Church, which at some point led him to embrace the idea of the diaconate. This is how he described his exile in an autobiographical moment:

> In 1933 I was working in a small Catholic parish in the south of my native Hesse; but early in the next year, I, like countless other officials, was transferred to the Protestant region of North Hesse. The Nazi Government thought in this way to negate the influence of Catholic officials in Catholic parishes, but in this they erred. Many who had been transplanted in this latter day Diaspora began only now to discover their apostolic spirit. It must have been in the designs of God's Providence that I should have taken up residence with my family in the building containing the room that served our little band of exiles as a "chapel". The priest came every Sunday from the town, 12 miles away, to say Mass and was our guest. An inevitable consequence of this was that we became more acquainted with the life of the Church, that we had to do the duties of sexton, organist and Lector and that we were permitted to take an active part in the Divine Liturgy in a way that would have been impossible in an organized Catholic parish.[13]

Inspired by Father Otto Pies' groundbreaking 1947 article, "Cell Block 26: Experiences of Priestly Life in Dachau," Josef Hornef began to write on the diaconate that same year and finally managed to have his first article published in 1949.[14] It was the beginning of a prolific and profound contribution to the literature on the diaconate. Over the years, Hornef became the first unofficial historian of the movement and one of its most authoritative and persuasive apologists.

The New Vocation is the classic work of Josef Hornef's life. Taking his cue from Father Schamoni's *Married Men as Ordained Deacons*, Hornef treated the diaconate as the most effective means to alleviate the spiritual deprivation felt by an ever-increasing number of the faithful due to the critical shortage of priests in parishes and missions.[15] And like Father Schamoni, Hornef understood that the essential role of the permanent deacon would be to assist the priest in his liturgical-sacramental ministry.[16] All other diaconal ministry flowed from the deacon's presence near the priest at the altar of sacrifice. If Father Schamoni's work was a pioneering argument on behalf of the rebirth of the ancient office of deacon for the modern world, as a part-time ministry for married men, Hornef's was an exhaustive elaboration and critical assessment of Father Schamoni's work that elevated the entire debate on the diaconate to a new level of intellectual and theological integrity. Hornef, a layman and a jurist, delivered a very frank and forthright treatment of a matter that was still very much in its infancy at the time he wrote *The New Vocation*, and that consequently needed the maturity of thought and spirituality he was able to provide out of his personal experience and considerable meditative examination. His book appeared just in time to help keep alive the hope for a restored diaconate as the Church entered a new era with the pontificate of John XXIII.

Of particular interest is Hornef's analysis of the following: the Sacrament of Order; the meaning of ordination; the nature and functions of the diaconate; the training of deacons in both Christian Doctrine and social service; the diaconate in the Protestant churches; the alliance of deacon with the parish community; the social apostolate of the deacon (a significant advance on Father Schamoni, who thought that charity could be left to the deacon's wife);[17] the opening up of minor orders to married men; the contentious issue of celibacy; the link between the diaconate and the increasing demand for liturgical reform; and the diaconate in the missions. Hornef was exhaustive, meticulous and very readable in his rendition of each one of these issues.

However, the questions of whether deacons should be full-time or part-time and whether they should receive remuneration for their apostolic work vexed Hornef to an inordinate degree. As we know, most dioceses quickly and quietly resolved both issues at the start of their respective diaconate programs: the vast majority of today's deacons are in part-time ministry, and deacons do not receive payment of any kind unless they are directly employed in diocesan administration or are hired by government agencies in an official capacity, such as a hospital chaplain.

On the matter of the relationship between the bishop and the deacon – so fundamental to our present understanding of the permanent diaconate[18] – Hornef is silent. That may appear strange, but for him, and for many of his contemporaries commenting on the diaconate, the essential focus was on the nature of the one priesthood of Jesus Christ and the three hierarchical degrees of participation in that priesthood by means of the Sacrament of Order:

> We have already said that there is only *one* priesthood; and likewise there is only *one* Sacrament of Orders, even though it is conferred in stages.
>
> Now this *oneness of the priesthood* and the oneness of the Sacrament of Orders means that there is also a *oneness of function*, that is to say, that all who have received the Sacrament and participate in the priesthood are entrusted with the same Divine commission, with the proviso, of course, that certain things are, in accordance with the mind of the Church, withheld from the lower orders and reserved to the higher by virtue of their higher participation in the priesthood. This is what is called the *Principle of Subsidiarity*. In the bishop is vested the fullness of priestly power. He hands on priestly power by conferring the Sacrament of Orders, and exercises the power of jurisdiction and supreme teaching authority in his diocese. The priest (in the narrower sense) is the one who offers sacrifice and is the ordinary minister of the Sacraments. All other priestly tasks not reserved to the bishop or priest are also imposed upon the deacon. His ordinary service, therefore, embraces all the many-sided tasks which go to making up the care of souls.
>
> The purpose of all priestly activity is to *bring Christ to the people*, and this is done in a number of ways.[19]

According to Hornef, those ways are three in number: liturgy, the Word and charity.[20] This is all very orthodox. Interesting is Hornef's lengthy treatise on charity, what today we call service.

It reads as if it were written for a manual on the modern diaconate, but it was fated to go unappreciated. Why? Until the discourse on the diaconate discovered and accepted the defining relationship between bishop and deacon, the development of the charity or service aspect of a deacon's ministry, known and practised as diocesan ministry, would remain largely dormant. As previously mentioned in regards to Father Schamoni's *Married Men as Ordained Deacons*, the shift in emphasis in diaconal service from word and liturgy to diocesan ministry did not begin until after the Council had restored the permanent diaconate.

Lastly, also absent from *The New Vocation* is any reference to those Scriptural passages that confirm the existence of deacons as officeholders in the Apostolic era. Father Schamoni wrote about Acts 6:1-7, Philippians 1:1 and 1 Timothy 3:1-13. Hornef knew about these passages, of course, but he did not feel obliged to refer to – let alone elaborate on – what he considered a well-known fact about the Scriptural origins of the diaconate. Instead, he simply assumed it, and on that assumption proceeded to discuss and defend the need for deacons as officeholders in the mid-twentieth-century Church. He saw no need for the past to justify the present, although he knew, along with everyone else who was writing on the diaconate, that if there had not been deacons as officeholders in the Apostolic Church, there would have been no discussion about deacons as officeholders in the twentieth century. It would take a new generation of writers on the diaconate, following the Council and continuing well into the restoration, to explore every reference and description of diaconal service in Apostolic, post-Apostolic and Patristic sources right up to the end of the sixth century. The main pedagogical reason for taking this approach was (and remains) tied to the perceived need to justify and explain to the Catholic faithful that the diaconate is primarily a ministry of charity or service, in light of Jesus as the first deacon, who "came not to be served but to serve" (Matt. 20:28).[21]

In the final analysis, *The New Vocation* was perhaps the best book-length introduction to the then novel idea of a permanent diaconate that was produced in the 1950s. In hindsight, one could comfortably say that it would have been of immense help to those commissioned by national episcopal conferences to report on the advisability of the introduction of the permanent diaconate in their respective countries, and to those diocesan committees entrusted with the same task in their respective jurisdictions. Within a Canadian context, this did not happen. The Canadian episcopal committee, which began its deliberations on the diaconate in 1966, either chose to ignore or was unaccountably unaware of Hornef's magisterial work, while, oddly enough, citing several of Hornef's articles (see Chapter III). In either case, one is left wondering why.

Father Karl Rahner, SJ

We are getting ahead of ourselves. Let us return to the 1950s and focus on Father Karl Rahner, SJ. Father Rahner entered the Jesuit novitiate in 1922 and was ordained ten years later. Except for a brief period near the end of the Second World War, when he was pastor of a church in Lower Bavaria, he spent his entire priestly life teaching, researching, writing and editing. He may have been the most original Catholic thinker of his day, described by many of his contemporaries as a systematic theologian and by others as a transcendental theologian. Not much escaped his inquisitive and critical eye. His output was prodigious and legendary. The bulk of his writings have been published in *Theological Investigations*, a multi-volume work that began to appear in 1954.[22]

No other theologian imparted so much erudition and legitimacy to the argument on behalf of the restored diaconate than Father Rahner did, both before and after the Second Vatican Council, and no other theologian had the "political clout" to bring the matter in a decisive fashion to the attention of the Church Fathers at the Council. His patronage was crucial to the intellectual underpinnings of the diaconal movement, as it carved out a place for itself on the stage of the Second Vatican Council, and proved itself resilient enough to withstand the sometimes combative process whereby the Fathers recognized and restored the diaconate's proper place in the Sacrament of Order, in *Lumen Gentium*, "A Light Unto the Nations" (otherwise referred to as the Dogmatic Constitution on the Church).

Father Rahner's most significant contribution to the discussion on the diaconate, prior to the Council, was an article titled "Die Theologie der Erneuerung des Diakonates." Divided into seven sections, it was published in *Diaconia in Christo* in 1962 and was translated into English as "The Theology of the Restoration of the Diaconate" in 1966.[23] His argument in favour of the opportuneness of restoration – the present time was the right time – was an in-depth exploration of the intimate connection between the office of deacon, diaconal ordination (sacramental transmission to that office) and sacramental grace received upon ordination.[24] This took up the first three sections. Stripped down to its bare minimum, the argument went this way: (1) the already existing office of deacon, in which married and unmarried men were doing the work of deacons, was a permanent and important calling because they were assisting in the apostolic work of Church leaders; (2) as such, their diaconal work, their participation in the office of deacon, was sufficient justification for the Church to restore the sacramental transmission of that office; (3) with ordination would come the sacramental graces proper to the exercise of the diaconal ministry. What the Church should restore because it was in her mandate to do so was not the office of deacon but the sacramental rite – diaconal ordination.

On the distinction and right relationship between the office of deacon and diaconal ordination (sacramental transmission), Father Rahner wrote:

> These are not identical entities, nor are they... absolutely inseparable entities, at least in the case of the diaconate. They are mutually related realities in the sense that the sacramental rite of transmission of the office receives its ultimate justification from the office and not vice versa... no matter how true it may be that in certain circumstances there may be an office in the Church which can be, but is not necessarily, transmitted sacramentally, the ultimate reason for the opportuneness of a sacramental transmission of office will always be the opportuneness of the office itself. For a rite of the transmission of an office – a rite which is a sacrament – is not intended to be anything else than the sacramental conferring of the office itself and the sacramental distribution of

the grace required for this office. Hence, by its very nature, the transmission of office finds its ultimate significance and reason for its opportuneness in the office itself.[25]

Central to Father Rahner's entire thesis on the diaconate was his claim that the office of deacon already existed. Proof for this was furnished by the fact that there were plenty of deacons, although not known by that name, who were busy doing diaconal work:

> The office of diaconate exists in the Church, and this even (if not almost exclusively in reality) outside the ranks of ordained deacons. For there are full-time, professional catechists, and full-time, professional "welfare-workers" (in the widest sense of the word), who have taken on the full-time job of fulfilling the Church's mission of charity, who give lifelong service to the hierarchy and who certainly think of the job for which they have been explicitly commissioned by the hierarchy as fulfilling an essential task for the Church. This is a task which belongs not only to the Church in general (so that it can be fulfilled from the outset and quite obviously even by lay people) but belongs quite peculiarly and specially to the office-bearers of the Church, to the hierarchy as such, so that this charitable work really possesses the formal nature of a real diaconate. There is in the Church a full-time and professional administration, which represents a real auxiliary function for the fulfillment of the task of the hierarchy as such. We can speak of an office of deacon at least where these functions are exercised, to a fuller extent, by an explicit commission received from the hierarchy, under the immediate direction of the hierarchy and as a direct assistance to the task of the hierarchy, as a permanent and enduring function – even in those cases where this office has not been transmitted by sacramental ordination.[26]

(Curiously, Father Rahner seems to have anticipated at least one element in the current screening process for candidates to the diaconate. In a majority of dioceses in North America, including the Archdiocese of Toronto, when a man applies for admission to the diaconal program, one of the first questions he is asked by the director is, "And what kind of diaconal service are you doing right now?" Such a question assumes that a person's participation in the work of the diaconate precedes ordination to the diaconate, although it does not guarantee it. Also, by stressing the relationship between deacon and hierarchy, Father Rahner moved away from the position of both Josef Hornef and Father Wilhelm Schamoni that understood the deacon as a helper of parish priests.)

On the opportuneness or timeliness of the restoration of diaconal ordination, Father Rahner has this to say: "The decisive reason consists in the fact that (1) the office already exists, (2) a sacramental transmission of his office is possible and (3) such a transmission, at least where the office exists, must be regarded basically and from the outset, if not as something necessary yet as something fitting and opportune."[27] He called this "a governing principle of the Church's practical attitude in her sacramental practice."[28] The restoration of the ordination of deacons, then, rested on the power of the Church given to her by Christ from its very foundations, and on the practical application of that power at a time when it was a good thing to confer ordination on those men involved in the work of the office of deacon. There was no time like the present time – no impediment to delay. And no need to delay.

By way of summation, Father Rahner wrote:

> In summary, it can be said quite simply that there exists in the Church a sacramental, grace-effecting rite of transmitting the office of the diaconate, at least as a possibility *iuris divini* in the Church; the office to which this sacramental rite of transmission is objectively adapted already exists in the Church to a sufficient extent and in a sufficient manner; there is a general law of the nature of the sacramental order of grace which states that a sacramental rite which is possible should also be really applied to the communication of grace signified by it, wherever and whenever this communication is demanded; an office existing in the Church (even though to some extent only anonymously) requires

the help of God's grace for its exercise, for the salvation of its holder and for the benefit of the Church.[29]

Father Rahner devoted the remaining four sections of his article to celibacy and the diaconate, office and grace of office, full-time and part-time diaconate and practical norms for the restoration of the diaconate. We should note that only once did Father Rahner refer to Scripture in this essay, under the subheading "Remarks about the Mutual Relationship Between the Individual Offices in the Church." He wrote at length about "the election and constitution of the Seven," without ever mentioning that he was referring to Acts 6:1-6.[30]

"The Theology of the Restoration of the Diaconate" was one of thirty-nine articles devoted to the diaconate in *Diaconia in Christo*. It boasted authors from seventeen different countries and several who were not members of the Catholic Church, making the 650-page book an international and ecumenical enterprise. A copy was presented to Pope John XXIII in September 1962, a month before the opening of the Second Vatican Council. This was an astute political move. Since Father Rahner was not only a contributor but also an editor, his fellow contributors hoped that the presentation of such a massive amount of scholarship on the diaconate would ensure that the topic stayed alive as the Fathers decided on the substance of the Council's deliberations. In essence, it was an appeal to the Council.[31]

Hannes Kramer

Also presented to John XXIII, in the lead-up to his reception of *Diaconia in Christo*, was an extraordinary petition on the diaconate signed by eighty-three Catholic theologians. Among the signers were Josef Hornef, Father Wilhelm Schamoni, Father Karl Rahner, Father Yves Congar, OP, Father Michel-Dominique Epagneul, FMC, Father Bernard Häring, CSSR, Herbert Vorgrimler and Paul Winninger.[32] Nine members of the International Circle of the Diaconate, led by Hannes Kramer, a layman, organized the petition. A copy was sent to every Church Father, including Archbishop Philip Pocock of Toronto.[33]

Born in 1929, Hannes Kramer, an accomplished forest ranger in Germany's Black Forest, abandoned his profession to become a deacon. The social and economic chaos of postwar Germany convinced him that the Church in Europe needed to incorporate what we now call social justice within the apostolic work of the hierarchy. In his opinion, one that was shared by a small but not insignificant number of Catholic laymen, the restoration of an ordained diaconate was the best way for that incorporation to take place, one that would ensure its legitimacy within the Catholic Church and its ability to survive and mature into a permanent feature of Church life in the world.

In 1951, Kramer joined the Institute for Social Service in Freiburg-im-Breisgau. After attending a seminar sponsored by the German Catholic Social Services Conference (Caritasverband), also in 1951, Kramer and six other social workers formed the first Deacon Circle. Their intense love of Jesus as the Good Shepherd and their adaptation of Franciscan spirituality gave them hope that one day there would be ordained deacons as an integral part of a servant Church. On 1 May 1952, the group published the first issue of its newsletter, "Diaconate Circle Working Paper." In this and subsequent issues, the group promoted four essential ideas: the Church and the world needed an ordained diaconate; there was to be no obligation of celibacy for the restored diaconate; the Church's ministry is concerned with the total welfare of all people; and the ordained diaconate was instituted by Christ to serve the temporal-material needs of people.[34] In other words, charity, rooted in service to others, was the primary role of the ordained diaconate, which was an essential element of the Church hierarchy.

In 1955, Kramer moved to Munich and founded a Deacon Circle there. Soon, other circles were formed in Cologne, Aachen and Rottenburg. In 1956, the "Diaconate Circle Working Paper" published Father Rahner's initial views on the diaconate, which on refinement and further inquiry he turned into an article, "Preliminary Dogmatic Remarks for Correctly Framing the Question about the Restoration of the Diaconate."[35] In return, Father Rahner invited members of the Deacon Circle to contribute articles to *Diaconia in Christo*.[36] Hannes Kramer was the author of two of those articles.[37]

The petition wasted no time making its point. On the first page, it put forth its central claim: "Well-known theologians have studied the matter [of the permanent diaconate] from the historical, theological and practical points of view, and have arrived at the consensus that the proposed restoration (1) is possible, (2) would bear great fruit in the interior life of the Church, and (3) would do much to foster the cause of unity among Christians which Christ so dearly desires."[38] On the same page, the petition went on to announce the imminent publication of *Diaconia in Christo*, claiming that it presented every angle of the argument on behalf of restoration, and to remind the Fathers, ever so gently, that several preparatory commissions and the Central Preparatory Commission for the Council had given favourable consideration to the permanent diaconate. The petition was a plea not to let the matter die on the order paper, so to speak.

The remaining four pages of the petition answer seven questions in encapsulated fashion:

1. What are the essential features of the proposed restoration of the diaconate? *Answer:* "The Church would ordain as permanent deacons men found to be called and suited to this office, including married men. By virtue of ordination these men would belong to the hierarchy of sacred orders in the Church as ministers of a lower rank, after the bishops and the priests. They would perform tasks proper to the restored diaconate: the work of assisting in the liturgy, the ministry of the word and offices of charity. These are tasks which seem to require the grace bestowed by sacramental ordination. Thus they could fittingly be performed by ordained deacons."[39]

2. Is there any basis for the project to be found in Scripture, Tradition, theology and the history of the Church? *Answer:* Yes. To support its claim, the petition gave a skeletal version of the evidence in each of the four categories. For example, from

Scripture, it referred to Acts 6:2, 8; Philippians 1:1; 1 Timothy 3:8–12.

3. Why is such a restoration needed today? *Answer:* "Reports on the pastoral situation throughout the world, plus actual apostolic experience show that the works mentioned above, namely the administration of the sacraments plus the care of both the supernatural *and* temporal needs of souls, have multiplied and diversified to such a degree that they cannot be performed by the bishops and priests alone. Because of their dual nature, both temporal and supernatural, these works require specialized knowledge and intensive training, as well as the grace and authority which flow from sacramental ordination. Both these requirements would be met by the restoration of the diaconate in the manner described."[40]

4. What position would the deacon occupy in the structure of the Church? *Answer:* As a link between priest and people, he would be essential to the rejuvenation of parish life.

5. What of the question of celibacy? *Answer:* The petition argued in favour of a married deaconate.

6. What kind of man would be suitable for this office? *Answer:* To be fit for the office of deacon, a candidate must be aware of the dignity of his calling, accept a life of selfless service to the Church and world, possess the virtues of charity, simplicity, modesty, humility and his conduct in marriage and family life must be impeccable.

7. How would the project get started, if it were approved? *Answer:* "In order to guarantee general unity of practice throughout the Church, certain fundamental principles and guidelines would have to be drawn up by the Supreme Authority of the Church. Then each individual Ordinary, in conformity with the Holy See, could judge (1) whether the restoration of the diaconate is desirable and feasible in his diocese, (2) if so, exactly how the guidelines of the Holy Father with regard to the training of candidates, etc. are to be locally implemented, and (3) what

special tasks are to be assigned to the deacons in the particular diocese in question."[41]

The petition ended by asserting the petitioners' "faith in the sacramental grace and power of the diaconate"[42] and their reverential obedience to Holy Mother Church. However, after having requested in the most humble manner that the Fathers not only consider but also approve the restoration of the permanent diaconate for the reasons given, and do so in the manner described in the petition, the petitioners went overboard in their humility and inserted that the restoration take place "at least in the nature of an experiment."[43] That could have sunk the entire enterprise before it had a chance to sail. When one is asking a higher authority to give its blessing to a major change or shift in practice and thinking, one should never offer a second choice or minimize one's request. Happily, the Fathers ended up treating the topic of the diaconate as an all-or-nothing proposition within the context of a dogmatic constitution rather than a decree, declaration or pastoral constitution.

Conclusion

There matters stood on the eve of the Second Vatican Council. The movement on behalf of the permanent diaconate in the Latin Rite Church had made its case and placed its most fervent hopes into the hands of the Church Fathers gathering in Rome. As we have seen, there were three basic arguments in general circulation. They were not mutually exclusive by any means, but each one tended to stress a particular aspect of the whole picture devoted to the subject of the diaconate. First argument: deacons were needed to assist overworked priests in their liturgical and sacramental ministry. Second argument: the restoration of the ordination of permanent deacons should be allowed because the office of deacon already existed. Third argument: deacons were needed to bring the presence of Christ to the material-temporal order of human society.

In addition to the discussions, articles and books, the work and witness of the International Circle of the Diaconate and the 1962 petition, there were other voices at public events in the 1950s that acted as a backdrop to the movement's momentum, steadily reinforcing and reinvigorating it as time went on. Here is a sampling of events. In 1954, Father Johannes Hofinger, SJ, of Manila, spoke on the diaconate at the International Liturgical Meeting; in 1956, the Dutch Bishop Willem van Bekkum, who was stationed in Indonesia, gave a vigorous defense of the restoration of the diaconate at the First Liturgical Congress on Pastoral Liturgy in Assisi; on 5 October 1957, Pope Pius XII addressed the issue at the Second World Congress of the Lay Apostolate, telling the delegates that the time was not ripe for a permanent diaconate, but if that day were to arrive, the diaconate would take its place with the priesthood, which effectively put an end to the then current notion of a lay diaconate; and in 1959, Archbishop Eugene D'Souza of Nagpur, India, delivered a major address on "Permanent Deacons in the Missions" at the International Study Week on Missions and Liturgy in Nijmegen–Uden, Holland.

Regardless of the voice or the platform, the message was clear – the time had come for the universal Church to renew the diaconate for the sake of the Church and the world. How the Church Fathers would receive the demand for the diaconate was anyone's guess.

2

SECOND VATICAN COUNCIL: TRIUMPH AND HOPE

Introduction

In Chapter One we traced the history of the idea of the restoration of the permanent diaconate in the Catholic Church by examining the intellectual and practical labours of five of its major proponents in the post–Second World War era. Our timeline began at Dachau during the war and ended on the eve of the Second Vatican Council. We must keep in mind, however, that there was a Conciliar precedent concerning the diaconate prior to the Second Vatican Council, that is, the sixteenth-century Council of Trent. (The First Vatican Council, 1869–70, was able to complete only two constitutions: *Pastor Aeternus*, on the infallibility of the pope, and *Dei Filius*, on the faith. The Council had to adjourn due to Italian occupation of Rome, which was the last stage in the unification of Italy.)

In this chapter we will be Janus-like, looking in two directions. First, we will take stock of Trent, which treated the diaconate as a constituent element of the Sacrament of Order, and assess the long-term fallout from the Church's failure to implement the intentions of the Council Fathers, who hoped that the diaconate would be returned to its "pristine usage."[1] That did not happen until the Second Vatican Council, when the debate on the role of the deacon in the

Church was finally resumed at the level of an ecumenical council and this time brought to a fruitful conclusion in *Lumen Gentium* #29. In a very real sense, the Second Vatican Council fulfilled the promise of Trent on the diaconate within the framework of a more integrated understanding of the Sacrament of Order, which gave rise to the Council's acceptance not only of a permanent diaconate that was inspired by the testimony of the Early Church but also of a diaconate open to married men. In both respects, *Lumen Gentium* #29 signalled an end to a static perception of the diaconate and the beginning of a dynamic theological and pedagogical process whereby numerous episcopal jurisdictions, including that of the Archdiocese of Toronto, have developed and nurtured a stable and thriving permanent diaconate in tune with local needs and conditions.

The Second Vatican Council also dealt with the permanent diaconate in a major way in *Ad Gentes Divinitus* #16 (Decree on the Missionary Activity of the Church), effectively adding a fourth element to the classical description of the diaconal ministry. For this reason we will examine it. Lastly, the Council made passing references to the restored diaconate in *Sacrosanctum Concilium* #35 (the Constitution on the Sacred Liturgy), *Dei Verbum* #25 (Dogmatic Constitution on Divine Revelation) and *Orientalium Ecclesiarum* #17 (Decree on the Catholic Eastern Churches).

But all the greatness and goodness of the teachings of *Lumen Gentium* and *Ad Gentes Divinitus* would have come to naught in the practical life of the Church if Pope Paul VI had not issued two Apostolic Letters, motu proprio (translated, this means "of his own hand"), on the restoration of the permanent diaconate. They were *Sacrum Diaconatus Ordinem*, dated 18 June 1967, and *Ad Pascendum*, dated 15 August 1972. Both Letters established general norms for the order of deacons. Also issued by Paul VI on 15 August 1972 was another Apostolic Letter, *Ministeria Quaedam*, which formally recognized the specific roles of the laity in the liturgy and by inference distinguished them from those exercised by deacons.

Chapter Two is about precedent, as exhibited by the Council of Trent; it is about process and perception, as the Second Vatican Council restored the ancient office and dignity of deacon for the modern world; and it is about papal directives concerning the Council's teachings on the diaconate. This chapter is not about a victory of progressive liberals over conservative reactionaries; nor is it about the fulfillment of the needs of the Church in the Third World. The permanent diaconate took root and flourished, not in Asia or Africa or in Central and South America, with the notable exception of Brazil, but in North America and Europe, where the Church continues to shrink in numbers and public influence. The irony is inescapable. Rather, this chapter concerns the Second Vatican Council's understanding of the one Sacrament of Order – bishop, priest and deacon – and consequently its willingness to give new life to a permanent diaconate open to married men. The triumph was the restoration. The hope was that a restored diaconate would play a major role in the reform of the Church.

Council of Trent

The Council of Trent met in twenty-five sessions during three distinct periods of time: 1545 to 1547; 1551 to 1552; and 1559 to 1563. It opened on 13 December 1545, in Trent, Italy, and closed on 4 December 1563 in the same city. In 1557, it met for sessions nine, ten and eleven in Bologna. Three popes presided over the Council. They were Paul III, Julius III and Pius IV. Being the Church's official response to the Protestant Reformation, the Council's primary "objective was the order and clarification of Catholic Doctrine, and legislation for a thorough reform of the Church."[2] Never numbering more than 255 at any given session, and quite often far fewer than that, the Council Fathers made formal declarations in the form of canons and decrees on the following: Sacred Scripture, Original Sin, Justification, the Sacraments in general and each one in particular, including three treatments of the Holy Eucharist (on its own terms and then in relationship to Holy Communion and the Sacrifice of the Mass), Purgatory, Saints, Relics and Indulgences. The Fathers also issued ten specific reform declarations titled "On Reformation."

On 9 September 1562, at the end of the twenty-second session, the Council concluded its teaching on the Eucharist and the Sacrifice of the Mass, perhaps its most magisterial accomplishment, and on 15 July 1563, which closed the twenty-third session, it issued its teaching on Holy Orders. That the session on Holy Orders followed immediately after the one on the Eucharist and the Sacrifice of the Mass was not a mere coincidence. The Council Fathers at Trent understood the Sacrament of Order only in terms of the Sacrifice of the Mass. There was an indestructible bond between the two.[3] This understanding would have a profound impact on the Council's approach to the diaconate and the formulation of its teaching on it.

The debate on the diaconate began on 23 September 1562. That it took place at all, according to Father Edward Echlin, SJ, was an achievement in itself.[4] But it would be incorrect for us to imagine that in its brief deliberations on the diaconate the Council Fathers at Trent had in mind what we call a permanent or active diaconate, or that they ever intended to air the additional subject of a married diaconate, regardless of the testimony of sacred Scripture and the practice of the Early Church. If the Church had sanctioned a married diaconate, it would have been a major concession to the Reformers, who had spent a great deal of theological and political capital in their denunciations of clerical celibacy. The debate, then, was more along these lines: to what extent did the Council desire to enrich the role and expand the number of functions proper to deacons as they prepared for ordination to the priesthood? In other words, although the diaconate would remain in essence a necessary transition to the priesthood, and not a stage of ordination independent of the priesthood and the Sacrifice of the Mass, how would the Council define the work of the deacon during that transition period: as something passive or active, and how long would that period last?

The Council had within its ranks many Church Fathers who were hostile to any notion of treating the diaconate as anything more than a step upwards in the hierarchy of Order. They did not seem too inclined to entertain appeals to Scripture, the Church Fathers or the Early Church. The diaconate existed not for the faithful but for the man seeking ordination to the priesthood. This was the prevailing view, the result of centuries of tradition and practice bolstered by the teachings of leading theologians such as St. Thomas Aquinas.

So strong was their collective opposition that even the modest proposal to recognize the right of deacons to preach was handily defeated.[5]

However, there *were* other voices at the Council whose opinions on the diaconate were more generous and expansive within the traditional framework of the Church's understanding of the diaconate. Prominent among these voices was that of the bishop of Ostuni, whose diocese was located in southern Italy. In June 1563, he challenged the Council to restore the functions of subdeacon and deacon:

> I desire the function of the subdeacon and deacon, diligently collected from the writings of the fathers and decrees of the councils, to be restored and put to use, especially the functions of deacons. The Church has always used their services, not only in ministries at the altar, but in baptism, in care of hospitals, of widows, and of suffering persons. Finally, all the needs and concerns of the people are mediated to the bishop by deacons.[6]

The bishop continued by proposing that the period of transition from deacon to priest last from three to four years.[7] Although this proposal on its own was hardly radical, it did reveal the bishop's deeper appreciation of the diaconate. He was aware that the Church Fathers and the early councils had addressed the role of the deacon, that his role extended beyond ministry at the altar to include a wide range of ministry to the faithful, in particular those who were suffering, and that the deacon was the intermediary between the bishop and the faithful. If a deacon were truly a deacon, he would need time to be a deacon before he became a priest, and hence the proposal for a three- to four-year transition period. In a momentary flight of historical fancy, one might want to conclude that the bishop of Ostuni had a notion, however indirect, of the permanent diaconate, but one should be careful not to read the present into the past.

What is more helpful to the historian of the diaconate is the fact that there must have been other bishops at the Council who were in sympathy with the bishop of Ostuni, for how else can one explain the marvellous schema (proposal) of 6 July 1563? It displays an understanding of the diaconate at once so sympathetic and so rich in detail that one cannot help but be struck by its intuitive grasp of the diaconate's vast potential in the reform of the liturgical and charitable life of the Church. (Interestingly, it is the same schema quoted in part by Father Wilhelm Schamoni in his *Married Men as Ordained Deacons*, and referred to by Josef Hornef in his article "The Order of the Diaconate in the Roman Catholic Church.")[8] Father Echlin provides the following translation of the entire proposal:

> It is clear how many and necessary and sacred were the services committed to the order of deacons which is distinct from other orders and the next to the priesthood. They are the eyes of the bishops and special ministers of the church whose office of celebration of sacred mysteries and care of the church should never be lacking. And in the holy sacrifice they offer at the altar the oblations received from the subdeacon. They care for the table of God. They announce the gospel to the people. They assist the consecrating priests. They admonish the people about the solemn rites to be observed in church. They ought to exhort that these raise their hearts and prepare their souls for prayer, and to warn those who intend to be present at the sacrifice to have no adversity among themselves, not hatred, not wrath nor ill will, but mutual charity. The ministry of deacons should be diligent in governing the church. Their office is to guard the preaching bishop lest he be approached by vicious enemies or the divine word be reviled by insults and despised. When the bishop so directs [,] it pertains to deacons to baptize and preach, also to reconcile to the church public penitents in case of necessity and in the absence of the bishop and priests, providing they reconcile without solemnity. Deacons should seek out and care for with real zeal whatever pertains to the corporal assistance of widows, of students, of orphans, of incarcerated, of sick and all afflicted persons, and provide for the spiritual help of the faithful. They have loving concern for all the faithful in works of mercy, especially for those in whom they observe a greater need for their charity.

Therefore this sacred synod considers all these things so necessary that bishops should take care that those things which have been done to this day should be holily and religiously continued. Let them restore with zeal those which were interrupted by negligence, so that the faithful, with the help of God, may more easily attain eternal beatitude.[9]

There is no evidence, however, that the Council of Trent adopted this schema in any of its canons and decrees. Pressed for time because the Council was drawing to a close, and unable to modify what was a prevailing medieval conception of the priesthood, the Council Fathers let pass an opportunity to revitalize the diaconate in a concrete way as part of its reformation of the Church. One can only wonder what the Church might have become if the schema *had* been adopted.

But all was not lost. Something of the intent and, dare we say, spirit, of the schema found its way into Chapter XVII of the "On Reformation" section of Trent's teaching on Holy Orders, dated 15 July 1563:

That the functions of holy orders, from the deacon to the janitor [doorkeeper] – which functions have been laudably received in the Church from the times of the Apostles, and which have been for time interrupted in very many places – may be again brought into use in accordance with the sacred canons; and that they may not be traduced by heretics as useless; the holy Synod, burning with a desire of restoring the pristine usage, ordains that, for the future, such functions shall not be exercised but by those who are actually in the said orders; and It exhorts in the Lord all and each of the prelates of the churches, and commands them, that it be their care to restore the said functions, as far as it can be conveniently done, in the cathedral, collegiate, and parochial churches of their diocese, where the number of people and the revenues of the church can support it; and, to those who exercise those functions, they shall assign salaries out of some part of the revenues of any simple benefices, or those of the fabric of the church – if the funds allow of it –

or out of revenues of both together, of which stipends they may, if negligent, be mulcted in a part, or be wholly deprived thereof, according to the judgment of the Ordinary. And if there should not be unmarried clerics at hand to exercise the functions of the four minor orders [doorkeeper, acolyte, lector and exorcist], their place may be supplied by married clerics of approved life; provided they have not been twice married, be competent to discharge the said duties, and wear the tonsure and the clerical dress in church.[10]

The restoration of the functions of the deacon down to the doorkeeper, and the invitation to laymen to carry out the duties of the four minor orders, never took hold to any significant degree in any Catholic diocese because there was no papal directive on Chapter XVII. Pope St. Pius V implemented many of the Council's teachings. He issued the Roman catechism (1566), a revised Roman breviary (1568) and a revised Roman Missal (1570). Pope Clement VIII issued a revised version of the Vulgate Bible (1592). Also, these two popes and many of their successors vigorously promoted the Council of Trent's teaching concerning the establishment of diocesan seminaries for the training of priests according to established norms for intellectual and spiritual formation, keeping the Church's focus on the vitality of the priesthood. In these five areas, Trent imparted shape and substance to the catechetical, liturgical and intellectual life of the Church that lasted largely intact until the 1960s. But there was no papal implementation of the Council's obvious desire to restore the "pristine usage" of the diaconate. Except for the 1917 Code of Canon Law,[11] the Church would not return to the subject of the diaconate until the Second Vatican Council.

Second Vatican Council

Pope John XXIII declared his intention to convoke an Ecumenical Council on 25 January 1959, a mere three months after his election to the papacy, and he formally convened it with the publication of the Apostolic Constitution *Humanae Salutis*, on 25 December 1961. He died in June 1963, leaving to his successor, Paul VI, the task of shepherding the Council to its end and implementing and defending its many teachings. The Council met in four sessions over four years: 11 October to 8 December 1962; 29 September to 4 December 1963; 14 September to 21 November 1964; and 14 September to 8 December 1965. At one point, more than 2,500 bishops were in attendance. By the close of the Council, the Church Fathers had issued four Constitutions, nine Decrees and three Declarations. The Council's resolution of the debate on the permanent diaconate is found in *Lumen Gentium* #29 and *Ad Gentes Divinitus* #16.

The work of the Council on all matters, including that of the permanent diaconate, comprised three phases: antepreparatory stage, preparatory stage and the acta of the Council, the debates and votes. The antepreparatory stage was a block of time during which the bishops submitted ideas – their personal wish list – for schemata that they wanted discussed by the Council or, on the negative side, their opinions about what the Council should not discuss. In all, they made 8,972 proposals. Of these, 101 pertained to the diaconate, with only eleven opposed to its restoration. Of the remaining ninety proposals on the diaconate, thirty-seven of them, representing 283 dioceses, supported the restoration (one bishop could speak for many bishops, and the bishops from a particular country could act as a bloc); another thirty-seven, representing 138 dioceses, subscribed to a diaconate without the obligation of celibacy; and sixteen, representing seventy-one dioceses, listed the prerequisites and functions of deacons.

Under the category of prerequisites, the bishops spoke about the age of maturity for ordination to the diaconate (forty years old) and the candidate's need to show evidence of Christian spirit, knowledge of dogmatics, morals, scripture and liturgy and experience in catechesis. Under the category of a deacon's functions, we find reference to preaching, baptism, marriage and burials, to distribution of Holy Communion and Viaticum, and to the deacon as assistant at the Eucharist, as presider at exposition of the Blessed Sacrament and as administrator of the Church's temporal goods. Surprisingly, there was also a suggestion to give deacons the right to confer Extreme Unction in the absence of priests.[12]

Taken as a whole, the bishops' positive proposals set high the bar for admission to the diaconate and presented a comprehensive list of functions. The proposals also demonstrate an understanding of the diaconate that was largely tied to the authority of the parish priest and the sacramental needs of parishioners. The deacon's identity would be derived from the parish where he was appointed. No proposal at the antepreparatory stage described the deacon in terms of charitable service outside the bounds of a parish or commented on the relationship between bishop and deacon. However, what is important is that the diaconate *was* on the table, so to speak, and was supported by a range of bishops – from Africa, Latin America, Asia and Europe – that was wide enough to guarantee its inclusion in a schema at the preparatory stage.

The work of the preparatory stage was entrusted to ten commissions, which were overseen by a Central Preparatory Commission. They were created to devise appropriate schemata for the Council's consideration. The status of the diaconate and the minor orders was given primarily, but not exclusively, to the commission *De Disciplina Sacramentorum* (The Discipline of the Sacraments), headed by Cardinal Benedetto Masella. Assisting the commission in his capacity as a theologian was none other than Father Karl Rahner, SJ, the very visible and energetic promoter of the diaconate.[13] We must keep in mind, though, that the diaconate was only one of five topics covered in the commission's draft schema, *De Sacramento Ordinis*, which was presented to the Central Preparatory Commission, on 15–23 January 1962. The other topics were confirmation, confessions and reserved sins, marriage impediments and procedures and priests who had left the ministry.[14]

The Central Preparatory Commission debated the diaconate on 17 January. Cardinal Masella proposed the restoration of the diaconate in the Latin Rite Church and the reduction in the number of minor orders from four to two, lectors and acolytes. Diaconal functions would include liturgical, catechetical and administrative roles. Deacons would be allowed to preach. Ordination of deacons would be open to married men in specific areas where the determination of need would be at the dispensatory discretion of the Holy See. Deacons would be members of the clergy. However, there must be no relaxation in Church law on celibacy for priests. Masella was adamant on that point, in an attempt to obviate any fears that a married diaconate would open the door to a married priesthood. He argued that the rise of the lay apostolate, which was a good sign for the Church, and the decline in the number of priests, especially in mission territory, necessitated the immediate restoration of the permanent diaconate according to the ancient tradition of the Church.[15]

Objections to Masella's proposal on the diaconate were three in number and enough to sink the entire schema. First, a restored diaconate, either celibate or married, might have an unnecessary negative effect on the work of the lay apostolate. Second, a married diaconate might weaken the Church's stance on the law of celibacy for priests. Third, it might hinder vocations to the priesthood. These last two objections resurfaced during the Conciliar debate on the diaconate in October 1963. Of the fifty-six Church Fathers who voted on *De Sacramento Ordinis*, only sixteen voted *placet* (in favour) without any reservations.[16]

In the meantime, two other preparatory commissions submitted reports on the diaconate. The Commission for Oriental Churches, led by Cardinal Amleto Cicognani, submitted a draft schema titled *De Ecclesiae Sacramentis*, and the Commission for the Missions, led by Cardinal Gregorio Agagianian, drew up a schema that for clarity and assertiveness was unmatched by the other two schemata dealing with the diaconate. The Commission for the Missions clarified the distinction between the vocation of priest and that of deacon, asserted that marriage (i.e. a married diaconate) would not devalue priestly celibacy and demanded that diaconal functions should be entrusted only to those ordained to the diaconate. The commission also listed the works of charity as one of the responsibilities of a deacon.[17]

At the preparatory stage, then, any real hope of the diaconate's revival appeared to be dead in the water well in advance of the Council. The Central Preparatory Commission had voted down the schema *De Sacramento Ordinis*, and the work of the other two commissions, at least when it came to the diaconate, seemed unable to carry the matter forward. But was all hope lost? Curiously, the diaconate would make its way onto the Council's agenda via another preparatory commission, *De Doctrina Fidei et Morum*, with Cardinal Alfredo Ottaviani of the curia at its helm. Because the scope of its concerns was so vast, this commission broke up into sub-commissions. One of these sub-commissions drew up what became the first draft of the all-important schema *De Ecclesia*, the forerunner of *Lumen Gentium*, which was presented to the Council Fathers for debate that began on 1 December 1962 and ended six days later. Thus began the third stage of the Conciliar process in regards to the diaconate.

The first draft of *De Ecclesia* was divided into eleven sections, with an appendix on the Virgin Mary. But there was no mention of the diaconate! To what degree its absence was intentional on the part of the sub-commission cannot be determined. The fact that it was not included, however, was an omission too glaring to ignore and, ironically, ended up providing a fortuitous opportunity for the diaconate's supporters to lobby more aggressively and effectively on behalf of not only the diaconate's restoration but also its inclusion in any proposed Constitution on the Church. This marked the beginning of a shift in emphasis in the reasons given for the restoration, from the purely expedient (a shortage of priests) to a theological and historical recognition that, since the time of St. Paul, the diaconate had been a distinct element in the hierarchy of the Church. Any Conciliar teaching on the hierarchy would have to include a section on deacons, regardless of any practical problems or fears that might militate against its revival in the Latin Church.

Events turned in favour of the diaconate's supporters when the Church Fathers rejected the first draft of *De Ecclesia*. They did so prompted by a long list of concerns and criticisms, none of which had anything to do directly with the diaconate. Yet by insisting on a top-to-bottom rewrite of the schema on the Church, the Church Fathers unwittingly but fortuitiously breathed new life into the debate on the diaconate.[18]

After the Conciliar rejection of the schema on the Church, the centre of action shifted to the German bishops. They took ownership of the Council's desires. Working with them behind the scenes to rewrite and restructure *De Ecclesia* were Father Karl Rahner and Father Gérard Philips, a University of Louvain theologian and future historian of the Council. Meeting at Munich, on 5 and 6 February 1963, the German bishops examined Rahner and Philips's revised schema. It was a radical overhaul of the first draft of *De Ecclesia*. Of particular interest to us is the fact that Chapter III of that draft devoted only one paragraph to bishops, one to priests and none to deacons, as if to say that the hierarchy of the Church consisted only of bishops and priests. In response, the two theologians lengthened the section on the priesthood and added two paragraphs, one on the diaconate and one on the minor orders. The bishops approved.

In mid-February, the Rahner-Philips version of *De Ecclesia* was presented to John XXIII and Cardinal Ottaviani. The proposed section on the diaconate was retained, but the one on minor orders was stricken from the text.[19] But the inclusion of the material on the diaconate, a major triumph for the promoters of the restoration, did not go uncontested by the Theological Commission. Here is the text of Paragraph 15 of the second draft of *De Ecclesia* that alarmed so many on the Theological Commission and that would arouse such fierce debate among the Council Fathers:

> Bishops and priests are assisted by deacons, in a lower rank of the hierarchical order. They help with the celebration of the sacrifice (mass), they are the extraordinary ministers of solemn baptism and holy communion, and they may perform various tasks connected with public charity, preaching and administration, as shall be assigned to them by competent authority. Although in the Church today the diaconate is regarded for the most part as a step toward the priesthood, this discipline has not always been in force and is not everywhere in force today. The diaconate can in the future be exercised as a proper and permanent rank in the hierarchy, when the Church considers this advisable for the good of souls, either in certain areas or in all. In which case it belongs to the ecclesiastical authorities to decide whether such deacons shall be bound by the law of celibacy or not.[20]

Appended to the text was a footnote claiming that t
of Trent, on 6 July 1563, had desired something very sin
diaconate. In other words, Paragraph 15, written four hu
after Trent, was nothing new; rather, it was the resurrection of the
original intent of the Church Fathers of the Counter Reformation
to restore the diaconate to its "pristine usage."[21]

In the meantime, Father Rahner replied to the rumblings coming from the Theological Commission, in a special presentation
to the German bishops at Fulda, Germany, 26–29 August 1963.
Rahner's defense was accepted without amendment and sent as an
official communication to the General Secretariat of the Council
before the opening of the second session on 29 September 1963.[22]
This prevented any backdoor attempt to strike or amend Paragraph
15. In the end, the Theological Commission produced a second,
much improved, draft of *De Ecclesia* that was reorganized into four
chapters, with Chapter II dedicated to the constitution of the Church
with an emphasis on the episcopacy.[23] Paragraph 15 was inserted
into Chapter II.

On 1 October 1963, the Church Fathers voted 2,271 to 43 to
accept the entire schema *De Ecclesia* for discussion. The first full-
scale debate on the diaconate began on 4 October and ended on 16
October. It took place alongside the one on episcopal collegiality
and the voting on *Sacrosanctum Consilium* (The Constitution on the
Sacred Liturgy). From contemporary reports, and from historians
of the Council, it is clear that the debate on the diaconate was one
of the most vigorous of the entire Council, much to the surprise
of many observers, such as the American Catholic commentator
Michael Novak, who out of ignorance thought that the diaconate
was a minor matter and of little significance compared to the then
concurrent debate on collegiality, for example.[24]

But that was not how the bishops approached the question,
especially since the diaconate was intended by its promoters to be
treated as "a proper and permanent rank in the hierarchy," a theological novelty for the twentieth-century Church. The possibility
of a married diaconate was another novelty of no small significance,
because a married clergy at any level of the hierarchy in the Latin

Church was positively countercultural in the Catholic world. On both counts, plenty was at stake. Both supporters and opponents produced hard-edged opinions with little wiggle room from various quarters. Those bishops who suspected that the schema's introduction of the possibility of a married diaconate was a "Trojan Horse" threat to the Church's long-held discipline of priestly celibacy generated a great deal of heat in the debating chamber. But to Cardinal Francis Spellman of New York, who was the first to speak on 4 October, goes the distinction of delivering the most censorious rejection of the restoration. For him, the diaconate had no place in the Constitution on the Church.[25]

In all, twenty-five Church Fathers, representing eighty-two Conciliar colleagues, spoke against the restoration, focusing their concerns mainly on celibacy but also on practical matters such as the cost of building seminaries for deacons, and forty-five Church Fathers, representing 755 Conciliar colleagues, spoke in favour of Paragraph 15. They brushed aside fears about the supposed threat of a married diaconate to the Church's tradition of a celibate priesthood, and instead stressed the diaconate's place in the sacrament and hierarchy of Order and the needs of the faithful.[26] Supporters outnumbered opponents by such a wide margin, almost guaranteeing that the Council would approve of the restoration as a minimum measure. But celibate-versus-married diaconate would prove to be a stumbling block right to the end.

In the midst of all the back-and-forth of the debate, and galvanized by Cardinal Spellman's opening remarks, Cardinal Leon Suenens of Mechlin-Brussels, Belgium, delivered what turned out to be a pivotal intervention in support of the renewal of the diaconate, on 8 October 1963. He had ten minutes to make his point:

> I wish to speak in favor of restoring a permanent diaconate. Those who have spoken against it seem at times to have forgotten that this is a question touching the very structure of the Church.

1. We should not begin from a kind of naturalistic realism but from a *supernatural realism*, from a lively faith in the sacramental nature of the diaconate.

I do not wish to stress those issues which are still open questions, such as the pericope dealing with the election of Stephen and the other six (Acts 6:3-6).

However, some things are certain and clearly evident in the New Testament, from the first apostolic Fathers (especially from Clement of Rome and Ignatius of Antioch), from the constant tradition which followed, and from the liturgical books both East and West.

(1) From the time of the apostolic and sub-apostolic Church, certain of the charisms of the sacred ministry were attributed in a specific and fixed way to a grade distinct from the priesthood.

(2) This grade seems to have been set up especially to provide direct help for the bishops (a) in the care of the poor and the proper direction of the community (b) for what might be called the communitarian preparation of the local Church (especially by brotherly love), and for its liturgical preparation *in the breaking of the bread* (Acts 2:42; 4:32-35; Heb. 13:16) to build a real religious community.

If anyone does not see this task of preparation of the community to be a Church as something sacred and necessarily liturgical in its nature, apparently he does not understand the Church as she really is, founded on the sacraments, and this through charisms conferred by the sacrament of orders.

To say that the tasks which are suggested for deacons could just as well be given to laymen is not a valid argument against restoring the diaconate.

It is not a matter of giving these external tasks in any way at all or to any one of the faithful (tasks such as leading prayer, giving catechetical instruction, undertaking social work); these tasks should be given only to him who objectively and adequately has the necessary graces, so that in building a true community there will be no lack of supernatural efficacy. Unless this is true the Church cannot be a true supernatural society, the true Mystical Body of Christ, built up harmoniously on those ministries and graces which the Lord has foreordained.

Furthermore it is not enough to have those gifts and graces which even good laymen may possess through the sacraments of baptism and confirmation and an authentic supernatural spirit.

Since other gifts have been foreordained which are more specifically suited to fulfill the community ministry, they should not be neglected. The Christian community has the right to profit by such gifts which are part of the Church's heritage.

2. Taking these theological principles as a basis, let us see what the actual situation is in different parts of the world.

We hear opposite opinions on this issue. But the objections which have been made to the restoration of the diaconate, though they may have some force in certain circumstances, do not hold everywhere for all people.

Therefore, it is not up to this Council to make a decision which applies everywhere, or to say that the diaconate is or is not necessary for the whole Church. All the Council should do is explicitly envisage at least the possibility of such a stable ministry, not for the whole Church, but only for those regions in which (with the consent of the proper authority) the legitimate pastors consider this restoration to be necessary if the Church is not to decline but grow and flourish.

This is the question put to the conscience of each one of us, Venerable Fathers: will we, by a merely negative decree, refrain from excluding the possibility of this sacred order as a means foreordained by God, used by the Church for many centuries and now extremely necessary for the renewal of the Church?

According to God's plan, the bishop receives from God the fullness and supreme power of the sacred ministry and likewise receives the commission to establish all those supernatural communities which are necessary for his people.

Therefore the bishop has the power of giving to other ministers a share in his powers adequate to deal with the structure of his people and the circumstances of time and place.

The practical need of the diaconate is evident especially in two cases: (1) when there is a very small community forced more and more to live in the diaspora, *i.e.*, separated from every other group of Christians either because of a difference of religion or vast geographical spread or political circumstances; (2) when there are immense throngs of people, especially in the suburbs, for whom it is necessary to restore some awareness of the Church as a family.

There are situations, therefore, in which the Church is given an opportunity to show herself as missionary in the correct and full sense of the word, ready to allow different solutions for different regions as long as they are all compatible with the structures given her by God.

In such cases I would say that the good of the people is a decisive criterion.

3. What we have said so far is an answer to the principal objection against this proposal, namely, the fear that by opening the diaconate to married men, the law of sacred celibacy will be weakened and at the same time the number of vocations to the priesthood will decrease.

But if the diaconate is a gift, if it is a grace, and if the legitimate pastors think it appropriate and opportune to draw from this heritage of grace, then the restoration of the diaconate could in no way diminish the fullness of Christ in the Christian community, but rather should augment it.

The precious witness of clerical celibacy should certainly be protected, in accordance with the ancient and venerable practice of the Latin Church.

But a diaconate with a certain clearly defined relaxation of the law of celibacy is not contrary to this practice. Instead of the negative results which some greatly fear, we may instead hope for quite a few advantages: it is not evident why the number of vocations to the priesthood should diminish. This is an a priori assumption. On the contrary, priestly vocations might well increase in communities which are knit together more closely through deacons, prepared by them and more effectively vitalized by their charisms; priestly vocations themselves will consequently be more sincere and genuine and better tested; perfect chastity *for the kingdom of heaven* will be given greater luster and afford a fuller witness.

In order, then, to conclude on a practical note, I propose that the Fathers be asked to consider this suggestion: Where episcopal conferences judge the restoration of a permanent diaconate opportune, they should be free to introduce it.[27]

Cardinal Suenens's masterful speech effectively ended any significant theological opposition to the general idea of the *restoration* of the permanent diaconate – the diaconate would be restored – but his words failed to quell the misgivings about a married diaconate. His speech was bold and brilliant for his examination of the permanent diaconate in light of the structure of the Church, of history and tradition, of its role in the Eucharistic liturgy and the building of community, of the grace received at ordination, of the bishop's duty to share the fullness of his ministry with other ministers, including deacons, and of the people's right to share in the graces of diaconal work. His speech was less than reassuring in its claims that the restoration of the diaconate did not have to be implemented in every jurisdiction and that vocations to the celibate priesthood would not be adversely affected by a married diaconate.

Once again a confluence of events at the Council kept the matter of the diaconate on everyone's radar screen. Sensing that the Conciliar debate on Chapter II of *De Ecclesia*, which included the debate on the diaconate, might spill over into November, the Council moderators put five propositions to the vote of the assembly on 30 October 1963. Propositions one to four dealt with various aspects of the episcopacy, and proposition five spoke to the diaconate. It read: "that the draft should deal with the opportuneness of restoring the diaconate as a special and stable degree of the sacred ministry, as demanded by the needs of the Church in various lands."[28] The absence of any mention of either celibacy or marriage was deliberate. It allowed the Council Fathers a chance to vote on the broader issue of restoration without being blindsided, yet again, by what was essentially the narrower issue of celibacy.

The vote was decisive. Of the 2,120 ballots cast, 1,588 were *placet* (in favour of the proposition), 525 were *non-placet* (not in favour) and only seven were invalid.[29] After the voting, which also saw the four propositions on the episcopacy approved by huge margins, the Church Fathers returned the entire schema to the Theological Commission for another rewrite.

Eleven months later, the Theological Commission produced the third and final draft of the Constitution on the Church, now called *Lumen Gentium*. Chapter III on the hierarchy (what had been Chapter II in the second draft) was presented to the Church Fathers on 22 September 1964, the same day that the second and final round of debate on the diaconate began. The old sore about celibacy quickly reappeared. Bishop Franjo Franič of Split, in the former Yugoslavia, who had opposed a married diaconate from the very beginning, thundered one last time. He called it dangerous, a threat to the priesthood and priestly vocations. What alarmed him was a provision in the third draft that allowed for the ordination of young unmarried men to the diaconate without the obligation of celibacy. In other words, deacons would be allowed to marry before or after ordination, as they saw fit.[30] Bishop Henríquez Jiménez, auxiliary of Caracas, Venezuela, responded in the affirmative:

> Concerning the possibility of married deacons, the schema restricts itself to leaving the door open. It makes no recommendations. If many members of the assembly have envisaged bestowing the diaconate on fathers of families, few are inclined to confer it on young men without at the same time imposing celibacy.... In what concerns priests, let me affirm that there is no doubt, either theoretically or practically, that

we will not give authorization to ordain married men in the Latin Church....

Would the diaconate be a threat to priestly vocations? No, because they are two different vocations.[31]

A compromise on celibacy was necessary. It was achieved by a process that was applied to the entire text of *Lumen Gentium*. The moderators divided the schema into thirty-nine voting sections. The material on the diaconate, which was #29, was divided into five of those voting sections, 35 to 39, with each section asking a specific question. On 28 September 1964, the Council Fathers voted in the affirmative on Section 35, the office of the deacon, by a margin of 2,035 to 94, and on Section 36, the restoration of the diaconate, this time by a smaller but still impressive margin of 1,903 to 242. On 29 September, the Fathers voted in favour of Section 37, the right of episcopal conferences with the approval of the pope to establish the permanent diaconate, by a margin of 1,523 to 702, and of Section 38, the admission of mature married men to the diaconate, by a margin of 1,598 to 629. Although both votes were more than two to one in favour, the negative votes in each case demonstrated a sizeable hard-core opposition to the whole idea of married deacons. Also on the same day, the Council Fathers voted on Section 39, which dispensed with the law of celibacy for young unmarried men ordained to the diaconate. The assembly responded to this in the negative, by a significant margin of 1364 to 839.[32] In this fashion, the Fathers, mindful of the rancour over celibacy, maintained it for those candidates to the permanent diaconate unmarried at the time of their ordination.

The Council Fathers approved Chapter III in a two-part vote on 30 September 1964. After the Council had approved all eight chapters of *Lumen Gentium*, it was promulgated on 21 November 1964.

Lumen Gentium #29 reads as follows:

At a lower level of the hierarchy are to be found deacons, who receive the imposition of hands "not unto the priesthood, but unto the ministry." For strengthened by sacramental grace they are dedicated to the People of God, in conjunction with the bishop and his body of priests, in the service of the liturgy, of the Gospel and of works of charity. It pertains to the office of a deacon, in so far as it may be assigned to him by the competent authority, to administer Baptism solemnly, to be custodian and distributor of the Eucharist, in the name of the Church, to assist at and to bless marriages, to bring Viaticum to the dying, to read the sacred scripture to the faithful, to instruct and exhort the people, to preside over the worship and the prayer of the faithful, to administer sacramentals, and to officiate at funeral and burial services. Dedicated to the works of charity and functions of administration, deacons should recall the admonition of St. Polycarp: "Let them be merciful, and zealous, and let them walk according to the truth of the Lord, who became servant of all."

Since, however, the laws and customs of the Latin Church in force today in many areas render it difficult to fulfill these functions, which are so extremely necessary for the life of the Church, it will be possible in the future to restore the diaconate as a proper and permanent rank of the hierarchy. But it pertains to the competent local episcopal conferences, of one kind or another, with the approval of the Supreme Pontiff, to decide whether and where it is opportune that such deacons be appointed. Should the Roman Pontiff think fit, it will be possible to confer this diaconal order upon married men, provided they be of more mature age, and also on suitable young men, for whom, however, the law of celibacy must remain in force.[33]

What does *Lumen Gentium* #29 say about the diaconate? It says that the deacon is a member of the Church's hierarchy, albeit at a lower level, and that the laying on of hands at a deacon's ordination is for the ministry and not for the priesthood. At the time of his ordination, the deacon receives the sacramental grace commensurate to his diaconal work, and for that reason his work is on behalf of the People of God (*Lumen Gentium*, Chapter II), in union with the bishop and his priest. In other words, the diaconate is for the faithful, and no deacon carries out his duties on his own initiative but as one who participates in the fullness of the Sacrament of Order, which is exercised by the bishop.

A deacon's work covers three principal areas of activity: the liturgy, the Gospel and the works of charity. Moreover, the diaconate is an office, and to that office belong specific spiritual and practical functions proper to deacons: officiating at Baptisms, the distribution of Holy Communion, taking Viaticum to the sick, witnessing marriages, reading Sacred Scripture (the Gospels) to the assembled, instruction and exhortation (catechesis and preaching), presence at the altar and communal prayer, conducting funerals and burials, involvement in the Church's charitable works and perhaps even administration.

But it is ordination, not a list of functions, which establishes the deacon as a member of the Church's hierarchy. At the same time, if these functions are "necessary for the life of the Church," she is willing to restore the diaconate "as a proper and permanent rank of the hierarchy" (in addition to the diaconate as a transition to the priesthood); to give episcopal conferences the responsibility to decide the worthiness of a restoration for their respective jurisdictions, with the approval of the pope; and to allow married men to become deacons. The retention of celibacy remains for those unmarried at ordination. Such was the hard-won result of four years of debate, amendment and voting among the Church Fathers, and, before the Council, many years of hope, discussion, prayer, petition and publication of opinions and memoirs on the subject.

What Lumen Gentium #29 does not spell out is the defining or special characteristic of the diaconal ministry, the one feature that ties the deacon to the bishop, from whom he receives the imposition of hands, and at the same time distinguishes the diaconate from the priesthood. A hint as to what the diaconal ministry's defining or special characteristic might be is found in the quotation from St. Polycarp, who instructed deacons to walk "according to the truth of the Lord, who became servant of all."[34] In their active imitation of Christ, "the servant of all," deacons must be servants of all. The use of this passage from St. Polycarp in Lumen Gentium kick-started what has evolved into an intense and mostly positive dialogue within diaconate circles about the servant-character of their recently re-established ministry within the Church.

The history of the clarification of the meaning of the servant-character of the diaconate, rooted in the servant-character of Christ and the Church that he founded, commenced in the post-Conciliar documents on the diaconate. It was subsequently picked up by a small army of theologians and historians of the diaconate anxious to discover and elucidate every scriptural and Patristic reference to deacons as office-holders, in the hope of confirming the servant-character of the diaconate.

Nor did the Church Fathers have much to say, even indirectly, on the history, tradition or theology of the diaconate. In fairness to them, that was not their task, which was to deliver the Church's teaching on the one Sacrament of Order.

Lastly, the Church Fathers said nothing about the norms necessary for the restoration of the permanent diaconate, in particular the criteria for the selection of candidates for diaconal ministry, their formation and the Church's expectations of them as members of the clergy. All that would come later from Paul VI.

Complementing the material on the diaconate in *Lumen Gentium* was the final paragraph of *Ad Gentes Divinitus* #16:

> Whenever it appears opportune to episcopal conferences, the diaconate should be restored as a permanent state of life, in accordance with the norms of the Constitution on the Church. It would help those men who carry out the ministry of deacon – preaching the word of God as catechists, governing scattered Christian communities in the name of the bishop or parish priest, or exercising charity in the performance of social or charitable works – if they were to be strengthened by the imposition of hands which has come down from the apostles. They would be more closely bound to the altar and their ministry would be made more fruitful through the sacramental grace of the diaconate.[35]

Two points in this paragraph are of interest to us. First, in this passage we find that the diaconate is now a fourfold ministry. In addition to the liturgy, the Word and the works of charity, as found in *Lumen Gentium* #29, there is the governance of "scattered Christian communities," if deemed necessary. This reminds one of the thinking of Father Wilhelm Schamoni (see Chapter 1). The inclusion of governance of "scattered Christian communities" as properly belonging to the diaconal ministry, along with liturgy, Word and charity, created opportunities for a new era in local parish leadership, but ironically not to any significant degree in mission territories, the original concern. Rather, those opportunities would appear in parishes without priests in North America and Europe, and in the Church's concern for all those individuals or groups of people who, being on the margins of parochial ministry for whatever reason, are scattered communities in need of Christian ministry.

Second, diaconal ministry can and often does precede ordination, but the graces of sacramental ordination to the diaconate will make that ministry more fruitful. Or, to put it more strongly, it would be best if all those doing diaconal ministry were ordained to the diaconate. Father Karl Rahner would have approved.[36]

Paul VI formally closed the Second Vatican Council on 8 December 1965, the Feast of the Immaculate Conception. To him fell the enormous and perhaps thankless duty of initiating and sustaining the implementation of the Council's many teachings. Despite his initial opposition to the restoration of the permanent diaconate, as a member of the Central Preparatory Commission in 1962, Paul VI was responsible for giving the diaconate the papal direction and support that it needed if the restoration were to take place in a fruitful and meaningful manner for the faithful.

Post-Conciliar Documents

On 18 June 1967, Paul VI issued *Sacrum Diaconatus Ordinem*, which set down broad norms for the restoration of the diaconate in accordance with the mind of the Council Fathers in *Lumen Gentium* #29 and *Ad Gentes Divinitus* #16.[37] Where Trent had failed, the

Second Vatican Council would succeed. This is Paul VI's enduring legacy to the permanent diaconate as we experience it today.

After an introduction, in which the pope reaffirmed the indispensable role of episcopal conferences in the establishment of the permanent diaconate, he continued by listing the norms for the following areas: the work of episcopal conferences in union with the pope; the diaconate for young (unmarried) men; the diaconate for older (married) men; incardination of diocesan deacons and their maintenance by the diocese; diaconal functions; the character and qualities expected of deacons, their prayer life (Divine Office), continuing education and their relationship to the bishop; deacons in religious communities; and the forthcoming rites of ordination to the diaconate.

Special consideration should be given to the fact that Paul VI opened *Sacrum Diaconatus Ordinem* with references to passages from two of St. Paul's letters that expressly mention deacons: Philippians 1:1 and 1 Timothy 3:8-13. These passages firmly anchor the diaconate as an office in the Early Church to the witness of Scripture. If there had been no mention of deacons in Scripture, the Sacrament of Order would not include the diaconate.

Special consideration should also be given to the pope's use of two Patristic sources on the diaconate. The first is a quotation from the letter of St. Ignatius of Antioch to the Trallians. It appears at the end of this sentence: "[The diaconate] is not to be considered merely a step toward the priesthood but rather it is so enhanced by its own indelible character and particular grace, that those who are called to it can firmly dedicate themselves as 'dispensers of Christ's mysteries and servants of the Church.'"[38] The full sentence reads: "The deacons too, who serve the mysteries of Jesus Christ, must be men universally approved in every way; since they are not mere dispensers of meat and drink, but servants of the church of God, and therefore under obligation to guard themselves against any slur or imputation as strictly as they would against fire itself."[39] The second Patristic source is from St. Irenaeus's *Against Heresies*, in which he describes St. Stephen as "the first to be chosen by the Apostles for the ministry of service."[40]

Paul VI is making a point here. He is linking the office of deacon to the ministry of service, the latter framing our understanding of the former. As a result, he is cautiously intimating that the defining or special characteristic of the diaconate is service. He would be more explicit on this matter in his next Apostolic Letter on norms for the diaconate.

On 15 August 1972, Paul VI issued *Ad Pascendum*. Three characteristics of this Apostolic Letter are worth noting. First, it was far less prescriptive and a great deal more theological and even meditative in its approach to norms for the diaconate than *Sacrum Diaconatus Ordinem*.[41]

Second, it made extensive use of Patristic sources. After paraphrasing Philippians 1:1 and 1 Timothy 3:8-13 to show once again the diaconate's scriptural underpinnings, Paul VI either quoted or referred to the works of St. Ignatius of Antioch, St. Polycarp, St. Justin Martyr, Tertullian, St. Cyprian and St. Augustine and to the *Didascalia Apostolorum* and the *Apostolic Tradition* of St. Hippolytus. The diaconate was very much an integral part of the liturgical and charitable life of the Early Church.

Finally, Paul VI treats the theme of the servant-character of the diaconate by resorting to the Gospel of Matthew. The first instance is Matthew 20:26-27, which is quoted in the *Didascalia Apostolorum*: "Anyone who wants to be great among you must be your servant." The full text reads: "Anyone among you who aspires to greatness must serve the rest, and whoever wants to rank first among you must serve the needs of all."[42] The second is Matthew 20:28. The first verse in its entirety reads: "Such is the case with the Son of Man who has come, not to be served by others, but to serve, to give his own life as a ransom for the many."[43] These words are the summation of Paul VI's most categorical statement on the intimate and spiritually dynamic relationship between the Church's mission of service, the diaconate and the people of God, going so far as to use *diakonia*, which is Greek for service. (The Greek word *diakonos* means servant, and from it derives the English word "deacon." The infinitive is *diakonein*, which means to serve.)

The Second Vatican supported the wishes and requests that, where such would lead to the good of souls, the permanent diaconate should be restored as an intermediate order between the higher ranks of the Church's hierarchy and the rest of the people of God, as an expression of the needs and desires of the Christian communities, as a driving force for the Church's service or *diaconia* towards the local Christian communities, and as a sign or sacrament of the Lord Christ himself, who "came not to be served but to serve."[44]

The permanent deacon is many things, and as such is indispensable to the right ordering of the spiritual and material life of the Christian community. As a member of the one Sacrament of Order, he is situated not on the bottom rung of a ladder designed for ascending but between the bishops and priests, on the one hand, and the people of God, on the other, serving both in myriad ways. But he is more than just a go-between; he is an "expression" – an embodiment – of the needs and desires of the people; he is "a driving force for the Church's service" – a man of action and deeds, a leader, a problem solver in the everyday world; and he is a "sign and sacrament of the Lord Christ himself" – a living icon of the Deacon of deacons. The deacon is a servant in the Church and the world. Paul VI set the permanent diaconate on the high road of Catholic idealism, a road of self-discovery and practical implementation in the twentieth-century vineyard of the Lord.

To conclude the papal program for the restoration of the permanent diaconate, Paul VI issued *Ministeria Quaedam*, also on 15 August 1972.[45] By this Apostolic Letter, Paul VI stopped the practice of tonsure, reinforcing the teaching of the Council that "entrance into the clerical state is joined to the diaconate."[46] The minor orders are to be called ministries, and they "may be committed to lay Christians." They are "no longer to be regarded as reserved to candidates of the sacrament of orders,"[47] but they must be received and exercised for a suitable period of time by them prior to ordination. In the Latin Church, these ministries are acolyte and lector. Finally, the major order of subdiaconate was abolished.

One might be forgiven if one assumed that it took the above three Apostolic Letters from Paul VI to prod episcopal conferences to examine the Council's teaching on the permanent diaconate and to launch investigations on the feasibility of its introduction in their respective jurisdictions. Actually, there were episcopal conferences that commenced their investigations even before the appearance of the first Apostolic Letter, *Sacrum Diaconatus Ordinem*, in 1967. The Canadian Catholic Conference (now the Canadian Conference of Catholic Bishops, the CCCB) is counted among them. The CCCB took *Lumen Gentium* #29 very much to heart.

3

CANADIAN CONFERENCE OF CATHOLIC BISHOPS: 1966–1972

Introduction

After two years of intensive study and consultation, the episcopal ad hoc committee on the diaconate in Canada recommended to its colleagues in the Canadian Conference of Catholic Bishops (CCCB) that they re-establish the permanent diaconate in Canada for both married and non-married deacons on the basis of diocesan need. The committee delivered its recommendation at the Plenary Assembly held in Winnipeg, on 23–27 September 1968. Making the case on behalf of the committee were its two chairmen, Archbishop Albert Sanschagrin, OMI, of Ste-Hyacinthe, Québec, and Bishop Remi De Roo, of Victoria, British Columbia. During the course of their presentation, the two bishops outlined to the assembly the steps in the documentation produced by the committee by which it had reached its final recommendation. The primary document was the 126-page *Guidelines of the Episcopal Committee on the Permanent Diaconate*, which included a seven-part questionnaire. (Since this work was commonly referred to as the *Guidance Manual*, which appears on the cover, it will be referred to by that title here.) A copy of the *Guidance Manual* was delivered to every Canadian bishop in December 1967. Next, hundreds of copies were distributed to Catholics across Canada. These recipients were specifically asked to respond to the questionnaire. The tabulation of the results of their answers forms the second most important document produced by the committee.

The committee had thoroughly prepared the bishops for the vote they were about to take. Before it was taken, however, Archbishop Sanschagrin and Bishop De Roo suggested to the assembly that any restoration should proceed cautiously, beginning with several pilot projects, and that any pilot projects be carried out under the direction of one of the CCCB's commissions, such as the Commission for Clergy and Seminaries.

We are inclined to believe that these two suggestions, on the surface entirely practical and reasonable, were really aimed at assuaging any last-minute misgivings that the bishops might have had about the potential folly of rushing into something so new and obviously experimental, despite all the scripture, theology and Church history supporting it. People's instincts can be suspicious of anything novel, and there was little else more novel in the Church in 1968 than the proposition of a married diaconate.[1] To what degree, then, would the Catholic faithful, including Catholic opinion makers, interpret the introduction of a diaconate separate and distinct from the priesthood, *and* a married clergy – albeit limited to deacons married before ordination – as an "invention" on the part of the bishops to compensate in advance for the inevitable dearth in the number of diocesan priests? That niggling question, or different versions of it, must have bothered some of the bishops and made them pause.

At a time of seemingly constant change in the Church, one more new direction from the bishops, no matter how genuine, might prove too much for Church members, ensuring an early and ignominious demise for the diaconate. It died once before. It could die again, this time a stillborn in the hands of its episcopal midwives. The solution was simple. A thorough catechesis of priests and people on the sacramental nature of the diaconate would be necessary to obviate any such unfortunate outcome. But in September 1968, catechesis was not at the top of any episcopal agenda. What mattered most that year was the restoration of the diaconate as envisioned by the Church Fathers in *Lumen Gentium* #29 and in Paul VI's motu proprio

Sacrum Diaconatus Ordinem. The resolution of any problems, either anticipated or unforeseen, in the diocesan implementation of the episcopal will to restore the diaconate in Canada would flow from the fact of its restoration. This was in keeping with the approach of the Church Fathers at the Council, who restored the diaconate without too much thought about theology or practicalities.

In the end, Archbishop Sanschagrin and Bishop De Roo, if they ever worried about the outcome of the vote, need not have worried too much. After reminding their brother bishops that a two-thirds majority was required for the CCCB to seek confirmation of its decision from the Holy See, the assembly overwhelmingly voted for restoration. The final tally of the secret ballot was 57 *placet* (in favour), 7 *non-placet* (not in favour), and 3 *juxta modum* (in favour but with specific reservations). There was one spoiled ballot.[2] Given Archbishop Philip Pocock's subsequent enthusiasm for the permanent diaconate, it is safe to say that he was one of those fifty-seven bishops who voted *placet*.

The vote, well over the two-thirds majority, vindicated the rigorous work of the ad hoc committee and coincidentally guaranteed the Canadian hierarchy an honoured standing in the vanguard of the European-led diaconate movement. The bishops had given themselves, and by extension, the entire Catholic community, an unmistakable mandate to move forward on the restoration of an office in the Church that was at once both ancient and new. It was ancient because it had been central to the life of the Early Church, and it was new for twentieth-century Catholics because it had not been "a proper and permanent rank of the hierarchy" for more than a thousand years. Of all the many gifts that the Church Fathers of the Second Vatican Council, in concert with the Holy Spirit, bequeathed to the Catholic faithful, the institution of the permanent diaconate has proven to be one of the most enduring and fruitful.

But that was far in the future. Let us return to September 1968. In what can only be described as one of those events that turns everything upside down and rewrites the script for historians, the CCCB's decision to restore the permanent diaconate was buried under an avalanche of controversy caused by the "Winnipeg

Statement," which had nothing to do with the diaconate. The "Winnipeg Statement" was the response of the Canadian bishops to Paul VI's encyclical *Humanae vitae*, which was issued in July 1968. In the ensuing and oftentimes confusing debate over what constituted official Catholic teaching on artificial birth control, any chance of celebrating the diaconate's restoration, a truly historic moment in the history of the Church in Canada, was lost.

However, perhaps that was all to the good for the future chances of the permanent diaconate. Temporary obscurity can provide the right tonic for the right idea to flourish, quietly and steadily, far from the madding crowd of critics and commentators. As soon as Rome had given its approval of the CCCB's decision on restoration in January 1969, the ad hoc committee disbanded, and the Episcopal Commission on Clergy and Seminaries was given the assignment of overseeing the publication of interim guidelines on the diaconate for diocesan use.

This chapter will examine in detail the work of the ad hoc committee from 1966 to 1969, and then briefly that of the Episcopal Commission on Clergy and Seminaries from 1969 to 1971. The committee's two publications were absolutely essential to those bishops who chose, for their own reasons, to organize the permanent diaconate in their respective dioceses. During this period, few Catholics in Canada, including the clergy, knew much about the diaconate, its place of honour in the Early Church, the German and French thinkers and doers behind its renaissance during the years after the Second World War, or the theology justifying and sustaining its restoration at the Council and its subsequent acceptance by the CCCB. And no one in the Canadian Church, at this particular juncture, had any experience in the selection, education and formation of permanent deacons.

The Ad Hoc Committee on the Diaconate in Canada 1966 to 1969

Archbishop Albert Sanschagrin, OMI, and Bishop Remi De Roo were the prime movers of the two-year process that led to the CCCB's approval of the restoration of the permanent diaconate in Canada.[3] It began without fanfare. During the week leading up to the Plenary Assembly of 12–14 October 1966, the two bishops invited any interested colleagues to form a discussion group on the diaconate. As a result of their freewheeling exchange, the bishops agreed to present the following motion for the assembly's consideration:

> That a provisional committee be set up to undertake a study of the conciliar texts relating to the permanent diaconate and the implications for Canada in this respect.[4]

The bishops adopted the motion unanimously and directed Archbishop Louis Levesque of Rimouski, Québec, president of the CCCB, to organize a committee at his own discretion. On 19–20 January 1967, the administrative council of the CCCB ratified the nominations to the ad hoc committee on the diaconate in Canada. There were six bishops, three French and three English, and two theologians, both of whom were French. Archbishop Sanschagrin and Bishop De Roo became co-chairmen and were joined by Archbishop Joseph Wilhelm of Kingston, Archbishop James Hayes of Halifax, Bishop Lionel Audet, auxiliary of the Archdiocese of Québec, and Bishop Gérard Couturier of Hauterive, Québec. The theologians were Father Bernard Lambert, OP, of Québec, and Father J.M.Tillard, OP, of Ottawa. In April, two theologians were added to the roster: Father Tibor Horvath, SJ, of Toronto (Willowdale), and Father John Hochban, SJ, of Halifax. In all likelihood, Archbishop Hayes was responsible for bringing Father Hochban on board; he would be involved in the early days of the diaconate program in the Archdiocese of Toronto.[5]

Over two years, the committee met six times in four different cities – three times in Ottawa and one time each in Toronto, Ste-Hyacinthe and Montréal – and it produced five extensive reports and the *Guidance Manual*, the centrepiece of its investigations and a work of lasting significance. Also, the CCCB sent Archbishop Sanschagrin as its representative to a meeting in Rome of bishops from seventeen countries that were considering the diaconate, on 21–23 February 1967. Paul VI called them together to discuss the third draft of proposed canonical legislation on the diaconate. Some of their work found its way into Paul VI's motu proprio *Sacrum Diaconatus Ordinem* of 18 June 1967.[6]

The minutes of the ad hoc committee's first meeting, 27 January 1967, are extensive and surprisingly revealing. The members were able to thrash out some very basic notions of the task at hand and should be applauded for the clarity of their conclusions so early in their work as a committee. They aimed to concentrate "on the theology and history *of the structure and the form for the Diaconate in the 20th century and for Canada's needs*."[7] To that end, their stated objectives were to discover two things: "the exact nature and the mission of the Diaconate"[8] – the theological and theoretical – and "the service that it is called to give to this country and according to the needs of the dioceses"[9] – the practical, the here and now in the everyday world, the pastoral work of the local Church. The investigation of the theological and the practical went hand in hand.

And central to the committee's endeavours to discover these things was their upfront definition of the *specific characteristic of the diaconate*, that one vital feature that distinguishes the diaconate from the priesthood, and the diaconate from the apostolate of the laity, in terms of the service that each renders, in union with the bishop, to the spiritual and material needs of the world. (I put the phrase *specific characteristic of the diaconate* in italics in order to highlight a thematic thread that holds together the debate on the unique sacramental identity of the deacon.) According to Father Lambert, one of the committee's theologians, that *specific characteristic* must be defined as "service in the name of the community, service consecrated by a sacramental order."[10] As a member of the hierarchy of the Church, the deacon is at the service of the Church, and since the Church is at the service of the world, the deacon is also at the service of the world. The deacon is "the *minister* of a particular service within the ensemble of pastoral action of the local or universal Church."[11] What exactly a deacon's particular service might be was left unexplored at this preliminary stage of discussion. But the phrase "particular service of the deacon" would resurface in the *Guidance Manual* when the committee attempted to come to a more refined understanding of the *specific characteristic of the diaconate*.

To its credit, the committee never lost sight of its two main objectives – an exploration of the relationship between the theological and the practical, and the search for a more precise definition of the *specific characteristic of the diaconate* – and thus avoided falling into needless confusion and taking others with it. To a significant extent, the framework of the *Guidance Manual* rested on the preliminary insights generated by the committee meeting of 27 January 1967. When it came to the relationship between the theological and the practical, the *Guidance Manual* remained generally consistent with the committee's original intentions. But the same cannot be said for the committee's attempt to shed light on the *specific characteristic of the diaconate*. It went off in many directions and had to settle for a definition that, while of value in the ongoing and expanding dialogue on the diaconate, fell short of the kind of clarification that the subject needed and did not receive until Father Horvath of the committee published his "Theology of a New Diaconate" in 1968.[12]

In the lead-up to writing the *Guidance Manual*, the committee contacted and shared information with diaconal movements in France, Germany and the United States. One of its German contacts was none other than the pioneer Hannes Kramer of Frieburg-im-Breslau.[13] Correspondence with these groups, and any documentation forwarded by them, were archived in a separate file[14] and most likely were used by the committee when it wrote the "Historical Summary of the Restoration of the Diaconate." This served as the Introduction to the *Guidance Manual*. It displays an excellent knowledge of the leaders of the European diaconal movement and refers to many of their seminal publications.

At the same time, Father Tillard submitted his "Theological Notes on Council Texts Concerning the Diaconate" in advance of the meeting of the Plenary Assembly on 3 April 1967.[15] This essay became Chapter IV of the *Guidance Manual* and successfully jump-started the committee's work on the entire project. The result of considerable reflection and intellectual maturity on the subject of the diaconate, and obviously written in advance of the formation of the committee, "Theological Notes" was probably one of the reasons why Father Tillard was a member of the committee. He sums up the six essential characteristics of the diaconate:

1. A service in the name of Christ-the-Diakonos
2. Consecration by a participation in the sacrament of Orders
3. Performed for our Father and for men
4. Within the third degree of the hierarchy
5. As a minister of the liturgy, the Word and charity
6. With a view to the pastoral communication of the mystery of the whole Christ to the world.[16]

For good measure, Father Tillard reworked his six-point summation by focusing on the relationship between the bishop and the deacon and the all-important meaning of sacramental ordination for the diaconate:

> The ordination of the deacon is a sacrament. By the imposition of hands, the bishop recognizes in the name of the Church the call of the Holy Spirit. He consecrates the candidate to a sacred service in the ministry of the liturgy, the Word and charity. He unites him to the hierarchy and disposes him to receive the charisms necessary for the diaconal ministry.[17]

Next was a definition of diaconal ministry according to the official functions of a deacon in *Lumen Gentium* #29.

We will revisit Father Tillard's Chapter IV when we take another look at the nettlesome topic of the *specific characteristic of the diaconate*.

As for the *Guidance Manual* as a whole, the committee set two aims, which were similar to the stated objectives of its meeting of 27 January 1967, and divided the work into two parts. The first aim was "to set forth the true nature of the diaconate by separating essential elements from accidental solutions."[18] This process unfolded in Part One, which was the "theoretical exposition of the diaconate under its general aspects."[19] The members put the diaconate under the microscope of history, scripture and theology. Their treatment of each of these broad categories can be found in Chapter I: The Texts of Vatican II on the Diaconate; Chapter II: The Diaconate in the New Testament; Chapter III: An Historical Survey of the Diaconate in the Church from the 1st to the 20th Century; Chapter IV: Theological Notes on Council Texts Concerning the Diaconate; Chapter V: An Analysis of the Document of the Holy See on "The Sacred Order of the Diaconate" (motu proprio *Sacrum Diaconatus Ordinem*); and Chapter VI: The Introduction of the Diaconate into the Pastoral Activity of the Church. The next two chapters investigated the diaconate in relationship to the Orthodox Church, the Reformed churches, religious communities and secular institutes. The ninth and final chapter was a detailed recapitulation of Part One in question-and-answer format.

A few words should be said about Chapter III: An Historical Survey of the Diaconate in the Church from the 1st to the 20th Century. It was an early example of a type of historical survey of the diaconate that has become a staple feature of every major work on the diaconate.[20] Father Tibor Horvath wrote this chapter.[21] In it, he wanted to demonstrate the "historical development of the *functions* [my emphasis] of the diaconate"[22] by employing subject categories derived from documentary evidence from all available sources and presenting them and the supporting evidence in chronological order. His categories were for the most part diaconal functions as they evolved over the centuries: service of the bishop; helper in breaking the bread; teachers and prophets; distributing communion; administering sacraments; fourth-century polemics between deacons and presbyters; Eucharistic celebration; baptism; celibacy; maintenance of deacons; fifth-century missionary mobility; charitable works; liturgy; age of ordination; helper of the priest; and the modern-day restoration of the diaconate.

Highlights of the documentary evidence used by Father Horvath to support his categories include a wide range of scriptural, patristic and historical sources. They are Philippians 1:1 and 1 Timothy 3:3-13; the *Didache* #15; Polycarp, Letter to the Philippians; the *Apostolic Constitutions*; the letters of Ignatius of Antioch; *The Shepherd of Hermes*; the *Apostolic Tradition* of Hippolytus; Irenaeus, *Against Heresies*; Clement, Letter to the Corinthians; Justin Martyr, *First Apology*; Tertullian of Carthage, *On Baptism*; Cyprian of Carthage; *Didascalia Apostolorum*; *Pseudo-Clementine*, various works; the *Codex*

Canonum Ecclesiasticorum; Isidore of Pelusium; Clement of Alexandria; Cyril of Jerusalem; Council of Elvira; Council of Nicea; Council of Agde; Gregory the Great; and Leo the Great.

Father Horvath refined and reworked Chapter III to a considerable degree in the above-mentioned "Theology of a New Diaconate."[23] Included in the article are two intriguing assertions. First, the seven chosen by the Apostles in Acts 6:1-7 were not the first deacons in the Church, a tradition started by Ireneaus in the late second century that over time only grew in influence. The word *diakonia* (service) appears twice in this passage, but the word *diakonos* (servant) is never used to describe the seven. More likely, according to Father Horvath, the seven were "the first bishops of the Hellenistic Church which the Twelve visited from time to time to show their union with Jerusalem (Acts 8:14-25)."[24] By making this claim, Father Horvath sidestepped a growing and distracting controversy concerning the selection of the seven in Acts and the institutional origins of the diaconate.

Second, the commencement of the gradual decline of the diaconate in the fifth century coincided with

> the introduction of the presbyterate as a new form of diaconate or service to the bishop. The presbyterate was successfully adapted to a changed situation caused by the growth of the Church while the diaconate never had a similar re-creation adapted to the new situation introduced by the new "diaconal" presbyterate.[25]

In other words, in terms of service to the bishop, or as the bishop's helper, the presbyterate superseded the diaconate, over time reducing it from a permanent rank in the hierarchy to a temporary or transitional one, as the penultimate step on the way to priestly ordination. Although the Church Fathers of the Second Vatican Council restored the permanent diaconate, they left the difficult chore of finding a suitable working definition of its *specific characteristic* to theologians of the post-Conciliar era. That the establishment of such a definition was necessary to the viability of the permanent diaconate in the long run was without question a matter of some urgency.

The second aim of the *Guidance Manual* was "to discover how to bring about a confrontation of principles and actual pastoral solutions."[26] The word "confrontation" is rather odd because it implies a struggle between opposing forces that may or may not lead to a resolution. Perhaps the following phrase might have been clearer: "to discover the link between principles (theology or theory) and practice." In any event, the committee devoted Part Two, described as "the stages and means to be considered to arrive at practical results,"[27] to an examination of this second aim.

The centrepiece of Part Two was the seven-part questionnaire, which asked respondents for their opinions on the utility of the *Guidance Manual* and what, if anything, the committee should recommend to the bishops. In a sense, the answers given by the respondents, when broken down into simple percentages, became a necessary bellwether for the committee's final report to the bishops on 30 August 1968. But we will not deal with the questionnaire and its results until we have dealt with the fundamental theological concepts of the *Guidance Manual*, which will return us to our discussion of the *specific characteristic of the diaconate* and point the way to Father Horvath's resolution of that particular conundrum.

The fundamental theological concepts in the *Guidance Manual* are three in number. First, the diaconate belongs to the one Sacrament of Order and, as such, is a member of the hierarchy of the Church: bishop, priest and deacon. Second, the Church is a Servant-Church, modelled on Christ-the-Servant, who is Head of the Church. This is based upon Matthew 20:28 – "Such is the case of the Son of Man who has come, not to be served by others, but to serve, to give his own life as a ransom for the many." This has become a much-quoted text in diaconate circles. The introduction of the concept of the Servant-Church in the discussion on the diaconate anticipates Paul VI's motu proprio *Ad Pascendum* (1972), which also quoted this passage from Matthew as proof of the Church's servant character.[28] Third, because of the diaconate's participation in the one Sacrament of Order and its membership in the hierarchy of the Church, the diaconate takes as its model Christ-the-Servant, the Head of the Servant-Church, as it participates in the *diakonia* of the bishop – in the service of the liturgy, Word, charity and community (small parishes and missions), with a special emphasis on the pastoral works of charity.

What, then, is the *specific characteristic of the diaconate* that distinguishes the diaconate from the priesthood (which also shares in the *diakonia* of the bishop) and, for that matter, from the laity, which by virtue of their baptism are called to participate in the Servant-Church? The answer had to be something more than the mere word "service," because all Christians are called to service.

The *Guidance Manual* addressed this question in many ways. As we have already noted, it spoke of the diaconate's essential characteristics and the many duties of deacons.[29] It also spoke of the diaconate's specific official function,[30] its distinctive feature,[31] its special characteristic[32] and the particular service of the deacon.[33] At times, its use of the word "function" was quite confusing. Interestingly, the closest that the *Guidance Manual* came to defining the *specific characteristic of the diaconate* can be found in Father Tillard's Chapter IV, one of the earliest pieces written by a committee member:

> The People of God, in their entirety, have the mission to be in the midst of the world as a visible and efficacious sign of the salvation of humanity, that is to say of the love of the Father for men. The Church of Vatican II is a Church in which the entire community of the faithful is called to put itself at the service of the world. This does not mean that it is to be without one who has as his specific official function to bear witness in all his activities of the service of the love of Christ for his brothers. The *diaconate* is earmarked to the service of the manifestation of this charity of God toward the world. Thus is understood how the deacon has pre-eminently the task of developing the diaconal spirit of the whole ecclesiastical community, both on the corporate and individual level. The deacon gives witness of the Church as the world-in-Christ (which is the immanent aspect of its function of service.) It manifests also the Church as a

sign of the future Kingdom, that is to say, it bears witness to the difference between the Church and the world (which corresponds to the transcendental aspect of its service) and thus shows the Church as ideal for men.

One cannot say: to the priesthood the spiritual, to the laity the temporal, without falling into a dualism contrary to the plan of God. The diaconate serves as a liaison between the Church and the world, the clergy and the laity, and thus it exemplifies the charity of the Father for the Church and the world. To be a connecting link is part and parcel of the diaconal function. Certainly, the deacon has not like the priest or bishop the power to consecrate. His intermediary rôle is, as it were, a hinge, swinging between the descending mediation of the priest and the bishop and the ascending mediation which rises from the brotherhood [the laity]. He distributes the gifts of the altar to which he has been associated, but which he has not consecrated; on the other hand, he brings to the altar the fraternal service in which he has taken part as deacon.

Every priest, it is true, is mediator between God and man. The priest receives the offerings and offers them to God. He gives to men the gifts of God. The deacon also occupies a place in this dual relationship, but with a position proper to his rank. Thus he contributes to the mediating officiality of the priest. The intermediary between the Magisterium, the priesthood and the faithful as regards the Word, in all its forms – kerygma, didaché, didaskalia – intermediary between the love of God and the needs of men (especially the impoverished), is the means by which the deacon takes part in the hierarchical mediation of service. This intermediary mediation of the deacon's rôle distinguishes it from the general mediation of all the faithful who intercede for one another in all forms of service in the Church and in the world. The diaconal mediation contributes to the unity and complementarity of all meditative aspects in the single organism of the Church.[34]

In a word, the deacon is an intermediary – between the bishop and the faithful, between the priest and the faithful and between the Church and the world, with the pastoral works of charity the deacon's special, although not exclusive, domain in the life of the Church as it intersects with the world. That is what makes him a deacon. Being an intermediary distinguishes him from bishop, priest and the laity. That is Father Tillard's understanding of what we have been calling the *specific characteristic of the deacon*, even if he never employed that phrase, and we must assume that at the time of the printing of the *Guidance Manual* in 1967, the committee as a whole supported his theology on this matter. Implicit in his view is that diaconal ordination and membership in the hierarchy of the Church are necessary conditions of our understanding of what a deacon is.

Father James F. McDonnell would torpedo the theology of the deacon-as-intermediary in a 1976 thesis on the permanent diaconate, claiming among other things that the *Guidance Manual* assumed rather than demonstrated that the Church requires that the special function of the deacon is to act as an intermediary between those who minister and those to whom they minister, and that "if it be admitted that the deacon is himself a member of the body of ministers in the Church, then this special function appears as somewhat of a tautology, and very difficult to validate."[35] Be that as it may, the point is that the *Guidance Manual*, as a working document for a rather limited readership in the Canadian Church – bishops, theologians, heads of religious communities and anyone else invited to read it in connection with the questionnaire – made a valiant attempt to define the *specific characteristic of the diaconate* because its authors knew that failure to do so would doom the diaconate's restoration.

Coincidentally, Father McDonnell refers the reader of his thesis to Father Horvath's "Theology of a New Diaconate," describing it as "an extensive treatment of the specific function of the diaconate in light of the Christological and sacramental dimensions of the ordained ministry in the Church."[36] It certainly is. But because Father Horvath's work was personal and not official, and consequently did not fit into the thematic structure of Father McDonnell's thesis, Father McDonnell did not feel obliged to give it any space in the body of his own work. However, no such impediment prevents us from examining Father Horvath's approach to the question of the *specific characteristic of the diaconate.*

According to Father Horvath, the mission of Christ includes the spiritual and material (the other-worldly and the this-worldly) renewal of humankind. Christ entrusted this mission to the apostles and their successors, the bishops, as expressed in the one Sacrament of Order, so that the Church would be concerned with the whole of people's lives. The one Sacrament of Order "is the active sacramental-personal presence of the risen Christ in the midst of His people as Head of His Mystical Body"[37] and includes bishops, priests and deacons. Only the bishop enjoys the fullness of the one Sacrament of Order, with the priest and deacon participating in it according to their respective stations in the hierarchy of the Church. Likewise, to the bishop has been given the mission of *diakonia*, ministry or service: teaching, sanctifying and leading, in liturgy, Word and charity. Since the priest and deacon are the bishop's helpers, by virtue of their ordination at the hands of the bishop, they participate in the bishop's mission of diakonia, according to their respective stations in the hierarchy.

Therefore, Father Horvath continued, speaking of "the *sacrament of the diaconate*," we must recognize the following important distinction:

> *The specific characteristic of the sacrament of the diaconate as distinct from the presbyterate is the active sacramental-personal presence of the risen Christ, the Eternal High Priest in the world as reconciling and renovating man in his external or material (horizontal) dimension and through Him the whole visible and cosmic world, with God and in God. It differs from the active sacramental-personal presence of the risen Christ, the Eternal High Priest in the world as reconciling and renovating man in his internal or spiritual (vertical) dimension, with God and in God, peculiar to the sacrament of the presbyterate. These two aspects are united in the episcopate, to which Christ conferred the completeness of this mission.*[38]

This can be distilled in three statements:

1. As ordained ministers, deacons are mainly, though not exclusively, concerned with the material or this-worldly dimension of Christ's mission.

2. As ordained ministers, priests are mainly, though not exclusively, concerned with the spiritual or other-worldly dimension of Christ's mission.

3. Because bishops enjoy the fullness of the one Sacrament of Order, they are concerned with both dimensions of Christ's mission and exercise their episcopal duties in both dimensions with the help of deacons and priests, both of whom share in the one Sacrament of Order.

Moreover, the *specific characteristic of the diaconate* justifies the fourfold diaconal ministry of Word, liturgy, charity and community (administrator of small parishes and missions)[39] and all the duties that flow from this fourfold ministry. In addition, charity has a special place. It is absolutely essential to the ministry of a deacon as he works to redeem and renovate the world of the here and now, because "charity is not some kind of exercise of piety performed by some fervent Christians but an essential part of the mission of Christ given to His ministers."[40] The Early Church recognized this, and the Church Fathers of the Second Vatican Council restored it to the daily life of the Church when they restored the permanent diaconate.

In an interview almost forty years after the publication of "Theology of a New Diaconate," Father Horvath insisted that the most fundamental aspect of the Second Vatican Council's restoration of the diaconate "as a proper and permanent rank of the hierarchy" was that it completed the sacramental life of the Church.[41] It was not done for reasons of expediency, such as to counter the perceived shortage of priests, although such practical considerations always play some sort of legitimate role in the thinking of the Church. Nor was it done primarily out of a recognition – as relevant as that recognition was – that the diaconate was rooted in Scripture, functioned in Apostolic times and developed into an integral part of the mission of the Early Church, taking on its own servant character. That was a matter of history and was the essence of Father Horvath's Chapter III of the *Guidance Manual*. Instead, the Church Fathers restored the diaconate as a *sacrament* of service, and went so far as to open it up to married men in order for the Church on the local level to realize more fully its overall mission of sacramental service.

Regrettably, Father Horvath's "Theology of a New Diaconate," which came out a year after the CCCB printed and distributed the *Guidance Manual*, went unnoticed by the Archdiocese of Toronto when it began to weigh its options on the introduction of the permanent diaconate in 1970. Those in charge of the Toronto program waited until October 1990 to recommend Father Horvath's article as reading material for part of the preparation for a general review of the diaconate program.[42] Of course, it was just as relevant then as it was when it first appeared (and, indeed, as it is today).

The *Guidance Manual* was ready for distribution to the bishops and their consultants on 15 December 1967. A total of 1,220 copies were printed. Of these 764 were in French, with 280 sent to the French-language section of the Canadian Religious Conference (CRC), and 456 were in English, with 120 sent to the English-language section of the CRC. A subset of the total number of copies was reserved for consultants, 332 French-speaking and 200 English-speaking, who were requested by the ad hoc committee on the diaconate to respond to the questionnaire's seven questions by 10 April 1968.[43] A total of 220 or 64 percent of the French-speaking consultants responded, and 200 persons or 82 percent of the English-speaking consultants responded. These percentages included CRC respondents.

The consultants represented many aspects of Church life. They were diocesan vicars general and deans, directors of pastoral work, vocations and Newman Centres, university chaplains, members of Catholic Action and other lay groups, religious men and women, secular institutes, labour relations people, social workers, religious sociologists, welfare workers, priests with special ministries and people involved in the Catholic press.[44] The CRC, meanwhile, would undertake its own consultation process. All these people were what one might label "professional Catholics." Even so, missing from this list was any mention of Catholic teachers, in particular elementary school teachers, who were the front-line catechists in the separate schools, and Catholic business people, who had contacts in the world of banking, commerce and industry. And, not surprisingly, there was no attempt to gather the opinions of active rank-and-file Catholic parishioners.

The questions dealt with the following: (1) the utility of the *Guidance Manual*; (2) perceptions of the permanent diaconate as prejudicial, superfluous, useful, important, very important or no opinion; (3) the application of the opinions in (2) on the usefulness of the permanent diaconate in the areas of Word, liturgy, charity, Christian communities, and the introduction of Christian values into secular milieu; (4) chances of success for the permanent diaconate; (5) reasons for the opinions expressed as to the chances of success; (6) the CCCB and authorization from the Holy See to restore the permanent diaconate in Canada; (7) type of deacon – married, celibate, more married than celibate, more celibate than married or no opinion.[45] (Many respondents found this last question baffling, but had no trouble supporting a married diaconate.)

The ad hoc committee collected the results to all seven questions, plus the lengthy commentaries many respondents included in their answers, in an eighty-page report and submitted it to a panel of experts at their meeting on 22 April 1968. The panel responded in time for the committee's next meeting on 18 June 1968. Based on their comments, the committee unanimously agreed to recommend to the CCCB that it petition the Holy See to allow the restoration of the permanent diaconate in Canada. The committee cited eight reasons for its recommendation:

1. The results of the survey: French-speaking respondents were 57.2 percent in favour and English-speaking respondents were 65.4 percent in favour

2. The fullness of the sacramental life in the Church

3. The increasing demands on the priestly ministry in liturgy, catechetics and preaching

4. Growing needs of modern society

5. The impersonal character, the anonymity, of huge parishes and the increasing need to create smaller communities that would link the individual to large parish communities

6. The impersonal character of large hospitals and educational institutions

7. The rapidly evolving situation of the Church and the world in Canada

8. To permit those Canadian bishops who want to institute the permanent diaconate in order to meet the particular needs of their diocese.[46]

After the CCCB accepted the ad hoc committee's recommendation on restoration at the plenary meeting of 23–27 September 1968, the committee's work came to an end. The next move was to seek approval from the Holy See. This formality took place in Rome on 20 January 1969, when Cardinal Carlo Confalonieri, of the Congregation of the Sacraments, officially recognized the CCCB's desire to restore the permanent diaconate, in a manner thought fit for the needs of the Canadian Church. The CCCB then looked to its Episcopal Commission on Clergy and Seminaries to take the process to the next level of implementation.

The Episcopal Commission on Clergy and Seminaries

The Episcopal Commission on Clergy and Seminaries began its work in January 1969. Its chairman was Bishop T.J. McCarthy of St. Catharines. Attached to a letter to Bishop McCarthy from Father Everett MacNeil, general secretary of the CCCB, is a list of five recommendations:

1. [That] the Board appoint a small ad hoc committee to prepare more detailed initial guidelines for those dioceses which might wish to proceed with the establishment of the Permanent Diaconate.

2. That two or three pilot projects in the restoration of the Permanent Diaconate be undertaken as soon as possible or as soon as dioceses can be found which would be interested in

this. It would be preferable if one of these were in a large urban diocese, one a diocese in a medium-sized city which has a major seminary, and the third a diocese which does not have a major seminary and has only limited resources in theology and Sacred Scripture.

3. That each of these three dioceses appoint a priest-director of the Permanent Diaconate, which priest will be expected to keep in contact with the ad hoc committee at every stage of the implementation of the program. In this way he can both help and be helped.

4. That careful evaluation of recruitment, instruction and guidance, and pastoral practice programs be constantly made and shared for the benefit of all three projects and the information of the whole conference [CCCB].

5. That there be begun at once a sustained sharing of ideas with people and especially priests on this matter of the Permanent Diaconate.[47]

Since it is not clear to what extent the commission had any influence with individual dioceses over matters mentioned in recommendations 2 to 5, we will concentrate on recommendation number one – the production of guidelines on the permanent diaconate. The National Education Office of the CCCB took on this task and was very busy from 1969 to 1972, turning out various versions of guidelines for diocesan use.

By November 1969, the National Education Office had produced what it called the first draft of a forty-nine-page document titled "The Restoration of the Permanent Diaconate in Canada."[48] It was divided into four major sections:

1. Vatican II (Objections and Difficulties, The Deacon and the Layman, The Deacon and the Priest, Religious Deacons, and In Defense of Deacons – An Anglican Point of View)

2. The Role of Deacons

3. New Attempts to Clarify Role

4. The Training of Deacons.

The document concluded with three Appendices. The first was an application to a permanent diaconate program; the second was an interview sheet; and the third was a sample curriculum.

The *Guidance Manual* of 1967 was highly theoretical and historical in nature and was intended for in-house use. "The Restoration of the Permanent Diaconate in Canada," although it lifted a fair amount of material from the *Guidance Manual*, was very practical in its orientation and was packaged as a set of guidelines for diocesan use.[49] For example, the fourth section – The Training of Deacons – reproduces almost in its entirety the diaconate program of the Archdiocese of Detroit, and was expanded in a booklet-size version of the manuscript in 1970 to include additional material on the Detroit program and the diaconate programs of Orchard Lake, the National Polish Seminary located in the Archdiocese of Detroit, and the Benedictine-run St. John's University in Collegeville, Minnesota. Perhaps for no reason other than considerations of space, the 1970 booklet version dropped the three Appendices. Despite that shortcoming, it was probably the first publicly distributed official document on the permanent diaconate in English-speaking Canada.

In January 1971, the National Education Office produced yet another version, with the addition of "Interim Guidelines" in parentheses in the title. The first three sections corresponded to the first three sections in the two earlier versions, but the fourth section – The Training of Deacons – was presented as a series of three different programs without any reference to the Archdiocese of Detroit, Orchard Park or St. John's University. There was also a fifth part that neatly summarized the basic elements of the restoration. It was followed by revised versions of the three Appendices that originally appeared in the 1969 version.

The committee on the permanent diaconate, established by the Senate of Priests of the Archdiocese of Toronto in 1970, relied to a great extent on "The Restoration of the Permanent Diaconate in Canada (Interim Guidelines)" as the primary investigative tool in its deliberations.[50] This third and perhaps final publication of the CCCB's National Education Office on the diaconate was the most authoritative and persuasive piece of supportive theology in the hands of the committee and of the other members of the Senate. As a result, it played a decisive role in the committee's recognition of the merits of restoration and in its recommendation to Archbishop Philip Pocock as to the establishment of the permanent diaconate for the faithful of the Archdiocese of Toronto.

By 1970, the idea of the permanent diaconate had travelled a long way, from the concentration camp at Dachau to Rome and the Second Vatican Council; from Rome to Ottawa and the Canadian Conference of Catholic Bishops; and from Ottawa to the Archdiocese of Toronto. All this occurred within a little more than a quarter century, a mere footnote in the vast and complicated history of the Church, but the decision of the Council Fathers to restore the diaconate "as a proper and permanent rank of the hierarchy," and that of Paul VI to graft the servant character of the restored diaconate onto the servant character of Christ and His Church, were truly epochal in nature and scope. It was now the turn of the Archdiocese of Toronto, led by Archbishop Pocock, a Council Father, to seize the opportunity to be a pioneer in the restoration of the diaconate in Canada, and in the ensuing process to prepare a path for other dioceses in the country to follow suit. The potential of the diaconate as an energetic and positive force in the renewal of the Church's mission to sanctify the world in the name of Jesus Christ was a gift of the Holy Spirit that came at just the right time.

4

THE PERMANENT DIACONATE COMES TO TORONTO: 1969–1977

Introduction

"There is a feeling that the Holy Spirit, at this time in history, has called us upon an uncharted course, a venture in creativity, based upon the needs of men and the needs of the Spirit."[1] These were the words of Bishop Ernest L. Unterkoefler of Charleston, West Virginia, who was the chairman of the U.S. Bishops Committee on the Permanent Diaconate. The occasion was a national conference on the permanent diaconate held in Chicago in December 1970. Bishop Unterkoefler's words were meant to reassure his audience – bishops, priests, deacons, candidates to the diaconate and observers – that it was the Holy Spirit that chose this particular time in the Church's history to breathe new life into the diaconate, making its restoration a necessary element in the overall reform of the Church. The bishop went on to remind his listeners that the promoters of the diaconate's revival were in unmapped territory at a time of much post-Conciliar upheaval and uncertainty, but that they were not to fear that they would fail at the task, because the Holy Spirit, having inspired the restoration, would guide them in its realization.

Everyone involved in the restoration, however, had to understand that the permanent diaconate was to meet the needs of the faithful, and that creative imagination at the diocesan level of implementation of diaconate programs was indispensable if the Church were to live up to the Holy Spirit's expectations. It was the duty of the local Church, then, to allow itself to be led by the Spirit as it grappled with the intricacies, challenges and pitfalls of restoring the permanent diaconate for the benefit of the faithful and all those who, for whatever reason, were on the margins of the Church or society or both.

In attendance at the conference were delegates from eleven American dioceses that already had functioning programs and were ready to share their experiences, from three dioceses on the verge of setting up their own programs and from several dozen other dioceses, still in the preliminary stages of investigation, that were there for an opportunity to judge for themselves the content and style of existing programs. Among the latter category of delegates were Monsignor John O'Mara and Father Paul Giroux of the Archdiocese of Toronto. Since they were members of the Senate of Priests' committee on the permanent diaconate, their attendance was natural and necessary.

This chapter will begin with the first on-the-record inquiry about the permanent diaconate in Toronto in 1969, and end with the first official review of the diaconate program, dated 26 April 1977. It will examine the process of discernment, discussion and debate that took place among the members of the Senate committee on the permanent diaconate. At times that process was painfully slow to produce results, but the committee's proceedings were always deliberate and focused. Its final recommendation, delivered via the Senate of Priests, was sufficient to convince Archbishop Philip Pocock of Toronto to restore the permanent diaconate.

Included in the narrative will be the major players in our story, those who participated in the process leading up to the restoration as well as those who by sheer effort and commitment, sustained and refined the initial training program, so that it could survive long enough for the diaconate to sink roots and begin to flourish. Very early on, candidates to the diaconate and then deacons themselves took a stake in the training and formation program, acting as mentors, co-ordinators and assistant directors. Another core element of the story is the effort by the deacons to establish a principal model of diaconal ministry and to develop its proper relationship with the apostolate of the laity. According to the Church, all the faithful are called to ministry by virtue of their baptism and confirmation. How, then, to reconcile in a positive and dynamic way the emerging ministry of the diaconate, as instituted by the Second Vatican Council, with the emerging ministry of the laity, which the Council Fathers also addressed in *Apostolicam Actuositatem* (Decree on the Apostolate of Lay People) on 18 November 1965.[2]

Intimately tied to this search was a second one, which sought to develop and maintain a distinctive and recognizable persona for permanent deacons as individuals no less than as members of a corporate body, not only within the archdiocesan hierarchy but also, and more specifically, within the threefold diaconal ministry of liturgy, Word and charity. In other words, the deacons needed to establish their own identity.

Particular attention will be paid to the ordination Class of 1974. They were the pioneers (or guinea pigs) in a lofty Church experiment: the program's success in its many ambitions could not be predicted, but everyone involved in the program sincerely believed it was the right thing to do. It was a transformative experience for the deacons and the archdiocese, giving as an inheritance inspiration and direction to each successive class of deacons.

The chapter will end with an examination of the structure, conclusions and recommendations of the 1977 Review of the permanent diaconate program, which was the last substantial act of the Senate of Priests in its oversight of the deacons. The Senate investigated the idea of the restoration, supported it in its recommendations to Archbishop Pocock and helped the program survive its first five years. Soon it would be time for the Senate to relinquish its direct involvement.

Archbishop Philip Pocock

In the heady days of 1969, there were not many bishops in Canada more willing than Archbishop Philip Pocock of Toronto to entertain the idea of the permanent diaconate or more eager to establish it as soon as he had made up his mind to do so. If the permanent diaconate were good for the Church, the archdiocese would have it, was his way of thinking.[3] On his return from the Council, he initiated a ferment of reflection across the archdiocese on the ramifications of the Council's many teachings. Out of that reflection emerged his desire to bring the permanent diaconate to Toronto.

In Archbishop Pocock's mind, it was a straightforward matter of giving substance to the Council's intention to restore the diaconate to its rightful place in the hierarchy, in light of the Council's theology of the one Sacrament of Order and according to its expressed desire to serve the many still unmet needs of both Church and society. The archbishop's restoration of the diaconate, undertaken when Canadian society was experiencing a seismic shift in the relationship between Christianity and culture, would redefine the meaning and range of Catholic ministry and alter, perhaps forever, the way the Church would see and present itself to those outside its doors in the Archdiocese of Toronto.

By the time that the Council opened in 1962, Archbishop Pocock was fifty-six years old and had been a bishop for eighteen years. He had come to Toronto in 1961, as coadjutor to Cardinal James C. McGuigan, after serving as bishop of Saskatoon and as archbishop of Winnipeg. He knew a great deal about leadership in the Church, when to consult and when to make a decision and how to live with the consequences of his decisions. He formed excellent working relationships with everyone in the chancellery, and, according to then Monsignor John O'Mara, he never took more than an hour to return a phone call when O'Mara was rector of the seminary.[4] Archbishop Pocock was thoroughly in tune with the *aggiornamento* of Pope John XXIII, and looked upon the Council as an extraordinarily fortuitous event in the history of the Church in terms of ecumenism, the liturgy and lay involvement.[5] The restoration of the permanent diaconate was a perfect fit. He gave his blessing to the program with an abundance of hope and enthusiasm, starting a tradition of strong episcopal support of the diaconate that remains in place today and is a principal reason why it has flourished so well and so consistently in the archdiocese for almost four decades. When Archbishop Pocock died in 1984, a deacon's wife commented in a letter to the *Catholic Register* that he "loved his deacons and their families and they loved him."[6]

Although any final decision on the permanent diaconate was Archbishop Pocock's alone to make, as a veteran of the episcopacy and a Council Father, he was not a bishop for whom the words "arbitrary" or "authoritarian" ever applied, either to his general personality or to his brand of Church politics. From the outset, he knew that no matter how right and justified, no matter how wise and prophetic, was the Council's teaching on the permanent diaconate in *Lumen Gentium* #29, the topic of the restoration of the permanent diaconate would quickly and quietly dissipate if it did not receive the support of his leading priests. The most basic configuration assumed that priests and permanent deacons would work together. Moreover, if a diaconate program were adopted, the priest-professors of St. Augustine's Seminary would be teaching the candidates. Since the seminary was the centre of theological and spiritual education in the archdiocese, there was no question that any diaconate program would be a seminary program.

To the priests, therefore, Archbishop Pocock delegated the task of investigating the suitability of the introduction of the permanent diaconate to the archdiocese and making a recommendation to him. The Senate of Priests, itself relatively new, was the consultative body that managed what was essentially an open-ended investigation, in which those on the Senate committee conducting the investigation enjoyed wide latitude in their work but were naturally required to stay within the Church's traditions. The focus of the committee's inquiry was the diaconate as understood by the Council. Archbishop Pocock kept abreast of the committee reports to the Senate of Priests, because he regularly attended its meetings, but he chose not to chair any sessions, leaving the members of the Senate free to be candid in their opinions and decisions.

A word about the origins of the Senate of Priests is in order. After considerable consultation involving several dozen priests and three bishops, Archbishop Pocock established the Senate in the autumn of 1966. It was his response to the Council's *Presbyterium Ordinis* (Decree on the Ministry and Life of Priests), dated 7 December 1965, and to Paul VI's follow-up motu proprio *Ecclesia Sanctae*, the Apostolic Letter issued on 6 August 1966 that provided guidance on the diocesan implementation of *Presbyterium Ordinis*. Around the same time, Archbishop Pocock set up a Pastoral Council for the archdiocese, in accordance with the Council's teaching in paragraph #27 of *Christus Dominus* (Decree on the Pastoral Office of Bishops in the Church), which was published on 28 October 1965. By 1969, of the two bodies – the Senate of Priests and the Pastoral Council – the former was already functioning at a high level of productivity and camaraderie, and was consequently far better prepared to handle the question of the permanent diaconate.

The earliest constitution of the Senate of Priests opens with two purposes:

1. To promote the spiritual, material and intellectual welfare of priests

2. To plan for changing pastoral needs and the welfare of the Diocese.[7]

It was the second purpose that gave legitimacy to the initial investigation into the permanent diaconate and that allowed the Senate of Priests, from 1969 to 1977, to oversee and influence the development of the program.[8]

The Work of the Senate of Priests

Curiously, the first mention of the permanent diaconate in archdiocesan documents, outside of the papers of Archbishop Philip Pocock, can be found in a letter of inquiry from Frank Isber, of Toronto, to Monsignor John O'Mara, then chancellor of the archdiocese. Mr. Isber's letter was dated 10 March 1969.[9] Enclosed in his letter to Monsignor O'Mara was a letter from Father Everett MacNeil, general secretary of the Canadian Conference of Catholic Bishops, in reply to Mr. Isber's request for information on the status of the permanent diaconate in Canada.[10] Father MacNeil confined his answer to a recitation of some basic facts: the Plenary Assembly of

Archbishop Philip Pocock, who attended the Second Vatican Council, established the diaconate program in Toronto in 1972, and monitored each stage of its early development.

Bishop John Boissonneau, Vicar of Deacons, Archdiocese
of Toronto, presiding at a diaconate ordination ceremony,
St. Michael's Cathedral, June 22, 2002.

Diaconate Ordination Class, Archdiocese of Toronto, June 22, 2002.

Deacon Bert Cambre sharing his vocation story with
a Rite of Christian Initiation of Adults (RCIA) class.

Deacon Terence Da Silva delivering the homily at Sunday Mass.

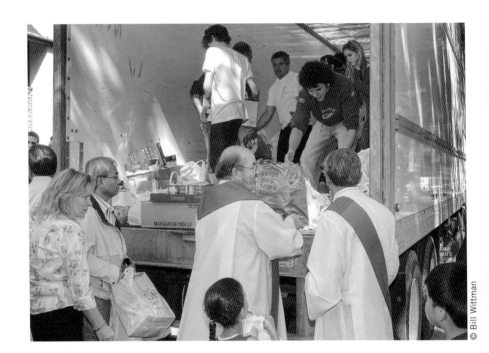

Fr. Scott Young and Deacon Terence Da Silva participating in a parish food drive.

Friends of Dismas. Catholic Deacons from the Archdiocese of Toronto provide material and spiritual support for persons returning to society after incarceration in the penal system.

Deacon Robert Kinghorn ministers to the spiritual needs of women at the Street Haven shelter, which is sponsored by ShareLife.

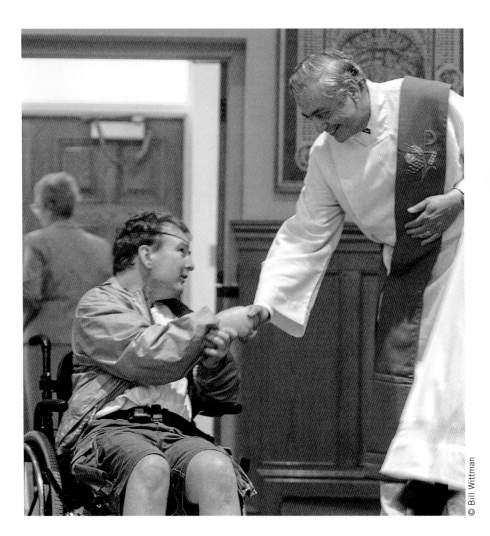

Deacon Bert Cambre exchanges the Sign of Peace
with a member of the parish community at Sunday Mass.

the Canadian Bishops had approved of the restoration; the Apostolic See had confirmed the decision of the bishops; and the restoration would be under the guidance of the Episcopal Commission for Clergy and Seminaries. He went on to point out to Mr. Isber that there were two categories of deacons – celibate and married – and that the decision of a diocese to restore the permanent diaconate rested on its ability to organize and maintain a suitable training program and to determine if a need existed for the diaconal ministry within its jurisdiction. Father Everett ended his letter by suggesting that Mr. Isber contact the archdiocesan chancery. This is precisely what he was doing when he wrote to Monsignor O'Mara.

But the chancellor did not have much to say on the subject because he probably did not know much more about it than the information that Father MacNeil had relayed to Mr. Isber, all of which was public knowledge for those who kept track of such developments in the Church. At the time of this exchange of correspondence, the Canadian bishops had produced only one document on the permanent diaconate, an in-house production called the *Guidance Manual*, in 1967. Its distribution was heavily restricted. A copy was sent to each Canadian bishop, including Archbishop Pocock, but he seems not to have shared it with anyone in the chancery or the seminary and not to have spent too much time with it. His copy looks brand new and untouched. In his reply to Mr. Isber, Monsignor O'Mara wrote:

> One of the biggest problems concerns the formal education of these men for the Permanent Diaconate and as yet no formal course of studies for deacons has been established in Canada.

> However, I believe that the Bishops are now studying the problems involved and I am sure that they will have some of them answered in the near future.[11]

There the matter rested. Frank Isber was never heard from again, at least not in writing, but his correspondence may have initiated a conversation in certain quarters in the archdiocese on the permanent diaconate. Perhaps that conversation initially took place at

St. Augustine's Seminary, where Monsignor O'Mara became rector on 27 June 1969, or perhaps on different occasions it surfaced in informal, off-the-record discussions among members of the Senate of Priests. In all likelihood, the permanent diaconate had appeared on different people's radar at the same time but in different settings, as is the case in the evolution of most new ideas and trends. Regardless, sometime in the autumn of 1969, Father Briant Cullinane, the chairman of the Senate of Priests, took the initiative and asked Father Noel Cooper, dean of studies at St. Augustine's Seminary, to form a committee whose mandate would be to determine the need for a permanent diaconate in the archdiocese and the feasibility of establishing such a program at St. Augustine's Seminary.[12] Since the matter involved the possibility of a major departure in the life and practice of the archdiocese, it is reasonable to assume that Father Cullinane's invitation was sent with the foreknowledge and agreement of Archbishop Pocock.

The first meeting of the Senate of Priests' committee on the permanent diaconate convened on 4 April 1970. Present were Monsignor John O'Mara, who enjoyed an excellent working relationship with Archbishop Pocock as well as the respect of his fellow priests, Father Noel Cooper, Father Robert Kennedy of Ottawa, Father Briant Cullinane, Mr. and Mrs. Fred Halloran, Mr. and Mrs. Joe Pitts, and Mr. Ed Brisbois.[13] The inclusion of these lay people was Monsignor O'Mara's doing. He knew them personally. More fundamentally, along with other priest-members of the committee, he realized upfront that any official discussion of the restoration of a diaconate open to married men needed to include, from its inception, married couples. The voices of the wives, even at this preliminary stage, had to be heard, and the opinions they expressed taken seriously. This in itself was a sea change for the local Church.

Fred Halloran worked in the chancery; Joe Pitts was a retired civil engineer who volunteered one day a week for the diocesan building committee, which was headed by Monsignor O'Mara; and Ed Brisbois was chairman of the Metro Separate School Board. Joining the committee at a later date were Mrs. Brisbois, Mike McDonald and Father John Hochban, SJ. Father Hochban, formerly of St. Mary's University in Halifax, was the registrar at the Toronto

School of Theology. He had been a theologian on the Canadian bishops' ad hoc committee on the diaconate, making him a vital link between the work of the bishops and the archdiocesan committee. Of all the members of the archdiocesan committee, Father Hochban had the best understanding of the essential theological and practical features of the permanent diaconate as worked out by the bishops' committee, and he would be able to articulate them to his fellow committee members.

The meeting of 4 April 1970 took place at St. Augustine's and was a freewheeling affair that lasted nearly six hours. Members were made aware of the *Guidance Manual* of 1967, of Rome's approval of the Canadian bishops' petition concerning the permanent diaconate in January 1969, and of the decision by some American dioceses to proceed with their own diaconate programs. The lay members felt that the Church was not penetrating society, and that priests, who were often overburdened and sometimes confused about their role, were unable to provide proper pastoral care for the people, many of whom had little contact with the Church. They went on to say that the present parish structure – never defined by anyone on the committee – needed help if it were to survive, and the schoolchildren needed better religious education.

There were two objections to the diaconate. The first was based on a purely functional understanding of the diaconate: there was no need to ordain men as deacons because, if given permission, lay people could do everything a deacon could do. Why not tap into the great potential of the laity and avoid adding members to the clerical state? The second objection centred on what the committee understood to be not only the historical but also the contemporary view of the diaconate – that the diaconate without ordination to the priesthood was incomplete and, concomitantly, that the diaconate could never provide effective ministry and sense of community, because by definition it was unable to provide the Eucharist, the heart of Catholic life.

These objections were hardly new. They had surfaced repeatedly, starting at the beginning of the modern debate on the restoration, for the reason that they had some merit. But in their repetition, they had gained a currency at the cost of a more nuanced appreciation of the Catholic theology of grace and ordination, the diaconate's place in the one Sacrament of Order and the relationship between bishop and deacon. (Such an appreciation could have been found, quite readily, in Father Tibor Horvath's 1968 article, "Theology of a New Diaconate," in which he addressed the seminal notion of the "*specific characteristic of the diaconate*." See Chapter Three.) The fact that these objections appeared at the start of the discussion in Toronto demonstrates their hold on the professional, no less than on the popular, perception of the diaconate as a collection of functions; it also reveals the extent to which such a perception fed on fears about the supposed pervasiveness of clericalism and authoritarianism in the Church and the concern that a restored diaconate as part of that clericalism would end up as a prop for the priest in the local parish church.

Comments in favour of the diaconate were rather opaque and couched mainly in negative terms. Nonetheless, some prescient insights did emerge. The committee talked about the value of the diaconate resting not so much on the deacon's administration of the sacraments, thus downplaying his liturgical role, as on his relationship with the community of believers. Members also were of the opinion that deacons should seek ministries outside the parish structure, a rather novel notion in 1970, and "provide a credible Christian statement to the growing number of people who are now alienated from the Church."[14]

The discussion proceeded with opinions on full-time versus part-time deacons, the education of deacons (with a parenthetical aside on the need for religious education for adults), social service, pastoral work and missionary outreach in a secular world. Absent in the "Minutes" of this meeting was any mention of a suitable ideal or model of the diaconate rooted in contemporary Catholic teaching on the ministry of Jesus Christ as servant of all. That happened at the next meeting, most likely at the initiation of Father Hochban, whose name appears for the first time as a member of the committee.

The committee met for a second time on 2 May 1970. After four hours of what must have been another intense exchange of opinions, the members concluded that the Church was not meeting important pastoral needs and that she had to find the right people to meet them. Who were those people? There were members of the committee whose initial inclination was "to entrust this work to lay people without changing their status."[15] But, as time went on, a majority was willing to accept permanent deacons as long as they avoided "the taint of clericalism and authoritarianism, by seeing their life in terms of service based upon the model of Jesus Christ as servant. Ordination would be seen as a deputation from the community for leadership and ministry."[16] This was a major breakthrough in the committee's understanding of the essence of the diaconate. The members then agreed that if the archdiocese were to initiate a diaconate program, it could not wait for "the conclusion of the present evolution of theology concerning the priesthood (and so also the diaconate)."[17] They were wise not to wait for the theologians to catch up to them. Other items discussed by the committee were the need to educate the faithful on the diaconate, the selection of candidates and their training and on-the-job testing.

Nothing too concrete on any of these matters materialized, however, and everything was left for future consideration. But the meeting did not end without a firm, if somewhat poorly worded, recommendation to the Senate of Priests:

> That the Senate of Priests request the Archbishop to authorize the development of a program for education of the people and selection and training of candidates for the permanent diaconate in the Archdiocese of Toronto.[18]

Appended to the bottom of Father Cooper's copy of the "Minutes" of the meeting of 2 May 1970 (he was the secretary of the committee) was a clearer rewrite of the resolution, probably written by him, which included a reference to the pastoral council:

> [That the Senate of Priests request the Archbishop to] authorize the committee to develop a program for education of the people re: permanent diaconate and to develop a means

of selection and training of the candidates for such a permanent order, pending consultation with pastoral council.[19]

This rewrite never made it to the Senate of Priests. Perhaps it was one person's private clarification. Also, there was never any consultation with the pastoral council. This is not surprising since the council was not functioning to the degree whereby its opinions on the diaconate would have been informed sufficiently to assist the deliberations of the committee on the diaconate.

Of even greater interest, however, is the fact that the members of the committee were not of one voice. While the committee was unanimous in its conviction that "the pastoral needs of a great many of our people are not being met and cannot be met under present conditions of diminishing numbers of priests and increasing complexity of urban life,"[20] a sizeable minority (numbers were never mentioned in the "Minutes") felt strongly that the Church should mobilize the laity for ministry instead of increasing the ranks of the clergy in an age of increasing anti-clericalism. This was a legitimate opinion, one that would resonate later in the debate on the right relationship between a restored and functioning diaconate and the emerging apostolate of the laity. At this point in its deliberations, however, the committee wisely chose not to get bogged down in the matter.

Regardless, the committee presented its proposal to the Senate of Priests at the Senate's meeting of 12 May 1970. Before the meeting began, members of the Senate received a five-page summation of the committee's deliberations, and at the meeting each one was given a copy of the sixty-seven-page preliminary version of the work on the diaconate issued by the Canadian Conference of Catholic Bishops.[21] Joe Pitts and Fred Halloran argued vigorously on behalf of the committee's recommendation. The ensuing discussion resembled those held by the committee on 4 April and 2 May 1970, a sign that the debate was running out of steam.

The Senate took no action on the recommendation, ignoring for the time being minority concerns about the laity. Instead, each member was given a month to examine the CCCB's sixty-seven-page work on the diaconate, in preparation for a second round of discussion at the next meeting of the Senate. In advance of that meeting, the committee on the diaconate held its own meeting on 13 June to prepare material on candidate selection and a training program.

The Senate of Priests met on 16 June 1970 and passed the following motion by a vote of 11 in favour, 3 opposed and 1 abstention: "The Senate approves in principle the restoration of a permanent diaconate for the archdiocese."[22]

Father John Hochban, SJ, Father Noel Cooper and Fred Halloran made the case for acceptance of the committee's recommendation "in strong and well defined language."[23] To solidify their case, they referred to the CCCB's "Final Report of the Committee on the Diaconate" of 30 August 1968. It included the results of the "Final Report of the Cross-Canada Survey on the Restoration of the Permanent Diaconate," dated 18 June 1968.[24]

The survey reported overwhelming support for the restoration in both French Canada and English Canada. Along with the survey results, the Senate was given four additional reasons in support of the permanent diaconate:

1. When we view the Sacraments as an expression of the functional life of the Church, the diaconate gives that life fuller expression.

2. The increasing demands on priests.

3. Vatican II viewed the changing society as demanding new remedies, and viewed the deacon as being closely in touch with the changes.

4. Anonymity in a large city parish; the need for smaller communities, and the possible formation of smaller communities within the Parish structure to achieve a sense of belonging.[25]

Archbishop Pocock thought that the motion was worth bringing to the Canadian Conference of Catholic Bishops when the time came to petition the CCCB for permission to set up a permanent diaconate program. However, Father Clement Schwalm and Father

Bernard Black, CSB, added a wrinkle to the process when they put forth a two-part amendment to the motion:

> The Senate recommends that the existing committee be approved to continue investigation to further the permanent diaconate, and that the minority opinion outlined by Fathers Hochban and Black re multiplication of priests be brought to the attention of the C.C.C. [CCCB] at the same time.[26]

The amendment passed with 7 in favour, 5 opposed and 2 abstentions.

The first part was innocuous. It recommended that the current committee continue its work. This was a practical matter that made a great deal of sense. It is the second part that strikes us as curious since it undercut the raison d'être of the Senate's own committee on the diaconate and moreover was doomed to failure. The "multiplication of priests" sounds very much like code for married priests. Those members of the committee and the Senate who wanted to test the waters with a proposal for married men as priests seemed to have had as their rationale a logic that made them ask this question: Why go halfway (married deacons), when it might be possible to go the full measure (married priests)? It was a radical shift from a desire on the part of a minority of the committee to have the archdiocese mobilize the laity instead of restoring the diaconate – as revealed at the committee's 2 May 1970 meeting – to one that wanted the CCCB "to consider the thought of ordaining laymen to the priesthood, not the diaconate; men who are perhaps married, already established in their field of work; men who are noted for their faith and moral values. As priests they would be vastly more valuable than as deacons."[27]

How odd that Father Hochban was involved in this amendment. He was the only member of the committee to have contributed to the production of the CCCB's *Guidance Manual*; he helped to make the case for the restoration of the permanent diaconate in the archdiocese at the Senate's meeting of 16 June 1970; two years later, he would deliver one of the most coherent and succinct lectures on the permanent diaconate.[28] No other member of the committee on the diaconate could match his theological understanding of the subject. How inexplicable, then, that he felt obliged to promote an amendment the second part of which called for the Canadian bishops to entertain the idea of a married priesthood. Perhaps it was meant to ameliorate the feelings of those who sincerely believed that the real goal of the committee's investigation should be married priests, on the perfectly legitimate understanding that the Eucharist would continue to be the centre of the Catholic community. We will never know for sure.

Be that as it may, that part of the amendment on married priests was bound for a dead end in Ottawa. Once again, the archdiocese saved itself from being derailed and managed to stay on track. The sole subject at hand was a permanent diaconate. It would be open to "men who are perhaps married, already established in their field of work; men who are noted for their faith and moral values,"[29] to borrow language from the amendment on married priests. And the sole aim of the committee's deliberations remained the same: to discover the feasibility of instituting the permanent diaconate in Toronto.

Which brings us to an intriguing subtext in our narrative. We are speaking of the offstage turbulence on behalf of deaconesses in the Church that surfaced in the 1970s and the reason that the committee on the diaconate never seriously debated it, at least in the manner that the mobilization of the laity and married priests was – in each case, a minority opinion given for the record. The simple answer is Archbishop Pocock.

On 5 October 1970, there was presented to the Canadian bishops a three-page brief petitioning on behalf of the restoration of the sacramental order of deaconess. It was a well-written, cogently argued piece that deserved the hierarchy's attention. Authors of the brief were Sister Margaret Butts, Sister Marie Walter Flood, Carole Gaudet, Jane Kenny, Sister Sabina Majeau, Sister Bernard Malone, Mary Schaeffer and Linda Spear.[30] Both Sister Sabina Majeau and Sister Bernard Malone [later and better known as Mary Malone] were members of the Order of the Faithful Companions of Jesus, and Mary Schaeffer was an art history teacher at Scarborough College.

She was the organizer of the movement. For his part, Archbishop Pocock quickly acknowledged receipt of his copy. In a letter of thanks to the archbishop, Mary Schaeffer promised to keep him informed of the petitioner's activities.[31]

She kept her word. From October 1970 to October 1973, she sent a steady stream of material to the archbishop. It included copies of *Diakonia*, a newsletter dedicated to the restoration of the diaconate for women, and several scholarly papers, among them being "The Deaconess" by Sister Marie Walter Flood and "The Early Christian Office of Deaconess as a Sacramental Order," author unknown. In November 1970, there was a *Catholic Register* article on what was described as a Movement for the diaconate for women. It quotes Bishop Remi De Roo's response to the idea that the Church revive the order of deaconesses. He said, "It's under consideration."[32] This must have been news to Archbishop Pocock. After reading the *Register* story, Margaret M. McCarthy, who was not associated with the authors of the brief and claimed to have no aspirations to the diaconate, wrote to the archbishop that she hoped and prayed that women who felt called to this particular service in the Church would be able to realize their calling.[33]

What Archbishop Pocock thought of all this activity must be left to cautious conjecture. He was polite to Mary Schaeffer and her friends in the Movement, quietly tolerating their pursuit of their agenda, while neither encouraging nor attempting to silence the authors of the brief. He let them alone, perhaps hoping that the subject would evaporate over time. Archbishop Pocock's attitude was dictated by the fact that as a bishop, and moreover as a Council Father, he knew that the diaconate for women was absolutely out of bounds for any kind of official consideration; if it were introduced as a serious topic of discussion during the proceedings of the committee on the diaconate, it would only impede its work and, if allowed to persist, might even torpedo it.

It is safe to say that the archbishop wanted the permanent diaconate for Toronto, because the Council and therefore the Church wanted it, and he wanted the Senate of Priests to understand that he wanted it (but he did not attempt to engineer the outcome of the committee's deliberations nor the Senate's endorsement of them). Any committee-level talk of deaconesses, then, had misadventure written all over it and was even a greater hazard to the committee's work than had been posed by either the laity-versus-deacons conundrum or the troublesome topic of married priests. The first was a false opposition and the second an act of overreaching.

As a result, the diaconate for women was never an issue, let alone a stumbling block for the committee. When it did come up in conversation, it had little traction to go anywhere. And it was hardly a problem for the first generation of deacons.[34] Even when a 1977 professional survey of archdiocesan lay people, clergy, pooled parishes and the Catholic Women's League, on the admittance of women into the diaconate, among other questions, revealed strong support for their admittance, the concept of ordaining women to the diaconate remained a non-starter in the Archdiocese of Toronto.[35] This was in contrast to the Diocese of Sault Ste. Marie and the Archdiocese of Montréal, where in both cases the question of deaconesses did turn into a thorny and divisive debate.

As mandated, the committee on the permanent diaconate continued its work. Unfortunately, the documentation for the period of June to December 1970 is almost non-existent. (And there is very little for 1971 and for the first five months of 1972.) From the little that we do have, we understand that the committee set three tasks: to agree upon a profile of the desired type of candidate for the diaconate; to plan a program of education for candidates; and to work out the proper place of the deacon within the parish structure.[36] We also know that Monsignor O'Mara and Father Paul Giroux, the director of pastoral education at St. Augustine's Seminary and a recent addition to the committee, attended the Chicago conference on the permanent diaconate in December 1970. It was conducted in an open and positive atmosphere that encouraged participants to share information. It was a listening and gathering experience for the two men. They examined in detail the literature of diaconal programs, looking for strengths to incorporate into the Toronto program and for weaknesses to avoid, and they questioned program directors for first-hand accounts of the diaconal experience in their respective dioceses. This approach allowed them "to cherry-pick the good stuff"[37] and to remain mindful about not making the same mistakes that other dioceses had made.

Two core propositions on the diaconate surfaced at the conference; these were subsequently appropriated by Toronto and had a profound and lasting impact on the program. The first proposition concerned the type of candidate for the diaconate: "We should search for an 'ambrosian model.' The recruiting of outstanding laymen is better than ordaining volunteers. The merely pious and those who welcome signs of office should be dropped immediately. We want intelligent selfless men who will serve where they are needed...."[38] The second gave sensitive consideration to wives of diaconal candidates and their families. "The wife must be given some vision of the program so that she can see and anticipate how it will affect the life of the family. There must be days of Christian sharing for the husbands and the wives with lots of room for questions and answers. This sharing should be applied to classes, liturgy and nights of reflection."[39] This envisioned the spouse as fully integrated into the process of her husband's educational and spiritual formation as a deacon candidate. She was not to be relegated to the role of uninvolved spectator. Rather, she was expected to accompany her husband every step of the way to ordination and, by implication, with him along the path in his life as a deacon.

After the Chicago convention, the committee met on 13 January 1971. The nine-point agenda was an incredibly ambitious one:

1. Do we want to initiate a Permanent Diaconate Program? What are our needs? What is our potential? What will the New Deacons do?

2. What type of men do we want?

3. Public Relations – Priests; laity; brochures; newspapers; organizations; meetings; sermons, etc.

4. Goals of Program.

5. Screening and selection of candidates.

6. Curriculum and faculty.

7. Pastoral activities.

8. What written material is available on the Permanent Diaconate?

9. How large should our committee be?[40]

No "Minutes" for this meeting have survived, thus making it impossible to determine to what extent the committee was able to resolve any of these issues prior to reporting to the Senate of Priests at its meeting on 19 January 1971. Moreover, the Senate "Minutes" on the permanent diaconate program are frustratingly brief. We are given the names of the priest-members of the committee, including those of two new members – Father Cy Robitaille and Father Michael Grace – and told that the committee was considering work in the following areas:

1. Goals and Purpose of the Program.

2. Qualities and characteristics of the candidates.

3. Information and Education.

4. Curriculum.

5. Recruitment and Screening.[41]

Despite another dearth in documentation, from this skeletal list we can be fairly sure that at this stage of its work the committee had made up its mind to recommend to Archbishop Pocock that he give his blessing to a permanent diaconate program. The committee must have intuited the direction in which he was leaning. Why else would it have taken on such a huge responsibility? It appears that the committee had moved its focus from an investigation into the feasibility of the permanent diaconate in the archdiocese to the commencement of detailed work that privately assumed the diaconate's restoration in advance of a formal referral to the archbishop. Such work must have proceeded during 1971, to the point where the committee was confident to approach Archbishop Pocock with a positive recommendation on the establishment of the diaconate, in line with the Senate's original intentions of 16 June 1970. Monsignor O'Mara and Father Paul Giroux met the archbishop in January 1972, and he agreed to the committee's request, on the understanding that no more than twenty-five candidates would be accepted into the program.

Toronto's commitment to the permanent diaconate was now a reality. So, we ask, what did the committee accomplish as the archdiocese prepared to accept its first class of candidates for September 1972? We know that the committee accomplished at least three major things: it produced a training program tailored to the needs of the diaconate; it developed a general profile of the type of candidate it hoped to attract; and it initiated a recruitment and selection process for candidates to the permanent deacon program.

The first proposal for a two-year training program for candidates to the diaconate was academic in structure, if not in expectations, and naturally used priestly formation as an inspiration. It may have been the handiwork of Father John Hochban, SJ.[42] It was not a curriculum or a listing of courses of study. Rather, it was a syllabus. The classroom was the main setting. (It was also incomplete, with no mention of the winter/spring and Monday evening sessions for the second year.) The "academic year" was divided into two major sessions: a two-week summer session in August (11 days, 25 classes), with wives and children for Sunday liturgy and lunch; and a winter/spring session to be held the first weekend of October, November, February, March and May, with five classes each weekend. Supplementing the weekend classes would be two-hour Monday evening classes, ten in the autumn and fifteen after Christmas. The second year would begin with another two-week session in June or July (11 days, 25 classes), with the remainder of the year supposedly resembling that of the first year. Classes would cover the following subjects or units, with five classes devoted to each unit:

1. first summer session: introduction to spirituality; science of scriptural interpretation; the person of Jesus in the New Testament; Christology and redemption-atonement

2. winter/spring session: general moral theology; theology of sacraments in general, theology of the Church; law of marriage; psychological theory and pastoral training

3. Monday evening sessions: Old Testament; unity and Trinity of God; Creation, original sin, Christian hope, life after death; particular moral theology

4. second summer session: theology of priesthood, Eucharist; liturgy, additional spiritual or inspirational sharing; more psychological testing.[43]

At the bottom of this one-page syllabus were comments on spiritual direction, individual consultation and the necessity of continuing education. The comments were followed by three questions. Was there enough formal education in the program? Would there be enough time to assess the dedication and suitability of the candidates? Would the program provide enough time to allow the candidates to develop spiritual values? Each of these questions were legitimate concerns, but answers to them would not begin to emerge until the program was up and running and had weathered a sufficient period of trial and error leading to correction and improvement. The program was an experiment, and, like all experiments, improvement came only by way of testing and revising according to the test results.

A later, and very different and truncated, description of the diaconal training program appeared in the committee's May 1972 brochure. There was no longer a syllabus of proposed lecture subjects. Instead, candidates and the curious read that there would be three twelve-week sessions of lectures and discussions each year for two years. Also, there would be renewal weekends for personal and spiritual development, sessions with wives to keep them informed of the program, and supervised fieldwork, which would take the candidates out of the classroom for different types of ministry. Each weekly session would be equal in time to that expected to be spent by the deacon in his weekly ministry, approximately fifteen hours.[44] The thinking was that part-time training for the diaconate would produce a part-time diaconal ministry.

As September 1972 approached, the training program was scaled down to a much more manageable and realistic proportion of the candidate's time. Father Giroux, the first director of the program, had a warm and encouraging personality. He realized that candidates would be working and that most of them would be married men with young children. One of the first unwritten rules for deacons in Toronto was that family and work came before service as a deacon. The program was still two years in duration but was now divided into ten weekend sessions of prayer and study each year. Each weekend began on Friday evening and ended on Sunday afternoon, with Mass followed by a potluck supper with wives and children in attendance. Since the program was (and remains) a program of St. Augustine's Seminary, all sessions took place at the seminary.

Two members of the Class of 1974 were responsible for the program's successful adaptation of the adult education techniques. Wilfred Maundcote-Carter, who worked in the Ontario Department [now Ministry] of Education, introduced the adult education model in the second year, and Colin Chase preserved and fine-tuned it as the program evolved. He quickly became the brain trust and mastermind of the program, introducing his fellow candidates to the works of Father Karl Rahner, SJ, which served as the theological model for the diaconate in Toronto, and to the writings of Father Bernard Lonergan, SJ, which provided a methodological basis for the program based on a more developed version of the "See, Judge, Act" approach of Catholic Action.[45]

There was, therefore, a heavy emphasis on readings of selected texts, follow-up discussions at the seminary and in candidates' homes, and individual tutorials that allowed each candidate to proceed at a pace suitable to his ability and to his work and home schedules.[46] There was no academic requirement for admission, and there were no tests, exams or essays. The men were candidates for the permanent diaconate, not seminary students for the priesthood, a vital distinction that had to be strictly maintained. At the same time, however, applicants were expected to have been involved in recognizable service to the Catholic community prior to their admission into the program. As second-year candidates, they were enrolled in the Deacon Internship Program, which was co-ordinated by the seminary and required that each candidate devote eight hours per week in one of thirty-three recommended placements. Supervisors in the field would assess their progress. This was the beginning of a candidate's education in service to others.[47]

The broad areas of "academic" study were the various categories of theology, Old Testament and New Testament scripture, liturgy, homiletics, a selection of Canon Law and sociology. Professors included members of the seminary staff: Father Aloysius (later Cardinal) Ambrozic, Father Charles Amico, Father Raymond Corriveau, CSsR, and Father Thomas Thottumkal. Two professors from Regis College were later additions. They were Father Attila (later Bishop) Mikloshazy, SJ, and Father Joseph Plevnik, SJ. Homiletics was a part of the program, but candidates were not necessarily being prepared to preach. The faculty of preaching was not automatically given. This matter caused some confusion and frustration among the candidates, and was addressed at least in part when the second year was restructured to follow the readings of the liturgical year.[48]

Of course, the spiritual formation of each candidate, in particular the regularity and richness of his daily prayer life, was an indispensable condition in his discernment of whether he had a vocation to the diaconate. This, then, was the gravitational centre of his training and education. There was a three-day retreat for prayer and reflection at the beginning of the year in September, and a specific period was allotted for discernment at the end of the year in June. Father John English, SJ, a well-known retreat master, and several of his Jesuit confreres, supplemented the spiritual formation work of Father John Moss, the spiritual director at St. Augustine's.

Finally, admission to the program did not automatically guarantee ordination to the diaconate. This came as a complete surprise to several candidates. They felt that since they were successful businessmen, they would be successful deacons — no questions asked, no doubts entertained. But that was not the meaning of ordination.[49]

A serious weakness to the training program in its first year was its ad hoc approach to the all-important monthly weekend sessions at the seminary. There was no systematic outline of study to follow from one month to the next, or for the entire year. Instead, there was always a rush to produce a booklet detailing activities for the upcoming weekend. Often, it was only ready by Friday of the weekend in question, when in fact it should have been ready for distribution a month in advance, so that the candidates would have had ample time to prepare in advance at home. Such on-the-fly preparation for the weekends was too amateurish for the task at hand, and was hardly the right way to train the candidates or to build up credibility for the program.

A more effective approach had to be found quickly, and Father Giroux provided one when he appointed Stan MacLellan, a candidate for the diaconate, as co-ordinator for the ordination year of the Class of 1974. He met with Father Charles Amico, Colin Chase and several other candidates, and together they devised an efficient and professional approach to the production of each month's booklet by agreeing beforehand on reading resources and teaching personnel and dividing the responsibilities among themselves for the choice and presentation of lecture topics for the monthly weekends.[50] The weekends were filled with lectures, and thus, for them to be effective, advance preparation on the part of the candidates was an absolute necessity.

Monsignor O'Mara and Father Giroux, as well as the other members of the committee on the permanent diaconate, hoped to attract the "right" candidates to the diaconate program. While keeping in mind that the diaconate would appeal to a range of personalities and experiences, they set up certain expectations for all applicants. They sought those who already had a spiritual life and were willing to build on it; who were attached to the Church, had some experience of Church-related service and were willing to develop a ministry of service; who were psychologically and emotionally mature; who had a stable marriage and a solid family life; who had a supportive spouse and children; who were financially stable; and who were willing to learn and take on leadership roles.[51] These were high expectations but not unreasonable ones. They were achievable ideals. As time would prove, there were plenty of Catholic men in the Archdiocese of Toronto who could live up to them and function quite well as deacons.

These unwritten expectations became "Qualities of Candidates" in the May 1972 brochure and were marked by a more practical tone. Candidates had to be at least thirty-five years old and in good health, which had to be certified by a doctor. They needed to be mentally and emotionally stable, possess a good job record, enjoy the respect of their fellows and be free of scandal. Since diaconal service would be part-time, they had to be financially self-supporting. A sincere interest in the welfare of the Christian community, as demonstrated by a personal history of service to others, was a prerequisite for admission. (As it turned out, many in the Class of 1974 lived up to this expectation, having been involved in one or more ministries: the Holy Name Society, the St.Vincent de Paul Society, catechism programs for public school children, Catholic Family Movement, charismatic prayer groups, Right to Life movement, Legion of Mary, marriage preparation and the Cursillo movement. Cursillo, in particular, was quite popular. It was a three-day spiritual renewal on the basics of the Christian faith. In September 1973, the class began the year with a Cursillo.[52]) Each candidate had to have a sound marriage – one that had stood the test of time – and the support and encouragement of his wife and children. Lastly, all applicants had to live within a reasonable travelling distance of St. Augustine's Seminary in east Toronto.[53]

By April 1972, Monsignor O'Mara and Father Giroux were ready to recruit and screen applicants for the permanent diaconate program. The first order of business was the compilation of a detailed brochure for distribution to the parish priests of the archdiocese. Since they would have to work with future deacons, they became the principal recruiters for the first class of candidates. (Father Basil Courtemanche was one example of an active recruiter.) We have already referred to this brochure in terms of the information it provided on the training and qualities of candidates. It also contained material on the authority behind the restoration of the permanent diaconate (Second Vatican Council, Rome and the Canadian bishops); a short list of suggested readings; and brief articles on the nature of community, the needs of the Church; and style of life expected of a deacon. It emphasized the service character of the diaconate and clarified one of the central tasks of the deacon – to promote the ministry of the laity. Over the years, these two themes would remain a constant in the program, fortified by an evolving theology of the permanent diaconate and reaffirmed by the deacons themselves in their various ministries in the parish and community.[54]

As soon as applications started to arrive, the process of screening began. It included a personal interview with each applicant; a social interview with the applicant and his wife, and, if thought necessary, a personal interview with the wife; and group sessions with applicants in order "to determine and clarify the learning objectives of the diaconate program"[55] and to allow the emergence of patterns of service among the applicants. The designers of the training program hoped to treat each applicant according to his own "threshold of knowledge,"[56] and they expected each applicant to have a spiritual director and to participate in days of reflection and prayer and Eucharistic liturgies with his family. The first year would be treated as a probationary period.

Thirty-three men were accepted for September 1972, of which twenty-eight were candidates from the Archdiocese of Toronto. Their inaugural meeting as a class took place at St. Augustine's Seminary on Saturday, 16 September 1972.[57] Billed as an orientation day, it was an informal and happy affair, more like a party than a meeting, with wives and children in attendance. Colin Chase appeared with one of his children on his shoulders.[58] Archbishop Pocock revelled in the whole scene and accepted everyone who showed up, even if an interview for admission had yet to be held, contradicting his original intention not to have a large inaugural class.[59] He went around the room and personally greeted each candidate, asking him why he wanted to become a permanent deacon. Thomas Cresswell's answer boomed around the room and is remembered by many to this day: "If you think the priest is going to play golf while I'm doing baptisms on a Sunday afternoon…."[60] The archbishop, appreciating the honesty of the answer, had a good laugh.

Archbishop Pocock looked upon permanent deacons as co-workers in the Lord's vineyard. He was optimistic about the future of the diaconate, and instructed the chancery to be generous in its financial support of the program, because he saw men who were ready to commit themselves to serving Christ's Church as deacons, and wives and families who were ready to accept new burdens and sacrifices as their husbands and fathers prepared for the diaconate. Whenever possible, he celebrated Mass with the candidates and their families at the seminary and joined them afterwards for a meal in the refectory. About those times, he wrote: "The sense of Christian community, which is always evident there, in sincere fraternal affection, in convivial collaboration and above all for me in the wholehearted simple joy of children and teenagers, is a promising pledge of the kind of collaboration the deacon's ministry will make to the people of God in Toronto."[61] He was not to be disappointed.

A Profile of the Class of 1974

Twenty-six men were ordained to the permanent diaconate for the Archdiocese of Toronto in five different ordination ceremonies in May and June 1974,[62] making Toronto the first diocese in English-speaking Canada to ordain permanent deacons and the second in Canada, after the Archdiocese of Québec, which had ordained ten deacons in 1972, six in 1973 and another four in 1974.[63] The first to be ordained for Toronto was Lawrence Rogers, on Tuesday, 21 May, at Chaminade High School, where he taught.[64] The remaining candidates were ordained on four consecutive Sundays in June:

> **2 June, Blessed Trinity Church**: James Clair, Thomas Cresswell, Alexander MacGregor, Patrick Matthews, Daniel Murphy and William Rankin
>
> **9 June, Holy Rosary Church**: Orval Mooney, Cecil Preyra, James Sanderson, Anthony Sandford and Nicholas Scandiffio
>
> **16 June, St. Leo's Church**: William Bannon, John Boudreau, James Cregg, Walter Gabourie, Corry Manne, Bernard Wilson and Ralph Yearsley
>
> **23 June, St. Boniface Church**: Colin Chase, Jed Côté, Stephen Kopfensteiner, Gerald Lennon, Stanley MacLellan, Wilfred Maundcote-Carter and Joseph McTeague.[65]

Twenty-four deacons were married and two were single and took a vow of celibacy, as required. The two unmarried deacons – Stephen Kopensteiner and Bernard Wilson – later became priests. Two of the married men – Thomas Cresswell and Lawrence Rogers – became priests after they had become widowers. The average age of the Class of 1974 was forty-five years. Five were in their fifties, with the oldest being fifty-five, and five were in their thirties, with the youngest being thirty-two.[66] On average, deacons had 14.5 years of formal education. Two deacons each had ten children, one had seven and only one married deacon had no children. The average number of children among the twenty-four married deacons was 3.6 children, a fairly accurate reflection of family size at the time.

The deacons came from many different walks of life – one of the aims of the program's recruitment efforts – to better reflect membership of the faithful, but there was a definite preponderance of middle-class professionals among them. There was one university professor, one lawyer, one civil servant and one assistant superintendent of a Catholic school board. Many candidates were managers of one kind or another: bank manager, mortgage manager, factory production manager, general manager of a large company, industrial engineering manager, district manager, manager of safety and security at a steel company, manager of operations at a television station, and manager of a paint company. There were two salesmen, a self-employed insurance agent, an insurance broker, an accountant, a supervisor at the Workmen's Compensation Board, a high school teacher and a social worker. One worked in financial services; another described himself as a skilled worker; one worked in a laundry after thirty-two years in the Air Force; another was a veteran of the British Navy. These deacons were successful men in the workplace, in many cases leaders of other men and women, who brought to the diaconate a wealth of workplace experience, perseverance and fidelity to the Church.

All deacons were given a liturgical base at a parish church. Immediately after ordination, the majority of them practised their ministry *within the parish*, in baptism preparation, catechetics, visiting the sick and the elderly, working with various prayer groups and overseeing the St. Vincent de Paul Society. One deacon assisted his parish priest in the construction of a new church. But there were deacons from this class who had a ministry *outside the parish*. One was the chief fundraiser for the Toronto School of Theology; three saw themselves as deacons at their place of work (high school, halfway house, school board); and there were deacons involved in marriage counselling at the seminary and in the Cursillo movement. One deacon's choice of ministry was a model of selection. Jed Côté was a long-time volunteer at Providence Villa. Following ordination, he was sent to the Villa for his ministry. In other words, he was selected because of his ministry at the Villa. Five deacons were assigned to specific tasks in the training program: three were described as program co-ordinators; one was a member of the screening committee for applications; and one was education co-ordinator. Only four of the twenty-six newly minted deacons intended to practise ministry in a hospital setting, chiefly as chaplains. The average number of hours per week for diaconal ministry was between twelve and fifteen, in accordance with the part-time nature of the ministry. When it came to the Sunday liturgy, the deacons assisted at the altar, distributed Holy Communion and preached, but only when called upon, at most once a month.

More deacons came on board during the next three years. Eighteen were ordained in 1975 and twenty-one in 1976. However, there was only one ordination in 1977 because the program was undergoing a major review at the time (which we will examine in detail below). The program was popular. Sixty-six men had become permanent deacons in five years, a rate of growth that was nothing short of spectacular. This good news prompted Archbishop Pocock to tell the Senate of Priests that he did not want deacons to outnumber priests in the archdiocese. Father Robert Clune assured the archbishop that that would never occur.[67]

The deacons' contribution to the spiritual life of the archdiocese was certainly impressive, according to an official report, but, as expected, there were growing pains. These were "caused mainly by the enthusiasm with which these men had thrown themselves into the work and by the unfamiliarity of the priests and the people with this new ministry."[68] Enthusiasm is not a bad thing; indeed, it is necessary to give life and support to what is apparently so radically new and different, but it soon became obvious to the deacons that many parish priests and parishioners had not been adequately prepared for their appearance in the sanctuary or at the back of the church after Mass. Reactions among the priests varied. Those who had actively recruited candidates to the program were receptive and made every effort to integrate the deacon into the parish. The more conservative priests generally did not have the will or energy to accept permanent deacons, because deacons were creatures of the Second Vatican Council. They wanted more priests, not newfangled deacons. Some priests simply felt threatened by the idea of married deacons having a role in the liturgy. And new pastors did not automatically accept the deacon who came with the parish, making him feel vulnerable and disposable.

There were occasions when the average person in the pew was confused about that "guy" reading the Gospel, or, even worse, preaching. "What right did he have to do that?" was the reaction of some who went out of their way after Mass to let the deacon know what they thought of his impertinence. To make matters worse, the phrase "lay deacon" was then in vogue and often resorted to when someone was trying to figure out who the deacon was, but there was no such thing in the Catholic Church. Such ignorance was a direct result of a lack of proper catechesis on the permanent diaconate.

After he had been a deacon for twelve years, Thomas Cresswell summed up the situation this way:

> Many of the deacons ordained for Toronto in the years '74, '75 and '76 were uncomfortable in the early years, for many of us felt that we were under a very large magnifying glass. Deacons, such as myself, who travelled across Canada, received a reaction from both priest and laity that was not what was expected. We were sometimes accepted, sometimes rejected and many times ignored.[69]

Not all problems concerning the early years of the permanent diaconate should be put on the shoulders of the priests and people. The deacons realized that, for all their enthusiasm, there were features lacking in their own training and preparation for the diaconal ministry that contributed to the initial suspicion and confusion. They did not have a specific ministry for which they had been trained and were expected to exercise; they did not have enough education in Scripture and homiletics; there was no program for continuing education; they did not know what role, if any, their wives were to play in their ministry; and they were not adequately prepared for ministry to the disadvantaged. As a result, more than one deacon turned himself into a mini-priest or a glorified altar boy, in the process becoming too caught up in his participation at the altar and in the pulpit. This was a serious misunderstanding of the *specific characteristic of the permanent diaconate,* which was principally one of service to the world beyond the doors of the parish church. If the training program were to allow such a misunderstanding to take hold, and if the deacon were to become almost completely attached to the sanctuary, the permanent diaconate would disappear once more, as surely it did in the fifth century.[70]

Happily, such a misunderstanding never took over the training program during its first five years. It failed to do so, because from the very inception in 1972, those in charge of the program, and all those called upon to assist in its administration, were wise enough to know that they had to keep fine-tuning the content and style of the program, so that everyone involved – seminary rector, program director, assistant directors, co-ordinators, mentors, candidates and the deacons themselves – would be able to discover and appreciate to the fullest the true nature of the permanent diaconate: that the deacon is the hands and feet of Jesus, "reconciling and renovating man in his external or material … dimension and through Him the whole visible and cosmic world."[71]

Five years in the life of the Church is not very long, but the first five years in the life of the permanent diaconate in the Archdiocese of Toronto was a long time indeed. From no deacons to more than five dozen deacons was a startling accomplishment, but these numbers, as impressive as they were, were hardly the whole picture of the diaconate, and by themselves they could not guarantee another five years for the diaconate, let alone a long-term future. A thorough review of the program was in order. The hope was that by means of critical examination a more mature theology for the program would emerge and thus clarify the nature of the diaconate for current deacons and future candidates.

The 1977 Review

In March 1976, the Senate of Priests established an Action Group on the Diaconate. (The Action Group will be referred to as the committee and their final report will be called the Review.) Father Raymond Corriveau, CSsR, was the committee chairman. Father Wilfred B. Firth, Father Harold O'Neill, rector of the seminary in 1976, Father Charles Amico, director of the diaconate program in September of the same year, and Colin Chase, the lone permanent deacon, were members. The Senate gave the committee a fourfold mandate:

1. To review the evolution and accomplishments of the Permanent Diaconate programme in the Archdiocese of Toronto since its introduction 5 years ago (September 1972).

2. To define more exactly the ministry of the permanent deacon as set forth in official church documents in relation to the ministry of the liturgy, of the word and of charity.

3. To reach a consensus through discussion on the role of the permanent deacon vis-à-vis that of the Christian lay person, the religious, the priest and the bishop.

4. Finally to decide whether the Archdiocese should continue with the existing Permanent Diaconate programme or replace it with a broader Training for Ministries Programme that would include women.[72]

Mandate Number 1: History of Changes in the Program

After giving a brief but informative history of the restoration of the diaconate in the archdiocese, the Action Group discussed changes that had already taken place in the management of the training program, the program itself and the deacons as a distinct community. Concerning the program's management, in 1973, Monsignor John O'Mara, Father John Moss, Father Paul Giroux and four candidates to the diaconate – Colin Chase, Dan Murphy, Patrick Matthews and Wilfrid Maundcote-Carter – formed a committee "to evaluate and supervise the program"[73] on a regular basis, in order to address problems in a timely fashion and to modify the program as circumstances demanded. The early days of the program were in a state of constant flux that demanded flexible and imaginative thinking. As time went on, this committee became a more formal governing entity with defined tasks. Commencing in 1974, it was charged with the recommendation of candidates for ordination and the ongoing evaluation of the curriculum. Other changes were the creation of the office of assistant director (Father Charles Amico was assistant to Father Giroux, and Deacon Colin Chase was assistant to Father Amico) and of the office of co-ordinator for each year. According to Deacon Tab Charbonneau, a co-ordinator was responsible for a host of important duties. He worked

> with the training staff on the planning of weekend study sessions. This included the subject matter, the preparation of the monthly study bulletin given to each candidate and the weekend schedule. He also dialogued with the mentors during the month on any problems that had surfaced, oversaw the study weekend to insure that it ran smoothly and was a member of the evaluation committee that met regularly to assess the candidate's progress.[74]

There were three major changes to the training program. The first was the introduction of peer mentors in 1973. The candidates were divided into groups of six, and each group was assigned a peer mentor. Prior to ordinations in 1974, peer mentors were candidates themselves; between 1974 and 1976, they were either candidates or deacons, and after 1976, they were deacons. They worked with candidates *and* their wives, giving guidance, support and encouragement and meeting with them weekly to study the assigned work. They also evaluated the progress of each candidate in their group and sat in on the monthly weekend sessions.[75] The role of peer mentor has changed little since its inception and is regarded by many deacons as one of the most innovative and essential elements in the training program.

The second change took root during the academic year of 1976–77, when candidates were exposed on a trial basis to the people and different environments of a detoxification centre, two prisons and a nursing home. Although quite a shock to some candidates, this experience allowed each one of them to explore to a greater degree whether these environments offered the possibility of a ministry suitable to their specific talents and interests.[76] This evolved into a requirement of the candidates, made official in 1977, that during their training they spend fifteen hours a month for six months in a ministry of service of their own choice, approved by the training program personnel and guided by an in-site supervisor. In this way, ordination to the diaconate would be a celebration of an already existing ministry.

On the surface, this might not seem so radical an adjustment in the program, but it was; it recognized in a practical manner the direction that the permanent diaconate had to take if it were to be true to its scriptural foundation and apostolic origins in a modern context, and to endure and thrive beyond the first bloom of the restoration. The opening chapter of a record of service had to precede ordination as a condition of the laying on of hands, and be understood and appreciated by the deacon and his family as an initiation into a life of diaconal service "'to the disadvantaged, those who have become isolated not only from the community of the Church, but from any human community, e.g., the sick, the addicted, aged, imprisoned – or any group cut off and in stress.'"[77]

This was a tall order covering a wide swath of God's people, perhaps the widest imaginable from the Christian perspective, but its scriptural origins are to be found in the Gospel of Matthew, Chapter 25, the Final Judgment, which is *the* call to service for the permanent diaconate. By expecting service from a candidate before ordination, those in charge of developing and fostering the diaconate in the archdiocese recognized not only the *specific characteristic of the diaconate* but also the need for such recognition as a foundation on which a theology of the diaconate could be erected, commensurate to the anticipated growth in the number of deacons and the hoped-for expansion and stability of their ministry throughout the archdiocese.

By the time of the 1977 Review, the committee reported that in addition to liturgical and administrative roles, permanent deacons were serving in the following areas:

hospitals, nursing homes, Cursillo groups, St. Vincent de Paul groups, pro-life programmes and many other phases of the life of the diocesan community. As the programme grows, the deacons are always discovering many ways to serve, so that in the future a great diversity of ministries can be expected. From the quality of men we have seen, service will be provided wherever need is identified.[78]

Service would be the diaconate's calling card in the Church and world.

There were many reasons subsequently given for this particular and prophetic understanding of the diaconate as primarily Christian service in the temporal order. On a foundational level, the program adopted the ideas of Father Karl Rahner, SJ, a leading and early champion of the restored diaconate. He wrote that the pre-eminent task of the deacon was one of "integrating the individual both into a humanized secular culture and at the same time in particular into the community of the Church."[79] His words proved inspirational and were often quoted in the program's literature, including the 1977 Review.[80]

On a more practical level, the program chose the model of deacon-as-servant, both inside *and* outside the Church, because it seemed closest to the way in which the diaconate functioned and flourished in the Early Church. Such a model had little room for the deacon as a mini-priest or for a new layer of clericalism in the Church, and came close to guaranteeing that the restored diaconate could not be used as a solution to the problem of a shortage of priests. The Church restored the diaconate in order to meet "needs that will always be present (ministry to the disadvantaged) and most easily neglected – needs at the core of Christian service."[81] One member from the Class of 1974 wrote,

> Over time, we [deacons] came to understand that we are called to a ministry of service: serving our Bishop, our local church and community. We bring to our ministries different levels of expertise in a variety of fields. We also bring the grace of diaconal ordination.... The role of Deacon is

to console, to offer sympathy, to help lift up and to care for those who are hurting. To be gentle with the alienated.[82]

The third change dealt with preaching. Although nearly every deacon in 1974 and 1975 had been given the faculty of preaching, all candidates were to be given more formal training in homiletics, starting in September 1977. This decision came about as a result of a meeting, either in late 1976 or in early 1977, between Archbishop Philip Pocock and Father Harold O'Neill, Father Charles Amico, Deacon Colin Chase, Deacon Tab Charbonneau and Deacon Alex MacGregor. They met in the chancery office. The archbishop said that since he had received many comments on the good homilies that the deacons were giving, he wanted to establish preaching as one of their regular duties. Father O'Neill and Father Amico had come to the meeting prepared to make a proposal for more rigorous homiletic training, which dovetailed nicely with the archbishop's desire.

Two questions then arose: Was a two-year program long enough to provide the kind of training in homiletics that was proposed? And should all future candidates be required to have a certain number of years of a university education? In the end, it was decided to institute a three-year program, starting in September 1977, and to limit enrollment to eighteen candidates. Then there was the matter of the Class of 1977. Its members were originally scheduled to be ordained in the spring of 1977, but their training period was extended for six months to allow more time for homiletics. Also, those who had not solidified a ministry were required to continue their fieldwork until they had done so. All candidates were interviewed and evaluated. As a result, ordinations for the Class of 1977 were staggered. Seven were ordained in January 1978, one in March, seven in May 1978 and one in January 1979.

That settled the first question. As for the second, it was decided that higher academic qualifications would be necessary in order for candidates to benefit from the expanded program in theology and homiletics. Father O'Neill, speaking in his role as seminary rector, strongly recommended four years of university work. Archbishop Pocock, however, refused to endorse his position, but no decision was taken. That was left in the hands of the members of the training program, who, after diligent and sometimes tense discussion, decided on two years of university work or its equivalent, as a basic requirement for admission into the program.[83]

There were some vociferous objections to the introduction of a three-year program and plenty of differing opinions on what should be considered the academic equivalent to two years of university studies. For the sake of the diaconate, however, people buried their differences. Soon, practically everyone saw that although a three-year program was more academic in tone, content and expectation, the addition of a third year allowed more time not only for better training in homiletics, one of the major reasons for expanding the program, but also for the candidates to work on liturgy and Canon Law and, in addition, to find and gain experience in a particular ministry, a requirement for ordination.[84] Many of the candidates who had been accepted for September 1977 reported that the extra time helped them to keep up with the demands of the course work, maintain a liaison with their parishes and participate in seminars devoted to pastoral training and other ministry programs.[85]

In 1975, the deacons took the first step in the formation of a corporate identity for themselves and their wives as a distinct and dynamic community within the Archdiocese of Toronto by establishing the Council of Deacons. The first election of executive officers took place in June 1976. They were Deacon Bernard Wilson, chairman, and Deacon John O'Connor, secretary, assisted by William Bannon, James Cregg, Tab Charbonneau, Andrew McNeil, George Morley, William Rankin and Gerald Lennon serving as members. The Council's Constitution stated that the Council was formed to promote the peace, unity and spiritual and material well-being of its members and associates. Its goals, three in number, were all-encompassing: one, "to foster a spirit of community among fellow deacons"; two, "to actively promote the Permanent Diaconate Programme and the continuing Education of its members"; and three, "to inculcate in its members a sense of duty and obligation to the People of God by working in close cooperation with the Archbishop, Bishop [that is, auxiliary bishops] and other clergy for the greater glory of God, the salvation of souls and the edification of its members."[86] Community was absolutely essential to the survival and success of the diaconate, especially during its infancy, and the deacons had to cultivate a sense of community for their own good and for the good of their ministry. In December 1976, the Council published its first issue of *Contact*, its official newsletter.

Mandate No. 2: The Ministry of the Permanent Diaconate in Church Documents

The committee commented on *Lumen Gentium* #29 (1964) and three post-Conciliar documents: *Sacrum Diaconatus Ordinem* (1967), *Ad Pascendum* (1972) and *Ministeria Quaedam* (1972), in order to arrive at a clearer and deeper understanding and appreciation of the Church's intentions for the restored ministry of the permanent diaconate. Such a thorough exercise was a first for the program in Toronto. Concerning each of these documents, which already have been examined in Chapter Two, this is what the committee had to say:

Lumen Gentium #29 (1964)

1. The Council mentions the ministry of service in the very first sentence.

2. The Council establishes the threefold ministry of the diaconate, which has remained paradigmatic: the ministry of the liturgy, of the word, and of charity.

3. In listing the particular duties of the deacon, the Council is almost exclusively concerned with the liturgical and sacramental ministries. At the time the only existing model of deacon was the transitional deacon, whose special duties indeed were exclusively liturgical and sacramental.

4. At this early stage there is no explicit mention of preaching among the duties of the deacon. The following are included: reading Scripture, instructing and exhorting the faithful.

5. Besides opening the door to the restoration of the permanent diaconate, the Council in 1964 did not offer any developed theology of the diaconate.

Sacrum Diaconatus Ordinem (1967)

1. [Similar to] the case with Vatican II the document contains no developed theology of the diaconate.

2. After repeating the sacramental and liturgical emphasis of Vatican II the document does add the functions of charitable, administrative and welfare work ... and the promotion and support of the lay apostolate.... This function of giving leadership in the lay apostolate is of special importance....

Ad Pascendum (1972)

1. Perhaps the most important point in the document is the opening paragraph's statement on the variety of ministries in the Church.

2. The document sows the seeds for emphases in the theology of the diaconate which grow into theological opinions, e.g., the deacon as the bishop's man, the deacon as intermediary between bishop and priest on the one hand and the laity on the other, and the deacon as the sign and catalyst of the *diakonia* of the entire Church.

Ministeria Quaedam (1972)

1. Although not explicitly bearing on the diaconate this letter of Pope Paul [VI] indirectly affects the theology of the diaconate in an important way. By acknowledging the ministry (even official ones) of the laity, the document steers clear of a subtle form of clericalism, i.e., that the only "real" ministries in the Church are the ordained ministries, whether of bishop, presbyter or deacon.[87]

Several features stand out in the committee's comments on these four Church documents. First, the Second Vatican Council gave general directives on the restoration of the permanent diaconate but very little theological insight on the diaconate itself. But, according to Father Charles Amico, "This proved very wise. The newly restored ministry needed time and experience to develop, both in continuity with tradition and in openness to new challenges."[88] So, we should look at the 1977 Review as a significant leap forward in local theological understanding of the diaconate. Second, of the three elements of the ministry of the diaconate – liturgy, Word and charity/service – charity or service emerges as pre-eminent, taking centre stage in the definition and evolving theology of the diaconate. Third, there is a fundamental organic link between the ministry of the diaconate and the apostolate of the laity.

Mandate No. 3: The Role of the Permanent Deacon in Relationship to the Laity, Bishop, Priest and Religious

By virtue of baptism, all Christians are called to the common apostolate of the promotion of the Kingdom of Christ. To each category of the baptized – laity, bishop and priest, religious and deacon – there is a specific apostolate: lay Christians promote the Kingdom of God in the temporal order; bishops as ministers of sacraments and of the Word and as builders of ecclesiastical communities; religious as eschatological signs and as agents of special service; and deacons as ministers of charity, the Word and liturgy (note the order, reflecting the primacy of charity).

Starting with the Apostolic Letter *Ad Pascendum*, in 1972, theological investigation into the specific apostolate of the deacon had produced five models for the diaconate: (1) Bishop's Man; (2) Intermediary; (3) Sign of Diakonia; (4) Catalyst (Stimulator, Animator); and, in a paraphrase of Father Karl Rahner's definition of the diaconate, (5) "Integrator of Marginalized into Humanized and Church communities."[89] While all five models were legitimate, the Archdiocese of Toronto explicitly chose the last two as the most appropriate and relevant for its diaconal program.

Mandate No. 4: Recommendations

The committee made seven recommendations in regards to the future of the program, touching on specialized diaconal ministries, the deacon and lay ministries, the deacon's ministry of charity, his liturgical base, preaching and the current state of theology of the diaconate. These recommendations became a blueprint for the program for many years to come and were often referred to by subsequent reviews in the 1980s and 1990s. They were:

1. The Committee recommends that the diaconate programme continue its existing programme, i.e. for those who feel called to ordination to the diaconate and for their wives.

2. Practically, to broaden this permanent diaconate training programme might jeopardize its specific orientation towards specialized diaconal ministries.

3. The conclusion in #2 is in no way meant to minimize the importance of lay ministries. The diaconate programme must constantly struggle to avoid exclusion of the laity from their active role in the Church. That is why this report has several times called attention to the role of the deacon in "promoting and supporting the lay apostolate" as catalyst and animator.

4. The main focus of the deacon's work should be on the ministry of charity or service. This will often but not always be on the parochial level. His functions in the Eucharistic community will reflect, promote and celebrate his ministry of serving in the community.

5. The deacon will always have a liturgical base, not necessarily in the parish. It could be in a hospital or prison chapel.

6. Preaching is one function of the deacon, especially in areas connected with his particular state in life and ministry. For this reason the diaconate programme requires at least two years of university or its academic equivalent.

7. The theology of the diaconate will continue to evolve. The development of this newly restored ministry should remain open-ended and flexible.[90]

Father Charles Amico and Deacon Colin Chase presented the findings and recommendations of the Review, dated 26 April 1977, to the Senate of Priests at their meeting in May. A full and spirited debate ensued.[91] At the Senate's next meeting, on 14 June, the Senate unanimously accepted the Review,[92] and in November, it authorized Father Amico "to use the Senate's report on the Permanent Diaconate in any way he chooses."[93] On 7 February 1978, Archbishop Pocock announced to the Senate: "the recommendations of the Senate committee on the Permanent Diaconate had been accepted and implemented."[94]

Deacon Stan MacLellan reported on the Senate's acceptance of the Review in the September 1977 issue of *Contact*. He told his fellow deacons matter-of-factly:

> The committee recommended that the existing program be continued. It commented on the importance of lay ministries; the deacon as animator; the ministry of charity or service; the need for a liturgical base; the preaching function; the continuing evolution of the theology of the diaconate.

> The report was accepted by the Senate. In short, nothing startling occurred. The body which initiated the discussions and investigations in 1969 wanted to know how the program was developing. It was pleased with the answers it received.[95]

In other words, thanks for the support and let the deacons get on with their work.

Contributing to the same issue of *Contact*, Father Amico, in his role as program director, took the time to highlight and expound upon the Review's insistence that the deacon's primary ministry was to the marginalized and to the promotion and support of lay ministries. There was to be no more ambiguity on this matter. He ended his brief discourse by making four points. First, the diaconate would always be needed because the marginalized would be with us in some form until the Second Coming of Christ. Second, the deacon's work must centre on Matthew 25. Third, the program would continue to attract the right kind of candidate. Fourth,

> We will be answering the objection of certain Canadian dioceses and of many African bishops who fear that restoring this ministry [the diaconate] will discourage or even annihilate lay ministries. In our model we will not multiply PDs [permanent deacons] unduly; we will not approach all active laymen and urge them to enter the program. What we will do is foster ministries among them, associate them with ourselves in our ministry to the marginalized.[96]

The opening five years of the permanent diaconate program in the Archdiocese of Toronto, 1972 to 1977, was a watershed of hope, experiment, hard work, good intentions, mistakes and errors, corrections and adjustments and plenty of prayer and patience. Those years came to a successful close with the submission, acceptance and implementation of the 1977 Review, which provided a much-needed measure of self-understanding and self-criticism. The Review was cathartic because it encouraged the committee to examine the past in a frank and intelligent way, and it was a tonic, because it laid the theological and practical groundwork for the future of the program, ensuring its viability for years to come. Sixty-six men had been ordained deacons. Not every one persevered in his vocation, but the vast majority remained active and true to their calling. Many more men would become deacons in the ensuing years, bringing the comfort and joy of Jesus to countless people hungering for God.

"Nothing in this life and particularly at this time is more difficult, or more toilsome or more fraught with danger than the office of bishop, priest or deacon," wrote St. Augustine. "On the other hand, there is no happier life as long as these ministries are carried out according to Our Lord's command."[97] Father Amico quoted these words in a January 1978 column in *Contact*. They were a New Year's challenge to the deacons and the current crop of candidates and to their wives and families to keep in mind that the diaconate was a worthy and beautiful calling from the Lord himself. The diaconate program would be true to its mission, now clarified and strengthened, and it would continue the grand adventure and good work initiated by Archbishop Pocock.

5

A MODEL OF SERVICE: 1978–1985

Introduction

The 1977 Review remains a foundational document in the history of the permanent diaconate in the Archdiocese of Toronto. It inspired and guided deacons in their ongoing endeavour to clarify the purpose of their vocations as ordained members of the hierarchy and as visible icons of Christ the Servant in a world always hungry to hear the Good News. It resurfaced at almost every study of the diaconate program. From among the five models of diaconate considered by the 1977 Review – bishop's man, intermediary, sign of *diakonia*, catalyst or animator of the lay apostolate, and service or charity to the marginalized of society – the committee made a deliberate decision to highlight the last two models and, upon further reflection, to emphasize the diaconate's ministry of service to the marginalized or disadvantaged as its primary focus. A regrettable consequence of this decision was the diminution of the status of the model of deacon as catalyst or animator of the laity, allowing the model to disappear from the collective consciousness of the diaconate community. It received a second life, however, in 1991, when its resurrection was seen as necessary to mollify criticism of the supposed narrowness of the terms of the 1977 Review's model of service. (We will discuss this in greater detail later.)

Beginning in 1977, ministry to the marginalized was the governing model, the primary ministry or mission, of the archdiocesan diaconate. It defined expectations for everyone involved in the diaconate, from the rector of St. Augustine's Seminary and the director and assistant director of the training or formation program, to the co-ordinators, mentors, candidates and their wives. It also determined admission standards, the length and scope of the training program for candidates and the post-ordination assignments and service agreements, which were the greatest assurance that the diaconate was holding fast to its chosen model.

Of course, the model of deacon-as-servant to the marginalized left ample opportunity for the deacon to participate in the ministries of liturgy and the Word, which were interpreted by the diaconate as a public and communal celebration of the deacon's ministry in union with the presiding priest and the worshipping congregation. Of much greater significance, though, is the fact that the model guaranteed that after 1977 very few deacons would be given a strictly parish-based ministry. Instead, it called for deacons to have a liturgical base, generally speaking in a parish, and, at the same time, *to work as deacons* in public institutions, such as prisons, hospitals and nursing homes that usually fell within the geographical jurisdiction of the parish where they celebrated the ministries of the liturgy and the Word. Subsequently, some deacons assumed diocesan-wide ministries, such as Pearson Airport Chapel or the ports of Toronto and Oshawa, which by definition transcended parish boundaries and occasionally allowed the deacon to have a liturgical base not situated in a parish.

This chapter will examine the Policy Statement on the Training Program (January 1978), the pioneering work of the Deacon Search Committee (1981) and the deliberations and decisions of the Advisory Board (1981–1983) that was set up to implement the recommendations of the Deacon Search Committee. It will end with an inquiry from Sister Anne Bezaire, OSU, on the Toronto diaconate program, and a response by Father Brian Clough, rector of St. Augustine's Seminary.

Policy Statement on the Training Program 1978

In retrospect, the 1977 Review was the cornerstone of a "re-vivified" diaconal program, bringing together for the first time all the theological and practical elements of formation and ministry, as well as vowing to attract the right kind of candidate. Archbishop Pocock gave it his blessing. But the Review, as a stand-alone effort, lacked the force of an official document. It was an act of profound self-understanding, but to be effective and authoritative it required translation into official policy of the Archdiocese of Toronto. As such, it would direct, confirm, and, whenever needed, explain decisions made by the Executive Committee of the diaconate-training program, the only archdiocesan committee authorized to deal with the activities of the permanent diaconate.[1]

The procedure of writing a policy statement on the training program began as early as May 1976, the date of the first draft. This was three months after the Senate of Priests set up the Action Group on the Diaconate, which produced the 1977 Review, and nearly a year in advance of the completion of the Review. The attempt to write a policy statement without the guidance of the Review, to build a house where there was no foundation, was bound to falter. The first draft, which drew heavily from an American diocesan source, listed twenty-one aspects of the diaconate, but had little to say on training.[2] Of interest to us are two items on this list. Number 12 offered a definition of a deacon's ministry of service: it "should be directed towards those persons on the fringe of society who need to be integrated into society and then into the ecclesial community and to those to whom the Church needs to render more effective witness."[3] Number 15 referred to the deacon as "a catalyst and animator of a particular need with specific responsibilities within the community,"[4] but it made no reference to the deacon's relationship to the lay apostolate.

The committee given the job of writing a policy statement met at least two more times, on 31 January and 25 April 1977, focusing on amendments. In the meantime, desiring to produce a more imaginative policy that reflected the needs and goals of Toronto's training program as he saw them, Deacon Stan MacLellan proposed a completely new approach to the undertaking. For the June 1977 meeting, he submitted a draft that outlined the objectives of the training program – the preparation of candidates for the threefold ministry of charity (service), liturgy and Word, *in that order* – and incorporated a year-old article by Deacon Colin Chase on the nature of the training program as one of constant discernment that took place in five specific educational phases over three years. It ended with sections on specific guidelines for admission and education of candidates; the consent of wives; signs of progress; ministerial relationships; a description of the diaconate's threefold ministry; and the need for support for deacons from the Catholic community.[5] After the Executive Committee edited and amended this draft, it became "(Policy Statement) Training Program for the Permanent Diaconate Archdiocese of Toronto" and was dated January 1978.[6] Copies were distributed in February after Archbishop Pocock acknowledged it as official archdiocesan policy.[7]

Having based the Policy Statement on the 1977 Review, the Executive Committee insisted that the ministry of service (charity) had absolute primacy in the threefold ministry of service, liturgy and Word. That was the model of diaconate as understood and practised in the Archdiocese of Toronto. Nothing had changed. Rather, the model was now policy, and the point of any policy in any organization is for its leaders to adhere to it. The Executive Committee would prove itself equal to the challenge. "The main focus of the deacon's work," quoting from the Policy Statement, "should be on the ministry of service toward the <u>marginalized</u>: those who have been pushed to the fringe of society by such things as poverty, sickness, crime and age. This ministry will often but not always be on the parochial level."[8] The words "should be" made room for exceptions to the model without committing the program to search for them.

So, what happened to the model of deacon as catalyst and animator of the lay apostolate? It was demoted, in a fashion, from serving as a model to becoming one of seven ministerial relationships, and was placed sixth among the seven. Quoting *Sacrum Diaconatus Ordinem* (no. 21), the Policy Statement declared, "One of the deacon's main duties is to 'promote and support apostolic activities of the laity.' He is a catalyst and animator of particular activities."[9] What activities in particular did the framers of the Policy Statement have in mind, ones that would be in harmony with the model of service now so firmly entrenched? They left that question for deacons to discuss in the future. Such a discussion seems not to have taken place, if only for the reason that no one in the diaconal community was in haste to pursue it in the absence of a development that deacons could not ignore, such as an episcopal request.

Like its predecessor, the 1977 Review, the 1978 Policy Statement enjoyed a long and distinguished life in the evolving organizational history of the permanent diaconate. For many years it was the first and only document of its kind. For that reason, it had an enormous influence on the direction that the diaconate program took, especially in terms of the service model, and the determination of the diaconate community not to stray from the path that it had chosen.

Deacon Search Committee 1980–1981

In April 1980, Deacon Tab Charbonneau and his wife, Mary, attended the annual convention of the National Association of Permanent Diaconate Directors in Kansas City, Missouri. They were the only representatives from Toronto, and their attendance was a first for the archdiocesan diaconate.[10] In his request to Bishop Robert Clune to send him to the convention, Charbonneau said that the primary reason for their participation would be to gather information on support programs for deacons in ministry. To date, the diaconate program had spent a great deal of its time and energy on pre-ordination training and formation, a legitimate and necessary exercise, but not nearly enough on the post-ordination life and work of the deacon. The program had evolved to the point where the number of deacons in the field far outnumbered the number of candidates in training, at a ratio of three to one and sometimes as high as four to one. It was time, therefore, to develop support systems for deacons, their wives and their families.

This was the first observation Charbonneau recorded in his notes on the convention.[11] It was a pressing problem for the well-being of the diaconate in many dioceses in the United States, and, in Charbonneau's mind, Toronto was no different. Two years shy of its tenth anniversary (1972), Toronto's diaconate program was barely out of its infancy. If it wanted to remain in good health and continue to grow and prosper, the deacons would have to treat this problem as a central component of the next phase of the program's natural development.

As soon as he typed up his report, Charbonneau delivered it to Bishop Clune and his fellow deacons. From there, things moved quickly. On 28 April 1980, a number of deacons convened to discuss the report, and, as a result, they proposed the formation of a Search Committee that would investigate all aspects of the current diaconate program with a view to the realignment of some of the program's support systems to the ordained. The committee would conduct its investigation within the framework of the needs of the diocese, the people of God, the deacon, and his wife and family. While only deacons would hold membership on the committee, Bishop Clune by right would chair the committee's sessions and by practical necessity would act as a conduit between the committee and Cardinal Gerald Emmett Carter.

The deacons laid out a threefold mandate for the Search Committee. The first mandate would be

> to review and identify the priorities and needs of the Archdiocese and its people and to identify in what areas the Deacon could fulfill his unique role of "service" to those not reached by the institutional church or who are considered "disadvantaged". And also where the Deacon can be the catalyst to draw out the Laity to their role of service.[12]

These two sentences look simple but say a great deal. On the one hand, this was fairly standard stuff. As a re-statement on the prevailing model of the deacon – as someone with a unique role to serve the disadvantaged – and on the deacon's second function as catalyst or animator of the laity, this mandate was in sync with the 1977 Review and the 1978 Policy Statement. There was nothing new here. On the other hand, the first half of the opening sentence was a bold initiative in ecclesiology. It would be a committee of deacons, and not the archbishop, that would identify the needs of the archdiocese and the faithful. Once identified, these needs would constitute one of the major determining characteristics of the modus operandi whereby candidates were selected and trained for a period of three years and then recommended to the archbishop for ordination.[13] It was naïve of the deacons to think this way, especially when the archbishop happened to be Cardinal Carter. They were not being disrespectful of the cardinal. Rather, they were so caught up in the administration of the diaconate program that they had become careless in their understanding of the governance of the local Church.

Fortunately for them, they corrected this blunder in the section on the identity of deacons in their final report to Bishop Clune. We do not know who insisted on the correction, but it would not be unreasonable to speculate that it was Bishop Clune, who would have been sensitive to the right of the Ordinary to administer his own diocese. The statement reads, "The ministry of charity or service is the essence of the Gospel call to care for the poor in body and spirit. The needs of the Diocese, both at the diocesan and parish levels, are to be determined by the Ordinary of the Diocese."[14] The deacons' assertion on the model of service is in the first sentence, and the counterbalance to that concerning the Ordinary of the diocese is in the second sentence, which seems as if it were inserted to corral diaconal ambitions and to remind deacons that they were the bishop's men. Appropriate affirmations, though, proved not to be enough. The presumption on the part of the deacons about their role in the identification of archdiocesan needs, in tandem with their right to define the appropriate model of service for the diaconate in the archdiocese, persisted, quietly and unofficially, until it caught the critical eye of Cardinal Carter vis-à-vis the William Hawkshaw ordination dilemma of the mid-1980s. The cardinal would challenge the diaconate on both counts.

The second mandate would be to evaluate the individual and ministerial needs of the deacon in terms of the skills required for diaconal service, his ongoing education and spiritual life, his relationship to his wife and family, his overall credibility in the community where he served and the effectiveness of his particular ministry.

The focus of this mandate was the deacon in the field, Deacon Charbonneau's primary concern and the impetus for the meeting of 28 April. Who better than deacons to determine and evaluate the needs of deacons in the performance of their ministry?

The third mandate would be to investigate the merits of setting up a permanent secretariat (an advisory board). This secretariat would co-ordinate the integration of the diaconate into the archdiocese, develop guidelines of accountability for deacons that would be used by the personnel committee (established in 1979), assess the compatibility of requests for diaconal ministry with the program's model of service and develop a public relations program that would increase the general awareness and understanding of the diaconate throughout the archdiocese. This was a tall order. But the deacons believed that for their vicar to oversee the effective administration of the diaconate program, he would need to consult an active and knowledgeable board of advisors who had the best interests of both the deacons and the archdiocese in mind when proposing policy.

The deacons took their initiative to Bishop Clune at the annual general meeting of the Council of Deacons on 2 May 1980, and he readily agreed to the formation of a Deacon Search Committee.[15] At the committee's first meeting, on 31 May, Bishop Clune used his opening remarks to elaborate on the purpose and scope of the committee's work, which was to be seen not as a threat to the existing program but as an opportunity to make it more effective and a source of satisfaction to the laity and lay ministries of service. According to the Minutes of the meeting,

> [Bishop Clune] emphasized the need to bring about a greater sense of community and unity, with respect to all who serve the Church, whether through an ordained covenant or lay apostolate. He made reference to field support to the Ordained Deacon, the continued involvement of wives after the formal training years at the Seminary, and stressed that while the committee was not a decision making body, they were certainly being asked to make suggestions and recommendations with respect to the overall Toronto Program.[16]

The purpose of the Search Committee was to investigate the diaconate from the inside. Its work would take place not in isolation but always within the wider context of service to the Church. This was an important caution. So too was the reminder that the committee was consultative in nature. It was authorized to recommend changes to archdiocesan policy on the diaconate program. The right to make changes to that policy was the prerogative of the archbishop.

The Search Committee had seven members from different regions of the archdiocese. They were Deacons John O'Connor, Brian O'Brien, George Morley, Tom Mason, Stan MacLellan and Thomas Cresswell, with Tab Charbonneau as the committee co-ordinator. They met on a regular basis, usually every two months, from May 1980 to October 1981. Their meetings were intense and productive, characterized by professionalism and dedication and driven by deadlines and a sense of urgency. The workload was distributed among six sub-committees: pre-ordination training program, personnel, continuing education, spirituality, field training and operations, and Council of Deacons. Each sub-committee was required to submit a written report with recommendations that would be incorporated into the committee's official submission. The sub-committees dealt with topics traditionally relevant to the diaconate and broad enough to invite thorough and critical scrutiny but not so broad as to invite submissions that said everything about the subject at hand. The first five of these sub-committees relied heavily (but not exclusively) on questionnaires to gather information, while the Council of Deacons preferred the camaraderie and collectivity of home meetings as their primary means of investigation.[17] Meanwhile, the committee-of-the-whole turned its attention to the identity of the deacon and the provision of an organizational structure for the program.

Over the course of its deliberations, the committee carefully edited the general framework of 28 April 1980, in which they would carry out their threefold mandate, calling them "Global Aspects." The changes to each of the four constituent parts were significant. They addressed the following topics:

1. the needs of the archdiocese as they relate to the "service" role of the deacon
2. the needs of particular parishes
3. the needs of the deacon before and after ordination
4. the needs of the deacon's family and the responsibility of the program to respond to those needs.[18]

Number 1: The needs of the archdiocese were no longer a stand-alone subject but were now directly linked to the model of the diaconate and its service role. Number 2: The needs of the people of God became the needs of particular parishes. Number 3: Although the needs of the deacon in the field were paramount in this review of the diaconate, the committee wisely chose to treat the deacon's need for support both before and after ordination as a single spiritual reality. Number 4: No longer would it be enough to identify the needs of the deacon's family. The program had a duty to respond to them.

The changes in Number 1 and Number 2 revealed unresolved tensions within the committee.[19] Concerning the revision to Number 1, the committee was unsure which should come first, the establishment of the needs of the archdiocese, which would indicate to a significant degree the kind of person suitable to the program, or the selection of people for the program, who, upon ordination, would be matched to the needs of the archdiocese. This proved to be quite a conundrum. Either choice might eliminate otherwise perfectly good people for the diaconate. The substitution of the phrase "particular parishes" for "the people of God" in Number 2 pointed to a lingering doubt in the minds of probably not an insignificant minority of deacons as to the suitability of the current model of the diaconate, as enshrined in the 1978 Policy Statement. They believed that, because the training and in-field programs concentrated almost exclusively on diaconal service to the disadvantaged, little emphasis was placed on diaconal service within the parish, which they considered to be an equally valid manifestation of the servant-deacon model and one worthy of the program's attention and promotion.

The committee allowed this sentiment to be aired in the spirit of vigorous debate.

The six sub-committees made a total of fifty-one recommendations, with the one for continuing education accounting for nineteen of them. A common concern for nearly each sub-committee and the committee-of-the-whole was a proposal to establish an advisory board to the vicar of deacons. In the short term, such a board would implement the recommendations, depending on their acceptance by Cardinal Carter, and in the long term, it would monitor the progress and problems of the entire diaconate program. Since it would be too unwieldy to list all fifty-one recommendations, we will highlight a selection of the more pertinent ones.

The training program sub-committee wanted a balanced program that would give equal time to theology, pastoral care, spirituality and family development and that would put in place a system for the ongoing monitoring of "the orientation of the training program, in light of any amendments to the model of deacon in the diocese, and any effective external connections with advisory groups or lay ministries programs."[20] A sore point with this committee was the change to the education criterion for admission into the program, from "two years of college [university] or its equivalent" to "two years of college [university] or its academic equivalent."[21] Deacon Stan MacLellan, speaking for the Council of Deacons, had already criticized this amendment in a letter to Bishop Clune, dated 18 September 1980. "The academic equivalent," he wrote, "is now to be measured by a test designed to determine the acceptability of one who *wants to enter university*, and not necessarily one who wishes to prepare himself for the threefold Ministry of Liturgy, Word and Service."[22] The training program sub-committee took up the cause, giving it an official stamp, and was supported by the personnel sub-committee, which stated that "the educational requirements are far too restrictive and that better tools are required to evaluate prospective candidates."[23] The committee-of-the-whole endorsed their plea, but it went nowhere. Many years later, the matter of "academic equivalent" remained a contentious issue for some of the veteran deacons.[24]

Aside from its opinion on the education requirement, the personnel sub-committee recommended, "a selection committee be formed under the vicar of deacons to develop standards for selection of candidates."[25] To that end, it proposed that the program incorporate the Deacon Perceiver interview, which had been recently developed by Selection Research, Inc. (SRI), of Lincoln, Nebraska, as one of several tools employed by the diaconate program in the candidate selection process.[26]

The majority of the nineteen recommendations made by the continuing education sub-committee concerned the management and supervision of the continuing education program, regardless of its specific content. But there were recommendations that aimed to reform the entire process and make continuing education a more credible and substantial part of a deacon's life and ministry. The continuing education sub-committee suggested specialized courses for specialized ministries, courses in prayer life, mandatory and regular attendance at continuing education sessions, invitations to wives at the beginning of each session, collaboration with the personnel committee in their meetings with deacons and the inclusion of a deacon's written commitment to continuing education as part of his work agreement with the program.[27]

The spirituality sub-committee strongly recommended the immediate appointment of a spiritual director for the program. Members of the Council of Deacons would assist the spiritual director in his work. Together, and in co-operation with the continuing education committee, the spiritual director and council members would devise and manage a program of spiritual formation for both candidates and deacons, encourage deacons to have personal spiritual directors and participate in retreats specifically for deacons, and set up annual dates for spiritual exercises.[28]

The recommendations of the field training and operations sub-committee called for the appointment of a field training co-ordinator, "who will be responsible to set up practical programs in specific ministries, in concert with the training program staff."[29] The sub-committee also wanted a greater emphasis on pastoral training in the course of studies and supported mandatory continuing education.

The Council of Deacons reaffirmed its commitment to foster and support a sense of community for deacons. In support of this responsibility, the council suggested that it concentrate its efforts on communications and social activities and interface with the committees on continuing education and spirituality. Addressing the many issues that the wives raised at the home meetings, the council proposed that it have two elected representatives for wives on the council, that they be invited to organize zone meetings and that they have their own spiritual director/counsellor/confidante.[30]

The Search Committee acting as a committee-of-the-whole addressed the perennial topic of the identity of the deacon. In the threefold ministry of the diaconate – charity, liturgy and the Word – the ministry of charity or service was paramount in importance, for it was primarily within the exercise of that particular ministry that the deacon would find his identity and become a more effective liturgical minister. It was important, therefore, that action be taken immediately to identify the service needs of the archdiocese, first on a diocesan level in public institutions such as prisons, hospitals, homes for the aged and handicapped, and in a variety of social action programs, and then on a parish level in work such as parish renewal, prayer groups, youth ministry on campus and in parishes, marriage preparation and baptismal catechesis. As soon as the needs of the archdiocese were identified, it would be necessary to identify the right kind of diaconal ministries to meet those needs and to develop criteria for their implementation throughout the archdiocese.

Following its examination of the diaconal ministry of charity, the Search Committee conducted similar examinations of the ministries of liturgy and the Word. Finally, it suggested the formation of an Advisory Board that would assess the committee's numerous recommendations and monitor the direction of diaconal ministry to ensure its fidelity to its original mandate to serve the spiritual and temporal needs of the disadvantaged. If there were any doubts as to the Search Committee's commitment to the model of the diaconate as set forth in the 1978 Policy Statement, they were dispelled by this statement of the committee, which was inspired by Father Karl Rahner: "The deacon should reach out in the name of Christ, to reinvigorate in both the civil and Christian community those marginalized by disadvantage or alienation, and inspire the faithful to do the same."[31]

The Search Committee's final task was to propose an organizational structure for the diaconate that would bring together for the first time and in one chart the various aspects of the pre-ordination training program and the post-ordination support system for the deacon in the field (see Appendix I). The chart was intended to present a comprehensive picture of the entire program, which contained both present and future features. The committee hoped that its proposal, if accepted, would lighten the workload of the vicar of deacons and promote the diaconate as an integral part of the life of the Church in the archdiocese. It also hoped that, because the chart would serve as a map or a blueprint, it would be of practical assistance to the vicar of deacons and his advisors in the implementation of the committee's recommendations.

The organizational chart featured twenty-five sections. They were arranged hierarchically to show lines of authority and relationship, with each section devoted to a particular function within the organization. In the text accompanying the chart, the committee gave "job descriptions" for fifteen of these functions. On the training program side of the chart, they were diaconate program director (executive director on the chart), pre-ordination supervisor, co-ordinators (theology, pastoral formation, spirituality and field education), training program co-ordinator, co-ordinators and mentors for the different years and a co-ordinator for wives and families of the candidates. For the post-ordination program, the functions were post-ordination supervisor, spirituality supervisor, continuing education supervisor and field supervisors. Other parts described by the Search Committee were candidate selection group, personnel committee, promotion (public relations), new ministries and the all-important advisory board. Included on the chart but not described were vicar of deacons, chairman of the Council of Deacons, individual spiritual directors, resource staff, supervisors for specific deacons, and zones and families, which fell under the supervision of the Council of Deacons.

Oddly, the chart did not include the archbishop or the rector of the seminary.[32] It was as if the Search Committee had chosen to forget its own words to the effect that it was the archbishop (through the vicar of deacons) who envisioned and directed the diaconate program and defined the roles of the deacon.[33] The absence of any mention of the rector of the seminary was also strange because the diaconate program had always been a program of the seminary, and nowhere in its "Recommendations" did the Search Committee advocate, or even hint at, the program's removal from the direction of the seminary. As troubling as these two lacunae were, they were not enough to sink the Search Committee's ambitious and thoughtful attempt to understand the diaconate in all its evolving intricacies. But these two missing elements seem to have been enough to prompt the Advisory Board in 1983 to take a second look at the organizational structure of the program.

The longer an organization survives and succeeds, the more it grows in complexity, and to manage that complexity, the more complex its organization becomes. Toronto's diaconate program was no stranger to this unwritten law governing the bureaucratic life of dynamic organizations. During the first nine years of its corporate existence, the program had survived the growing pains of its infancy; it had established sound policy for the training program, which set forth a model of the diaconate; it was attracting a regular flow of candidates, who felt that they could live up to that model; and with the Search Committee, which was an initiative of the deacons themselves, the program conducted a detailed examination of itself and produced a report that was both frank and hopeful. The diaconate was a success so far. How, then, to assure that that success continued well into the future, as circumstances and needs changed, for the greater glory of God in the Archdiocese of Toronto? The Search Committee's final report, "Recommendations," was a compass pointing to a future for the diaconate program that was filled with hope and promise and that rested on a firm foundation of practical and realistic advice.

Nothing would happen, of course, until an advisory board (a permanent secretariat in the words of the Search Committee's third mandate) was in place to deal with the committee's "Recommendations." But before we discuss that aspect of the diaconate's history, we turn our attention to an important addition to the personnel of the diaconate program. This took place in advance of the committee's submission of "Recommendations" to Bishop Clune in October 1981.

Sister Charmaine Grillot, CPPS, joined the diaconal community in September 1981 in response to the request of the wives of deacons for a spiritual director of their own. It was incorporated into the recommendations of the Council of Deacons to the Search Committee and was given unanimous support by both the council and the committee. Deacon Stan MacLellan, the former chairman of the Deacon Council, and Deacon Tab Charbonneau, at that time Bishop Clune's assistant, approached the bishop as early as June 1981.[34] He was very sensitive to the spiritual needs of the wives and to their constructive role in the diaconate program. Thus it comes as no surprise that he would pre-empt the work of an advisory board to correct what was probably a regrettable oversight. This was one instance in which process was willingly sacrificed for a long-overdue remedy. Bishop Clune lobbied Bishop Leonard J. Wall, the chancellor, to have the archdiocese hire Sister Charmaine, and Bishop Wall agreed.[35] When it came time to extend Sister Charmaine's contract and increase her salary, Bishop Clune went to the well with Bishop Wall once again and succeeded on both counts.[36]

Sister Charmaine was a member of the Sisters of the Precious Blood of Dayton, Ohio. She had been an elementary and secondary school teacher for fifteen years and dean of studies for her community for five years. After serving as president of her community for eight years, she took a sabbatical, starting in September 1980, and enrolled in the Spirituality Integration Program at the Jesuit-run Regis College in Toronto, where Father Alan Peterkin, SJ, was her professor of spiritual direction. Since Father Peterkin was providing spiritual direction to deacons and their wives in monthly retreat days and various workshops, Sister Charmaine was invited to participate in these gatherings. From the very beginning, the diaconate community, especially the wives, appreciated her presence and her advice. This led to her appointment, on a part-time basis, to minister to the wives of ordained deacons, which lasted from September 1981 to June 1982. Bishop Clune announced the news of her employment in a letter addressed to the wives.[37]

The archdiocese then hired her full-time as an assistant director of the diaconate program to minister not only to wives but also to deacons. In November 1982, she was named director of spirituality.[38] Working out of an office in the chancery, and reporting regularly to Bishop Clune, her immediate superior, Sister Charmaine conducted monthly days of reflection, yearly retreats, workshops on assertiveness training and personal development, and provided individual and group spiritual direction on a request basis. (She was not involved in the training program, but on occasion invited the wives of candidates to participate in her programs.) While she was in daily contact with those deacons – such as Tab Charbonneau, Stan MacLellan, Dan Murphy and Tom Mason – who were directly responsible for the ordained, she treated her work with the wives as a special component of her ministry. Sister Charmaine made it a priority "to bolster their self-esteem and their belief in their own goodness. They had a personality and goodness in their own right that was not dependent upon their relationship with their deacon/husband."[39]

Sister Charmaine left the program in November 1984 to become vice-president of Mission Services for the Catholic Health Association in St. Louis, Missouri. Her departure may not have been a surprise, but many deacons and their wives nonetheless were saddened by her decision to return to the United States. Philomena Andrews, Lucy Verschuren, Deacon Bob Ferguson, Helen Oneson and Deacon Dan Murphy and his wife, Jean, wrote open letters of appreciation, in which they extolled her listening skills, gentleness, wisdom and dynamism.[40] Her immediate successors were Sister Sadie MacKay, CSM, and Sister Rita MacLellan, CSM. These two members of the Sisters of St. Martha, who came from Halifax, worked diligently to continue the fine work begun by Sister Charmaine.

Advisory Board 1981–1983

In his December 1982 submission to the archdiocesan quinquennial report, Bishop Clune wrote that a Deacons' Advisory Board was presently considering the findings of the Deacon Search Committee. "This Board," he continued, "is made up of deacons, representatives of the Training Program and the Ministries Program, as well as priests, deacons' wives and laity. I feel that much has been accomplished because a forum has been provided for greater communication between the various parts of the Deacon Program, as well as with other members of the church community."[41] The board was struck in early 1982 and had fifteen members, a fairly representative group that proved to be remarkably productive and unified despite its large size. Besides Bishop Clune, who was the chair, there were six deacons (Tab Charbonneau, Colin Chase, Stan MacLellan, Daniel Murphy, John O'Connor and Barrett Simpson), three priests (Father Charles Amico and Father Brian Clough of St. Augustine's Seminary and Father Bernard Wilson, a parish priest who had been a deacon), two wives of deacons (Molly Callaghan and Alison Cresswell), one woman religious (Sister Charmaine Grillot, CPPS) and two laymen (Joseph Molinari and Bruno Scorsone).[42]

The board met for the first time on 23 March 1982. After listening to Father Amico's capsule history of the diaconate program, and to Deacon Tab Charbonneau's summary of the initiative behind the formation and work of the Deacon Search Committee, the Advisory Board defined its central purpose: "To review the recommendations of the Search Committee Report and to determine the feasibility and advisability of implementing these or other recommendations."[43] Put another way, the board would deliberate on policy for the diaconate program within the framework of the Search Committee's "Recommendations" of October 1981 and make recommendations to the archbishop. Bishop Clune reminded the board that it would operate in much the same way as the Senate of Priests or a parish council – it could advise but never make policy on its own. With this in mind, the board focused its efforts on the spiritual and educational needs of deacons in the field. It would also deal with the program's organization.[44]

The Advisory Board met eleven times from March 1982 to May 1983. The members spent a great deal of time on the following areas: continuing education; policies and procedures for personnel; spirituality; field training and operations; and organizational structure.[45] The subject of continuing education for deacons monopolized many of the early meetings and quickly became a vexatious issue. Its resolution was left in the hands of the first appointee to the new position of executive director.[46] The board had better luck when it came to the spirituality component of the program. Its main concern was the retention of Sister Charmaine. It proposed that she be given the position of director of spirituality and have her contract extended and upgraded accordingly. With her place in the program secured on a full-time basis, the board reasoned that the door was open for it to debate the program's organizational structure.[47]

We have already discussed Sister Charmaine's efforts on behalf of wives and deacons. Her presence was a great benefit to them and to the program as a whole. The Advisory Board was wise in its decision to support her work, and the archdiocese was generous to agree to the board's motion. This was the type of progress that was necessary to keep the program open to accommodating the evolving needs of the diaconate community as it matured and stabilized. Any other progress made by the Advisory Board, however, was limited to only two other initiatives: the adoption of the Deacon Perceiver interview and an organizational structure for the diaconal program. Happily, in each case, long-lasting positive change was the result.

The Deacon Search Committee had recommended the addition of the Deacon Perceiver to the selection process whereby candidates were accepted (or rejected) for the diaconal program and to the program's approach to the re-evaluation of the ministry of deacons when deemed necessary by the personnel committee.[48] In 1979, the National Association of Permanent Diaconate Directors (NAPDD) was looking for an objective and professional interview process that "would enable [diaconate] programs to predict the applicant's potential success in diaconal ministry."[49] The NAPPD turned to Selection Research, Inc. (SRI). Deacon Tom Mason attended SRI Perceiver meetings in Newark, New Jersey, in September 1980, in his capacity as a member of the Search Committee. He wrote up a lengthy report on the Deacon Perceiver, praising it but not without cautions, and proposing its adoption. Mason felt that the Deacon Perceiver was an excellent addition to the tools already in use for the selection or admissions process, because it could be extremely helpful in discovering servant-leaders among applicants to the diaconate. He saw this as fundamental to the preservation of the servant-leader model of the diaconate, which was favoured by the Toronto program almost since its inception.[50]

The topic of the Deacon Perceiver entered the board's discussions during its second meeting on 15 April 1982. Although the board recognized the obvious value of the interview in the selection process, it chose to dwell for the most part on its apparent usefulness in the determination of the needs and capabilities of deacons already in ministry and in the evaluation of the direction in which deacons were taking their ministry.[51] This approach did not change. Such an emphasis was probably a misreading of the intended purpose of the Deacon Perceiver, which we will discuss shortly, but it was in keeping with the Search Committee's understanding of the utility of the Deacon Perceiver.

No matter. In advance of the next meeting of the Advisory Board, Deacon Tab Charbonneau, Deacon Alexander McGregor and Sister Charmaine Grillot attended a two-day session of the Deacon Perceiver Academy, which taught and certified people to administer what has always been a copyrighted procedure. Based largely on their opinions, the board approved the Deacon Perceiver interview for the archdiocesan diaconate program at its meeting of 20 May 1982.[52] The board saw the Deacon Perceiver's benefit primarily as a development tool for ordained men, and only secondarily as an additional element of the selection process currently in use by the training program. (Other requirements included an interview at the seminary for the candidate and his wife, a letter from their pastor, references, a home visit by a deacon couple, psychological assessment, medical report, and lastly, separate interviews of the candidate and his spouse.)

The diaconate program wasted no time in incorporating the perceiver. Deacon Colin Chase reported to the board on a week-long perceiver training session in August at St. Augustine's Seminary. Those deacons who consented to take the interview gave favourable comments. They concluded that it helped them develop a profile of their strengths in diaconal ministry and would assist deacons moving from one ministry to another.[53]

What, then, is the Deacon Perceiver Interview? The basic operational assumption is that the selection of persons for any kind of church ministry "should be based on a priori talent assessment.... In other words, specific talents for the specific ministry are needed if the person is to be successful – not merely proof that he or she has the required background in education and experience."[54] The interview identifies talent in applicants and as such predicts, to a certain degree, the success an applicant might have in a particular ministry. For the diaconate, it looks for ability, willingness and desire to serve others in accordance with the model of servant-leadership. But talent is not synonymous with vocation in the Catholic meaning of that word. While talent obviously works in tandem with vocation, it is independent of it. Vocation is a result of personal motivation, and it is the formation process, after selection and prior to ordination, that will identify and enhance motivation.[55]

The interview discovers talent in nine different areas or themes. They are as follows: relator ("enjoys working with people"); helping ("active in helping other people"); teaming ("works to help others work together effectively with minimal conflict"); spirituality (prayer life and faith); accommodating ("always giving himself to others"); kinesthetic ("high energy level"); positive other's perception ("positive affirmation by others"); family ("high priority on family," "marriage vows are binding and sacred," "integrates his family into his work in the church, or on the job"); and purpose ("a strong belief system about the service that he has for others").[56] There are six questions for each of the nine themes, for a total of fifty-four questions. The interviewer presents the first question from each theme and then begins again with the second question from each theme and so forth until he has asked all questions. The interview is recorded, the interviewee's reactions are observed and his answers are rated by the interviewer. The tape and ratings are sent to SRI headquarters in Nebraska for verification. Officials there code the information, compare it against their computer model (the result of interviews of thirty hand-picked deacons), transcribe and rate the recording, comment on the variances in rating between Toronto and Nebraska and return everything for the program's files.[57]

The Toronto diaconate program continues to use the Deacon Perceiver. Although the perceiver's adoption by the Advisory Board in 1982 was founded on a belief that its application would be mainly for deacons in the field, today it is employed almost exclusively as part of the interview process for applicants to the program, in keeping with the intent of its SRI creators.

The Advisory Board's other significant initiative was its proposal for the organizational structure of the diaconate program. At its meeting of 15 November 1982, the board selected Bruno Scorsone, one of its members, to chair a special committee on organizational structure.[58] He was free to select additional members for the committee. They were Mary Matthews, a member of the Vatican's commission on the laity, Terry Delaney, a senior consultant with the Federal Government of Canada, and Father Bernard Wilson, a member of the board.[59] Scorsone also relied on the expertise of two people, who, although they could not participate directly in the deliberations of the committee, offered him valuable advice and guidance. They were Mario Galeazzi, a social worker at St. Stephen's Chapel, and Daniel De Matteis, manager of Methods and Procedures at Nestlé Enterprises.[60] Intense and productive discussions of the committee's work took place at meetings of the Advisory Board on 21 February and 14 March, and on 11 April 1983 when the report was completed.[61] It was dated 31 March 1983 and officially submitted to Bishop Clune on 9 May 1983.[62]

As we have discussed in the section previous to this one, the Deacon Search Committee produced a highly detailed organizational chart, covering both the pre- and post-ordination sides of the program, with descriptions for nearly every function or position mentioned on it. Its intention was to produce an all-inclusive picture of the program. But it was a very busy picture. However much the Advisory Board's special committee on organization appreciated this effort, and relied on it as a template of sorts, it approached the problem from a different and, it thought, more pertinent angle. It decided that its organizational chart would do two things: clarify lines of accountability and responsibility in the administrative organization of the diaconate program, and delineate between "the operations branch and policy-making branch of the deaconal system" in the Archdiocese of Toronto.[63] Consequently, the committee restored to the organizational structure the functions of the archbishop and the rector of the seminary, limited a mention of the training program on the chart to the rector and director of training, dropped the Council of Deacons but recognized the value of its purposes as set forth in its constitution, and proposed that the new Advisory Board assume the functions of the Council of Deacons and the personnel committee (See Appendix II).

The committee made five major recommendations:

1. The organization of the Permanent Diaconate in the Archdiocese would continue to be headed by the Vicar of Deacons, Bishop Clune, who would be accountable to the Cardinal Archbishop of Toronto.

2. There would be a full-time Executive Director reporting to the Vicar of Deacons and responsible for the conduct of the overall system. That office would include all personnel-related functions such as selection, counselling, field training, supervision of ministries, needs identification, assignments and evaluations.

3. The program's implementation and maintenance would be the responsibility of three full-time regional directors, each of whom would report directly to the Executive Director.

4. The Vicar of Deacons and the Executive Director would be assisted by a regionally elected Advisory Board whose membership would include 6 deacons (2 per zone), 3 deacons' wives and 3 others appointed by the Vicar. The Vicar's appointees would as much as possible bring experiences and skills from outside the deaconal system.

5. The responsibility for all pre-ordination training would remain with the Rector of the Seminary who, assisted by a Director of Training, would provide ongoing training resources and

advice to the Vicar and the Executive Director in a functional relationship.[64]

The committee appended an additional recommendation – that the proposed organizational structure be open to evaluation and, if necessary, to amendment to meet the changing needs of the Church. It also described in detail the functions of the executive director and the regional directors.[65] The first and fifth recommendations were not new, but their inclusion was necessary to the integrity of the proposal. The middle three recommendations – the appointment of an executive director and regional directors and the need for an elected Advisory Board that would give representatives of deacons and their wives a significant voice in the formulation of policy – were definitely fresh ideas.[66] On the official acceptance of these hung the worthiness of the committee's report, and, to a considerable extent, the value of the Advisory Board's good faith efforts to implement the "Recommendations" of the Deacon Search Committee.

The Advisory Board unanimously approved the recommendations of the "Report on the Organizational Structure."[67] The Executive Council of the archdiocese received a copy on 16 May 1983 and promised a response in two weeks.[68] Cardinal Carter replied in a letter of 15 June 1983. Impressed by the presentation of Bishop Clune and several members of the Advisory Board, he gave his blessing to recommendations concerning an executive director and regional directors:

1. The appointment of an Executive Director on a full-time basis for the purposes generally outlined in the "Report" which has been submitted. This person would have an office somewhere in the Archdiocesan complex and would receive such secretarial help as may be necessary.

2. The appointment of a volunteer in each of the Regions whose sole assignment as a Deacon, apart from his liturgical base, would be the service of his fellow Deacons under the general supervision of the Executive Director. In this manner a proper coordination and liaison should be established and should facilitate

the attainment of the objectives which have been mentioned in the "Report."[69]

Deacon Tom Mason became the first full-time and salaried executive director in September 1983.[70] The functions of the director, as described in a 1986 policies and procedures handbook, were:

(a) He will be the principal communications link with the Diocesan Bishop, the Vicar for Deacons, the Regional Bishops, the Regional Directors, the Training Program, the Continuing Development [Education] Committee and the Council of Deacons.

(b) He will, with the assistance of the [Executive] Board, develop instruments to assist the individual Deacon and the Board in evaluating the ministry, abilities, responsibilities, wishes and needs of the individual Deacon. These evaluations will be used as an aid in the assignment of Deacons and will be shared with the individual concerned so that each Deacon will have the opportunity to clarify the Board's perceptions and request changes. All the evaluations will be confidential. The Regional Bishop, Supervisor of Ministry, and Pastor of the liturgical Base will be consulted in this process of evaluation.

(c) He will inform and seek the counsel of the Regional Bishops, Vicar for Deacons, Regional Directors, and Director of Training concerning all vacancies or needs in the various Diaconal ministries as well as requests for new ministries or assignments.

(d) He will be ready to assume any other roles assigned to him by the local Diocesan Bishop/Vicar for Deacons.[71]

The Executive Board mentioned above took over the responsibilities of the personnel committee. Board membership included the vicar for deacons, the executive director and the four regional directors. The board's main concern was the assignment of deacons to a ministry and liturgical base and periodic reviews of their work.[72] (As a matter of interest in the death and resurrection of boards and committees in an organization's bureaucracy, it should be noted that the Executive Board was replaced by a reconstituted personnel committee set up at the discretion of the director of deacons.)[73]

Deacon Dan Murphy was appointed the second executive director in November 1989.[74] Deacon Bert Cambre succeeded him in March 2000. The office of director of deacons, as it is now called, has functioned without interruption since 1983, having successfully fended off a proposal in 1992 to amalgamate it with the priests' personnel office.[75] Its establishment remains the most effective and long-lasting achievement of the Deacon Search Committee and the follow-up implemental work of the Advisory Board.

Next in importance ranks the appointment of deacons as regional directors. The first directors were Tab Charbonneau (East), Stan MacLellan (Central), Barry Simpson (West) and Mike Robertson (North).[76] A fifth regional director was added in January 1991.[77] Their functions, also listed in the 1986 policies and procedures handbook, were five in number:

a. to advise in the preparation of evaluations, surveys etc. both of the Deacons and the Archdiocesan Permanent Diaconate Program

b. to confer in the matter of assignments of Deacons and their functions within the Archdiocese

c. to be accessible either individually or as a group to any Deacon who might wish to discuss his assignment, ministry, needs or wishes with this Regional Director or [Executive] Board as a whole

d. to visit with the deacons in their individual homes, place of ministry and/or liturgical base, to provide the Deacon with opportunity to discuss his situation in a regular and normal way; with [the Deacon's] wife, his Supervisor of Ministry, and his Liturgical Pastor, to acquire insight as to the Deacon's contribution to the ministries in which he ministers

e. to recommend any changes which might assist the [Executive] Board in the more efficient and comprehensive fulfillment of its mandate to serve the personnel needs of the Permanent Deacons of the Archdiocese.[78]

In January 1991, regional mentors replaced regional directors, with each mentor working with only one or two deacons. It was up to the deacon to ask a brother deacon to be his mentor. The mentor had no direct line responsibilities to the supervision of the deacon, as had been the case with the regional directors. The supervision was direct between the deacon and the office of the executive director and, of course, included the deacon's supervisor of ministry.[79] Commenting on the new set-up, Deacon Dan Murphy wrote to the deacons and their wives, "This will reflect an effort we are making to increase the support available to Deacons on an on-going basis, rather than when situations or problems arise."[80]

While Cardinal Carter approved the institution of an executive director and regional directors to the greater good of the diaconal program, he declined to address the recommendation of the Advisory Board's special committee on organization concerning a regionally elected advisory board that would take over the functions of the personnel committee and the Council of Deacons. The documentary evidence at hand does not reveal the cardinal's reasoning behind his decision. Deacon Tom Mason pushed hard in 1984 and 1985 to convince Bishop Clune and Deacon Dan Murphy, then the president of the Council of Deacons, of the merits of an elected advisory board, but he was unsuccessful.[81]

As we have noted, the personnel committee survived in the form of the Executive Board of 1986. The Council of Deacons, meanwhile, continued to operate and was a line item in the yearly budget of the office of the executive director. The council underwent a restructuring in 1988 following a survey of the previous year that listed three options facing members – close out the council, modify it or take a new approach.[82] The council decided to keep operating, and, in 1989, it changed its name to the Diaconal Association of the Archdiocese of Toronto.[83] Before too long, however, the council/association, which had been in existence since 1976, was experiencing what many members suspected was an inevitable death.

In March 1991, Deacon Dan Murphy, the executive director, invited thirty deacons and wives for a May weekend in Guelph to discuss the future of the permanent diaconate. In preparation for that meeting, an ad hoc committee of Phil and Theresa Dwyer, Al and Joan Moulton and George and Cam Newman proposed the creation of a co-ordinating board to take over the functions of the diaconal association. This board would have seven members: the vicar of deacons, the director of deacons, the co-ordinating director of the training program and four members of the diaconate community, who would be chosen by lot from those who had volunteered their names. (A member could be a deacon and his wife, but they would have only one vote.) Choosing by lot would allow volunteers to be elected by chance and thus avoid the appearance of running for election to the board. The board's duties would include, among other things, the management of retreats and days of recollections, social events and conferences, ongoing [continuing] education and upgrading, and involvement in community life, such as visits to the sick.[84]

Deacon George Newman, a member of the ad hoc committee, wrote that the Co-ordinating Board was established for the diaconate community "to bring together the ordained community and the formation program, and to address the needs of the community for Spirituality, Social Events and Continuing Education."[85] Deacon Dan Murphy interpreted the development in a less formal way. The Council of Deacons, according to his recollection of events, became the Co-ordinating Board "because we wanted the newer deacons to be part of the process rather than leaving it up to the 'old hands.'"[86] Regardless, Bishop Clune, who had been in favour of the idea all along, readily approved the change.

After more than seventeen years, the Co-ordinating Board continues to be a constituent part of the organizational structure of the diaconate program. It is an advisory board that consists of the vicar of deacons, the director of deacons, the director of the formation program and four elected representatives of the diaconate community. Its functions are wide ranging:

The Board assists the Episcopal Vicar of Deacons and the Director of Deacons by offering advice on all diaconal matters. The Coordinating Board is responsible for ensuring that advice is offered so that all aspects of diaconal life are encouraged and are working in harmony with one another. It includes such matters as the spiritual development of Deacons, their ministry, their continuing education, and the general well being of the Deacons, their wives and their families. The Coordinating Board has the responsibility to make recommendations to the Episcopal Vicar of Deacons, Director of Deacons, Director of the Formation Program, the Personnel Committee, and the diaconal community. The Board receives any recommendations, suggestions, and requests from individual deacons or wives that are presented to it, and acts on them in due course.

The Board is responsible for promoting communication among all parties involved in the Diaconate community within the Archdiocese. It also undertakes activities proposed for the ongoing benefit of the community, e.g. retreats, annual dinners, regional events. Such projects may require a committee to be solicited from among the Deacons and their wives within the community. If the needed expertise is not available within the Diaconate, it may be solicited outside the community.[87]

We end this section on the Advisory Board with an exchange of letters in March and April 1983 between Sister Anne Bezaire, OSU, president of the London Diocesan Sisters' Council, and Father Brian Clough, rector of St. Augustine's Seminary. This exchange, however brief, occurred when the Advisory Board was winding down its principal work in an atmosphere of confidence and hope. It is revealing, because it shows, on the one hand, some fundamental misapprehension of the permanent diaconate on the part of the Sisters' Council at a time when the Diocese of London was considering the establishment of the diaconate, and, on the other, it allowed Father Clough to summarize in a positive fashion the essentials of the diaconate program in the Archdiocese of Toronto in 1983. Indeed, it is a very robust summation of the reality and dynamism of a restored diaconate in Toronto, which, in keeping true to its 1977–1978 model of service, had accomplished so much for so many in only eleven years.

Sister Bezaire's questions are as follows:

1. Is the Permanent Diaconate being perceived as an "elite" group in the Church?

2. Is the deacon becoming a member of the clerical ranks, with a predominantly liturgical function, or is he involved in service to the poor and needy?

3. Is the fact that only men are admitted to the diaconate creating any problems for the women actively engaged in the same type of service?

4. Is the active role of the laity in the transformation of political, economic and social institutions being undermined by a concentration upon "Church" activities or is it being enhanced by dynamic leadership from the ordained deacons?[88]

Father Clough provided these answers:

1. The Permanent Diaconate is not an elite group in the Church in the pejorative sense of the word. They are men who have received in their diocese three years of specific training through a programme of study weekends and weekly home meetings. They certainly know more than the average lay person but the whole thrust of our programme has been to see them in the role of the Church's own good attempts to reach out to the poor and marginalized. They are to a great extent "bishops' men" because they are appointed to supra-parochial responsibilities, although they have a liturgical base in their own parish. Their dedication in this voluntary ministry is certainly edifying.

2. The Deacon is certainly a cleric but his predominant function is that of the ministry of charity. This would be in contrast to the Vatican documents, which go into great detail about his liturgical functions. Our programme is geared to the ministry of service with preaching and liturgical functions deemed to

be secondary. This was not so at the beginning but has been the case since the first three classes were ordained.

3. We have encouraged the wives of the candidates to follow as much of the programme as they wish. Following ordination some wives have remained with their husbands participating in the ministry. On the other hand there are many qualified lay women who are engaged in the same type of service as well as many religious women. I have not perceived that the restricting to men in the diaconate has caused problems for either group.

4. I find the question difficult to answer because of the presumptions in it. Our Deacons have been asked to see their role as including animation of the laity and they have not been asked to concentrate at all upon what you call "Church" activities. Certainly they are missioned by the Church, which recognizes their ministry, but we have not detected that the laity has decided to abandon its role to the deacons.[89]

That is where things stood in 1983, with the diaconate program at the beginning of its second decade of existence. It was a good place to be. The program had achieved a discernable measure of stability, direction and self-confidence as to its identity, purpose and place, the result, in part, of having the courage to examine itself in light of not only its own needs but also, and more importantly, the needs of the people whom its deacons were called to serve. It had every right to look forward to a bountiful future of service in the Lord's vineyard.

But, as if on cue, Cardinal Carter threw a spanner in the works three days after he had given his approval for an executive director and regional directors. The incident took place at the diaconate ordination ceremony on 18 June 1983. If there was one word that annoyed the cardinal it was "marginalized." He took umbrage at its use in a reprint of the diocesan diaconal policy in the ordination brochure, which stated that the ministry of the deacon is to the marginalized. It did not matter to the cardinal that the diaconal program had been operating on this fundamental belief about the purpose of the diaconate since 1977. He was irritated, and he let the deacons know just how irritated he was.

Apparently, some deacons were pleased by his remarks, while others were naturally chagrined. Bishop Clune, whose watch this was, was immediately put on the defensive. During the Episcopal Board meeting after the ordination ceremony, Cardinal Carter asked him what he intended to do to insure that diocesan policy on the diaconate was properly understood and implemented. "I told him," Bishop Clune reported to Father Clough,

> that we were all conscious of the difficulty of adequately and accurately describing the ministry of the Deacon and that I thought there was not that much variance between how he looked at diaconal ministry and those who see it as a ministry to the marginalized. The Cardinal agrees that the deacon is not to be a substitute for the shortage of priests, but that they are to have a definite diaconal ministry. I assured him that the Deacons' Advisory Board was working towards such a definition of ministry and that the different parts of the Deacon Program were working together very well, and that in the near future we would try to formulate a more accurate description of Diocesan Policy.[90]

Despite Bishop Clune's assurances that action would be taken, there is no evidence that the Advisory Board formulated a more accurate description of diocesan policy on the diaconate. In the absence of such a formula, it is safe to conclude that the board chose to adhere to its 1978 Policy Statement and to stay quiet. The cardinal's upset subsided; an imbroglio had been avoided. For the next two years everything went swimmingly. Such was the backdrop to what happened next.

6

REMAINING TRUE TO THE ORIGINAL VISION: 1985–2007

Introduction

At this point in our narrative, we must ask ourselves: Did the permanent diaconate of the Archdiocese of Toronto remain steadfast in its original vision of its primary ministry – its model of service to the marginalized – from 1985 to 2007? The simple answer is "yes." But the story of how the diaconate community managed to remain faithful to its model while it matured as a well-defined archdiocesan institution, never static or self-satisfied but always willing to grow and adapt to changing times, is a complicated and sometimes highly nuanced affair.

Our approach will be an in-depth examination of the internal operations of the diaconate program as it continued to undertake periodic reviews and self-studies. The program embraced self-examination as the best means to protect and enhance its specific model of the diaconate, to deepen its understanding of the theology of the diaconate and to chart a path that would keep it spiritually dynamic in its numerous individual ministries well into the twenty-first century. Deacons were never timid to look at themselves in the mirror, because they never worried about glory. Ironically, that was too worldly a notion for deacons who were firmly rooted in the world in many of the same ways that Jesus was rooted in his own public ministry. Rather, they constantly questioned who they were and what they were doing, because as a community they desired to keep pace with the needs of those on the margins of society as the Catholic population of the Archdiocese of Toronto grew along with that of the Greater Toronto Area.

This chapter begins with the Clune-Somerville-Carter correspondence (1985 and 1987), and goes on to examine in detail the work of the Diaconate Review Committee (1990–1991), which proved to be a cathartic reaffirmation of the program's model of service and essential identity, and an in-house publication called *Diaconate Self-Study* (2001). The chapter concludes with a portrait of diaconal ministry of service in the Archdiocese of Toronto, which will demonstrate the truth of our contention that the diaconal community never lost sight of its primary ministry.

The period of 1985 to 2007 was a joyful and at times painful confluence of events, challenges and changes that took place in the face of a steady resolve among deacons in their quest to stay true to their original model of service, by which it grew and flourished, not without faltering and failing at times, to be sure, but always steadily, always prayerfully, confident in its vocation to bring the Good News to everyone.

The Clune-Somerville-Carter Correspondence 1985 and 1987

The Clune-Somerville-Carter correspondence was a lively exchange of letters between Bishop Robert B. Clune, the vicar of deacons, Monsignor Peter Somerville, the rector of St. Augustine's Seminary who spoke for the Executive Committee of the diaconate training program, and Cardinal G. Emmett Carter, the archbishop of Toronto.[1] It opened with a letter, dated 5 March 1985, from Bishop Clune to Monsignor Somerville, concerning the peculiar predicament of William Hawkshaw, whom Bishop Clune had known since high school days. He stated that Hawkshaw entered the diaconate program in 1974, when the focus of diaconate ministry was mainly parish-based. His ministry was convert classes, now known as the Rite of Christian Initiation of Adults (RCIA), at St. Rose of Lima parish. Encouraged by his pastor, Monsignor Kenneth Robitaille, Hawkshaw intended to continue this ministry at his parish after ordination with the rest of his class in 1976. He was very good at what he did and wanted to stay with it. However, the evaluation committee of the training program would not recommend him, because the focus of the program had recently shifted to service to others in institutional settings outside of parish structures, and Hawkshaw would not abandon his ministry to conform to the shift.

When his case came up for review for a second time, in 1978, Father Charles Amico, the director of the training program, wrote to him: "service in catechesis did not fall within the scope of diaconal ministry now recognized in this Archdiocese." He continued: "Subsequent dialogue with yourself does not appear to identify that your principal ministry has the characteristic of service to the disadvantaged that is to mark the ministry of deacon."[2] Much the same reasoning was given in the formal rejection: "Your ministry as a catechist or adult religious educator is not considered to be a ministry to the marginalized, even though at times, per accidens, some marginalized persons may be present in your classes."[3]

That should have shut the door on Hawkshaw's aspirations, but ever the persistent optimist, he kept teaching RCIA classes and he kept knocking on the door of the diaconate. Over time, he became a cause célèbre for some deacons who openly sided with him. His purgatorial plight was enough of a thorn in the side of those in charge of the diaconate program that Bishop Clune received permission from Cardinal Carter, on 27 February 1985, to conduct a canonical investigation of Hawkshaw's status in the hope of finding a ready solution. Hence Clune's letter to Somerville.

As far as Bishop Clune was concerned, Hawkshaw should be ordained, because, after teaching RCIA at St. Rose of Lima for six years and concurrently at St. Dunstan's for the last two years, in addition to his training directors and sponsors of RCIA in other parishes, his catechetical ministry was no longer parochial but diocesan in scope and thus a valid ministry for the permanent diaconate. Clune went on to note that Father Marshal Beriault, the current pastor of St. Rose of Lima, and Father Neil Varley, the pastor at St. Dunstan's, supported Hawkshaw. Also backing him were Deacons Tom Mason, Michael Robertson and Stan MacLellan. In light of all this, Clune wanted the permanent diaconate training committee to consider recommending William Hawkshaw for ordination to the diaconate with the Class of 1985, or, failing that, because of the shortness of time, with the next group of transitional deacons.[4]

Monsignor Somerville's reply was the result of a "lively and serious discussion" at a meeting of the training committee on 15 March. It was not the conciliatory response that Bishop Clune was expecting.[5] The bishop, who as vicar of deacons was the link between the cardinal and the diaconate program, sincerely believed that he had found a valid solution to a prickly problem that would extricate everyone. He hoped that Monsignor Somerville and his fellow members in the training program would arrive at the same conclusion. They did not.

Seeking to safeguard the integrity of the diaconate program and the policy that guided it, the committee made a distinction between personality and policy. It never had any "objection to Mr. William Hawkshaw arising from his faith, his competence, his mental, emotional or physical health."[6] Rather, the difficulty was with the suitability of his ministry in light of the 1978 Policy Statement, which stated, "'the main focus of the Deacon's work should be on the ministry of service toward the <u>marginalized</u>: those who have been pushed to the fringe of society by such things as poverty, sickness, crime and age. This ministry will often, but not always, be on the parochial level.'"[7] Therefore, the committee concluded that the Policy Statement "does not leave room for a Permanent Diaconate ministry in religious education even in convert work."[8]

Monsignor Somerville went on to point out that the Policy Statement was an authoritative document. It was the work of the Executive Committee of the diaconate training program; it was based on a document produced by the Senate of Priests [referred to in Chapter Four as the 1977 Review], which made clear that "the main focus of the deacon's work should be on the ministry of charity or service;"[9] and it was approved by Archbishop Philip

Pocock.[10] The policy, moreover, was good and productive and should be retained for two reasons:

1. the first is [that] the very special need of the Church's reaching out to those who have been pushed to the margins of civil and ecclesial society might be jeopardized if the Permanent Diaconate were open to other ministries to persons less removed from existing parochial and diocesan structures. We rejoice – as one member of the committee wrote to me in response to an earlier draft of this letter – "the sick and elderly are being visited, those who are in prison do hear the Good News, those without hope have new hope…";

2. the second reason for maintaining a restricted or focused ministry is to protect the diaconate from becoming a "mini" priesthood or a "second class" priesthood.[11]

Although no formal vote was taken concerning Monsignor Somerville's reply to Bishop Clune's letter, each member had a chance to review his letter, and he was convinced that a majority would have voted in its favour. However, as Monsignor Somerville noted, "A minority position was expressed which included two points: the first was that the policy needed to be reviewed in the light of present diocesan needs and that one or two 'exceptions' would not jeopardize the programme or the ministry."[12] He ended by proposing that the training committee produce a one-page description of the ministry of the permanent diaconate. If it was felt that the ministry was still being defined too narrowly, the whole question should be open to broader consultation, although he feared that such a consultation would produce yet another committee. Enclosed in Monsignor Somerville's letter were six supporting documents, including a copy of the Senate of Priests' 1977 Report and the seminal 1978 Policy Statement.

Monsignor Somerville's reply unintentionally opened up a Pandora's box. What came tumbling out were two issues more complex and compelling than finding an answer to the question of a particular candidate's request for ordination, even if the search for that answer had already opened up the box. The two issues were, first, a challenge to the 1978 Policy Statement's definition of the model or mission of diaconal service, and second, a clarification of the relationship between the model of service, whatever it should be, and the determination of the needs of the archdiocese. In other words, who had the authority to define the model and establish the needs? In terms of everyday practice, right up to 1985, those priests and deacons in charge of the diaconate program had defined the model of service and determined the needs of the archdiocese. They had done so in good faith, assuring and reinforcing a very clear vision of the diaconate for the archdiocese, which accounted for a great deal of the program's success during its first decade. The reopening of the William Hawkshaw case proved to be the beginning of the end of that tradition.

Bishop Clune responded to Monsignor Somerville's letter by writing to Cardinal Carter, relating highlights in the history of the impasse over William Hawkshaw and the main reason for the seminary's refusal to ordain him to the diaconate: "because convert work is not considered to be a diaconal ministry according to the Policy Statement of our Archdiocese."[13] Bishop Clune defended the 1977 Review and the 1978 Policy Statement and Archbishop Pocock's acceptance of both documents. But, in a major departure from the diaconate training committee, he implied that these documents had to be revisited and revised because "circumstances have changed considerably in our Archdiocese."[14] Bishop Clune made it clear to the cardinal that he disagreed with the committee's decision not to recommend Hawkshaw for ordination. As soon as Hawkshaw had offered his services to Bishop Clune as a regional co-ordinator of the RCIA program, his ministry was no longer parochial but diocesan and consequently conformed to diocesan policy, as he understood it. The William Hawkshaw case was one example that fit Cardinal Carter's belief that "the ministry of the Permanent Diaconate should be broadened in our Archdiocese."[15]

Bishop Clune continued but took an entirely different track. He emphasized the current shortage of pastoral priests in the archdiocese and referred to Code 517 of the Code of Canon Law, which gave the diocesan bishop the right to appoint a deacon or some other person or community of persons to share in the pastoral care of a parish due to a lack of priests. This prompted Bishop Clune to recommend that William Hawkshaw be ordained to help with the RCIA in the region where his parish was situated and to assist Father Varley in the pastoral care of St. Dunstan's. He also proposed that a joint committee of the Senate of Priests and the diaconate update and broaden the 1978 Policy Statement.[16] Attached to Bishop Clune's letter to Cardinal Carter were Monsignor Somerville's letter and the six supporting documents. The matter was now in the cardinal's hands.

Cardinal Carter's response was to write a letter to Monsignor Somerville. He acknowledged receipt of Bishop Clune's letter and Monsignor Somerville's letter to Bishop Clune. Also, in passing, the cardinal mentioned that he had at hand Sister Charmaine Grillot's one-page statement on the diaconate. The cardinal did not quote her in his letter to Monsignor Somerville, but her opinion on the model of the diaconate, given at his invitation, influenced the direction that he took with Monsignor Somerville. For that reason, it is worth quoting from the letter:

> My understanding of [the] diaconate is that the deacons are the bishop's men. Hence, I believe that they are at the disposition of the bishop wherever there are needs. I believe that it is too confining to limit the service and ministry of deacons to the disadvantaged. It seems to me that, wherever there is a real need, those persons are disadvantaged; and the ordinary of the diocese should be free to send deacons there. I support your understanding of a broader aspect of service and feel definite steps should be taken to implement a new model of deacon. There are persons in the deacon community who would welcome such action.[17]

Sister Charmaine's statement was music to the cardinal's ears. "From my point of view a number of things had changed," he told Monsignor Somerville. "Particularly, I mention our concept of the diaconate as a permanent form of ministry, the nature of our society, our concept of who is 'marginalized' and I venture to suggest a more lucid view of the relationship between the bishop and the deacon."[18] His objections boiled down to two things: the use of the word "marginalized" and the right of the archbishop to decide on the needs of the diocese:

1. The concept of the "marginalized." I find in this expression a species of condescension which is somewhat unacceptable. To quote the actual text of the "Policy Statement" (page 1 A. Objectives) "the programme must therefore be designed to train the candidates to reintegrate into both the human and ecclesial community those <u>marginalized</u> by such things as poverty, sickness, age, crime, ignorance, or social injustice." How dare we suggest that those subject to the victimization of such situations are necessarily marginalized in the Church. I know some poor, some sick, some aged people, some victims of social injustice whose shoes I am not worthy to tie. They are much better Christians than I will ever be.

2. I cannot accept the concept that the committee, however enlightened, can make decisions in regards to the acceptance for ordination of candidates on the basis that the committee cannot find a mission for the individual. This is clearly not within the jurisdiction of this committee or any committee. It is not even within the jurisdiction of the Rector of the Seminary. The call to Orders both for the diaconate and the priesthood is clearly, as is traditionally, the onus and responsibility of the Bishop. It is he who decides whether the candidate can be fitted into the mission of the Church which has been committed to his care. He will, of course, if he has any sense, rely on the recommendations of those in charge of preparing the candidates for their estimate of the man's character and preparation. But to decide on the needs of the diocese is not something which the average bishop is ready to delegate.[19]

The cardinal then rewrote the offending text from the Policy Statement. It now read:

The main focus of the Deacon's work should be the ministry of service towards the dispossessed (disadvantaged): those who have been pushed to the fringe of civil society by such things as poverty, sickness, crime and age. This ministry will have the dimensions accorded to it by the Archbishop.

It is the Archbishop alone who, after consultation with those charged with the responsibility for the diaconate programme, will call candidates to the Diaconate. It is also he who in his discretion will decide on the needs of the Archdiocese in regard to the work to be done by Deacons after ordination.[20]

The cardinal was not prepared to amend the Policy Statement any further, although he was willing to listen to suggestions on that score, but he insisted that a Deacon's ministry include service to those who sought spiritual guidance. This was in accordance with the needs of the Church and the role of the Deacon. "Catechetical work, convert instruction, counselling, visiting of homes in parishes, all of these," the cardinal declared, "are fertile fields in which we need a great deal of assistance. To exclude our Deacons from these horizons would, to my mind, be a serious disservice to the Church."[21] He was aware of the danger of deacons being seen as mini-priests, and admitted that that was the reason why he did not institute the diaconate when he was bishop of London. Such a mistaken perception, however, was not going to influence his opinion that deacons were well suited to the task of assisting parish priests during this time of a shortage of priests.

The cardinal ended by saying that he wanted the amendment to the Policy Statement promulgated at the next meeting of the Council of Priests (formally called the Senate of Priests) on 1 May. He saw little ground for objection but was open to it.

Bishop Leonard Wall delivered Cardinal Carter's letter to Monsignor Somerville on Thursday, 25 April. The Council of Priests was to meet in six days. That gave Somerville precious little time to respond. He called for a special meeting of the training committee on Saturday, 27 April, and eight out of nine members came, including Deacon Alex MacGregor, who flew in from Ottawa. Their discussion waded into deep waters.[22]

Monsignor Somerville responded in a letter dated 1 May. Speaking for the committee, he readily agreed that it was the bishop who decided the needs of the diocese and the work to be done by deacons to meet those needs. There was no disagreement on this fundamental point of ecclesiology. This was the committee's first "concession." Nevertheless, that was hardly the whole story. Somerville proceeded to explain that when the committee refused to recommend candidates for ordination, it did so following the archdiocesan policy on the diaconate program. There was no point in having a policy if the committee were not going to follow it. While some committee members felt that the model of service was wisely restricted, others felt less so, but "all felt – until competent authority changed the model – that we should not recommend men who were not desirous of that closely defined ministry nor not suited to it by background, temperament and skills."[23] This was the committee's second "concession." It was the cardinal's prerogative to change policy, and the committee's duty to implement it.

If the cardinal's desire was to change the 1977/1978 model of service, the committee only asked that he entertain its concerns and objections before he proceeded. But the committee's first objection was rather odd. It hesitated to accept the cardinal's phrase "civil society" because "we are thinking not only of those who have been pushed to the fringe of civil society by such things as poverty, sickness, crime and age, but also those who are on the fringe of the Church community, the 'fallen aways', the unchurched, the alienated, etc."[24] This amendment to the cardinal's amendment to the Policy Statement was rich in irony. It unintentionally opened up the door to that broader interpretation of the model of service that Cardinal Carter favoured and was on the verge of adopting. He would seize upon the "fringe of the Church community" in his response.

Having opened this door, Monsignor Somerville spent the remainder of his letter doing everything to close it. The committee strongly felt that the "training program should not pre-empt its emphasis of caritative service to the disadvantaged."[25] (Dropped from the discussion was "marginalized.") If the model of diaconal service were expanded to include "'catechetical work, convert instruction, counselling, visiting homes in parishes,'"[26] the Church's preferential option for the poor would be undermined. If some deacon were assigned exclusively to parish-based ministries, such as marriage or baptismal preparation or RCIA, the perception of the deacon as a mini-priest would be inevitable and charges of clericalism would result. One of the main objections was entirely practical. The ministry of deacons was "limited," because the time allotted to the training program was restricted due to the fact that candidates were married and had jobs. "These limitations," Monsignor Somerville wrote, "have the value of ensuring that the training programme is focused and that the time is carefully spent preparing candidates according to a clear and closely defined model."[27]

Of course, there would be room for exceptions to the definition of the model of service, but only in the context of diaconal ministry: "If the evaluation team finds good reason to commend the virtue, the balance, the knowledge and the skills of a candidate who would otherwise not fit the primary focus of the programme, the Director of the Programme should discuss the case with the Archbishop or his delegate to see if the candidate might suit another need of the diocese."[28] In a nutshell, the committee believed that the policy on model of service should remain the same, but exceptional cases could be considered on an individual basis. Monsignor Somerville ended by reassuring Cardinal Carter that the deployment of deacons was the right of the archbishop.

The cardinal's next letter is dated 7 May 1985 and was directed, once again, to Monsignor Somerville. He apologized for the deadline that he set in his previous letter and was thankful to the cadres of the diaconate program, as he called them, for their opinions. He had four points to make. Point One: He was relieved that everyone agreed to the "ecclesiology presiding over the decision as to the work done by Deacons in general and a Deacon in particular."[29] He had no desire to pursue this point except to say that a structural change might be required to separate the training program from the assignment program. Point Two: He zeroed in on the committee's contention that the diaconate was also thinking of those on the fringe of the Church community: "My perception of the position of the committee in general is that you seem to have been thinking only of those pushed to the fringe of civil society. The criticism which I have of the Deacon Programme at the present moment is that it seems to think only of this group."[30] Point Three: He agreed with the committee that he did not want to see the deacon as a mini-priest and to limit his ministry to a parish: "But this does not prevent me from seeing the need for a ministry to the poor in spirit in many areas which we have not, to date, envisaged. The corporal works of mercy are of the highest importance, but the spiritual works of mercy have not been abrogated."[31] Point Four: He had trouble with the committee's use of the phrases "caritative service" and "diaconal ministry" in its description of the basic model of service: "I am convinced that we have been limiting the scope of our diaconal ministry over much. But assuredly every deacon should be aware of his responsibility to the dispossessed, however we may define this term."[32] This last statement was conciliatory in tone. Cardinal Carter closed with an invitation to continue the discussion with Bishop Clune and Monsignor Somerville.

What was the upshot of this remarkable exchange? Let us begin with William Hawkshaw. His request for ordination may have initiated the Clune-Somerville-Carter correspondence, but concern over his status faded the longer the exchange lasted. In the end, though, he was rewarded for his patience and perseverance and was ordained a deacon on 30 November 1985, at seventy-four years of age. His long-delayed ordination was one of those extraordinary exceptions to policy alluded to by Monsignor Somerville and an example of the Ordinary overriding the objections of the diaconate program. Deacon Hawkshaw served for many years as an RCIA instructor, dying on 13 June 2004.

More immediately, the Council of Priests did not deal with Cardinal Carter's amendment to the Policy Statement at its meeting on 1 May or at any meeting thereafter.[33] The model of diaconate service remained unchanged, as was revealed in a March 1986 letter from Father Keith Callaghan, pastor of St. Leonard's parish, to Cardinal Carter. Father Callaghan wrote to express his disappointment on learning that his request for a deacon to work full-time in his young and growing parish was denied on the grounds that the permanent deacon was "to exercise 'full' ministry to the 'marginalized community.'"[34] He had nothing against deacons working on behalf of the marginalized, but he wanted the ministry of the permanent diaconate to include work within the boundaries of the parish structure. The cardinal agreed with him: "You raise a problem which has intrigued me and, to some extent, disturbed me for some time. I have had many discussions about the exclusive use of our Deacons for the socially or economically marginalized as distinct from the spiritually and pastorally marginalized."[35] Cardinal Carter referred Father Callaghan's letter to Bishop Clune.

Lastly, Monsignor Somerville and the permanent diaconate-training program made good on their promise of 26 March 1985 to provide a concise description of the ministry of the permanent diaconate. Perhaps receipt of the Callaghan-Carter letters, via Bishop Clune, spurred the committee into action. After six drafts, Monsignor Somerville supplied Bishop Clune with a four-page report on 12 January 1987. It concluded that there were essentially two models of the diaconate existing side by side in the Archdiocese of Toronto. The first model was pastoral/parochial ministry, which had been the main model for those deacons ordained in 1974, 1975 and 1976. It was service within a parish under the direction of a pastor. The range of ministries included the following: regular preaching and assistance at liturgical functions; responsibility for the training and assignment of lectors and ministers of Holy Communion not only at Sunday Masses but also for members of the parish in hospitals, senior citizen homes and nursing homes; Baptismal preparation and celebration; wake and burial services; RCIA and marriage preparation; membership on the parish council and pastoral team; and perhaps home visitations; Legion of Mary and St. Vincent de Paul Society; and so forth. Working according to the pastoral/parochial model of service, a deacon was fully integrated into the pastoral, liturgical and charitable life of the parish and, depending on a parish's circumstances, could be of great assistance to the pastor.[36] Monsignor Somerville's memorandum to Bishop Clune did not mention what, if any, was the role of the deacon as a catalyst or animator of the laity as they performed their parish-based ministries.

The second model was service/diocesan ministry. It had been the model since 1977, was favoured by the training program and was not found wanting other than the fact that it would not provide much assistance to overworked pastors. According to this model of diaconal service, the deacon specializes in a particular pastoral care ministry independent of the needs of the parish where he has a liturgical base. His main work would take place in public institutions such as hospitals, prisons, senior citizen homes and nursing homes or among different identifiable groups, wherever they might be, such as troubled youth (i.e. Covenant House), divorced and separated people, alcoholics and drug addicts and the mentally and physically challenged. The deacon's "presence then at the altar of his liturgical base is a sign of that service on behalf of the Christian community to those dispossessed by reasons of poverty, sickness, race, age, crime, ignorance or social injustice."[37] His parish-based ministry, always secondary to that outside the parish, might include occasional preaching (every four to six weeks), assistance at some but not all major liturgical events and in the training of lectors and ministers of Holy Communion and, along with his wife, acting as a resource for marriage preparation courses. Monsignor Somerville did not speak directly about the deacon as catalyst or animator of the laity but at least referred to it elliptically in the fourth of five advantages of the service/diocesan ministry. Those advantages were:

1. the Deacon assists the Bishop in his ministry to those who are dispossessed and are unlikely to be spiritually cared for by the regular parish ministry

2. the Deacon specializes in one pastoral care ministry, allowing him to make best use of his talents and time

3. since the Deacon has a ministry for which he is specially trained, that is outside the regular scope of Parish activities, he is less likely to suffer a dramatic shift when the Pastor is reassigned

4. the Deacon in this model is then seen as both being sent out by the bishop and parish community to provide care to the dispossessed and to call forth the members of the parish community to minister to those in need

5. since the Deacon is clearly identified in a ministry of service to the dispossessed, he is less likely to be seen as a "substitute priest" in a parish ministry.[38]

Monsignor Somerville contended that the chief difference between the two models was not a theological one. Rather, it was "in the assignment of the deacon based on pastoral needs."[39] Although it was the right of the bishop to assign deacons to ministry in light of his determination of pastoral needs – a right acknowledged and respected by the training program – the members of the program thought that restricting the mission of the diaconate to service to the dispossessed would protect those institutional ministries already in place, which in their opinion would suffer if deacons were assigned to the supposedly more urgent and usually more visible needs of the typical parish.

Cardinal Carter's reaction? He accepted the service/diocesan model as "the normal pattern for the preparation and mission of the Permanent Deacons of the Archdiocese."[40] The pastoral/parochial model, therefore, was always an exception. But that was not his point. It was that there always should be room for exceptions as warranted by changing circumstances, his example being the airport ministry. As for a deacon's liturgical role, it was to be understood as his liturgical base and not as his assignment. Once again, the only exception was when a deacon was allowed to minister exclusively in the pastoral/parochial model. Finally, and this might have been the cardinal's prime concern from the very beginning in 1985, "It should be clearly indicated that the decision on the ordination of a Permanent Deacon and his assignment remains ultimately at the disposal of the Ordinary of the Archdiocese."[41]

Cardinal Carter was so insistent on these points because he wanted them included in an official declaration on the mission or mandate of the permanent diaconate to be drawn up by Bishop Clune and representative members of the diaconate community and submitted to him for his final approval. This was a good idea, for it would have put an end to any remaining doubts or confusion about archdiocesan policy on the preferred model of diaconal service. But the historical record does not reveal any movement on this matter. Apparently it was quietly laid to rest by bureaucratic rite.

The result of the cardinal's reaction? The 1977 Review and the 1978 Policy Statement remained the two most important documents on the diaconate in the Archdiocese of Toronto. Neither one had been altered in any official way. To that very important degree, the diaconate program's original vision of the type of ministry it should offer survived intact. But since the program accepted in writing the Ordinary's pre-eminent role in the ordination and assignment of deacons, and allowed for exceptions to the service/diocesan model of ministry, a future engagement on the model of ministry remained a distinct possibility. In the autumn of 1990, the issue was resurrected and taken up by the Diaconate Review Committee, which gave it a final airing. By then, Cardinal G. Emmett Carter had retired as archbishop of Toronto. He announced his retirement in dramatic fashion at a St. Patrick's Day Mass, 17 March 1990, at St. Michael's Cathedral. His successor, Archbishop Aloysius Ambrozic, was no stranger to the diaconate.

Diaconate Review Committee 1990–1991

At this point in our story, a brief statistical portrait of the permanent diaconate would be helpful. From 1974, the first year of ordinations, to 1990, when the Diaconate Review Committee came into existence, 139 candidates had been ordained deacons in the Archdiocese of Toronto. Of these, nine had died, fourteen had moved away, twelve were inactive or retired, six had become priests and ninety-eight were active in December 1990. The average age of these active deacons at ordination was 49.5 years, and their average age in 1990 was 57.5 years. By far the greatest percentage of active deacons (72 percent) was in the age range of fifty to sixty-nine years. Active deacons averaged approximately 6,500 hours of service per month, or 800 workdays. In 1990, there were nine deacons in full-time ministry.

If we compare the percentage of average hours per month spent in part-time institutional chaplaincy, liturgical ministry and general ministry in 1974 and 1990, we notice the pre-eminence of the service/diocesan model of diaconal ministry. (The other categories were other ministry, evangelization and sacramental preparation; the sample size was 82 percent.) In 1974, the average hours per month were 11.7 percent in part-time chaplaincy, 37.9 percent in liturgical ministry and 30.7 percent in general ministry. In 1990, the average hours per month were 41.1 percent in part-time chaplaincy, 28.4 percent in liturgical ministry and 0.4 percent in general ministry.[42] The tiny percentage of deacons in general ministry reflects the fact that prior to ordination each candidate was expected to have a ministry of service to which the Ordinary would appoint him. A service agreement would follow within three months after ordination. The deacon would be assigned (not appointed) to his liturgical base, in agreement with the pastor.

In the early summer of 1990, the diaconate-training program asked the board of governors of St. Augustine's Seminary, which oversaw the training program, to strike a committee to examine whether archdiocesan policy on the role and ministry of the permanent deacon faithfully reflected the theology of the diaconate and met the pastoral and social needs of today.[43] It was felt that such an official in-depth study "might help to alleviate some of the confusion and disagreement among priests, deacons, and laity as to the proper and most effective role for our permanent deacons."[44] Archbishop Aloysius Ambrozic chose Bishop Clune, still vicar of deacons, to chair the committee, and Bishop Clune selected Deacon Dan Murphy to act as secretary to the committee.

Along with Bishop Clune and Deacon Murphy, the committee members were Father (later Bishop) John Boissonneau, the vice-rector of the seminary; Father Tibor Horvath, SJ, a theologian who had written on the diaconate; Father Dan Donovan; Monsignor Kenneth Robitaille; Monsignor Leonard O'Malley; Father Don MacLean; Bishop Attila Mikloshazy, SJ, bishop of extern Hungarians and a seminary professor; Deacon Tab Charbonneau; Sister Rita MacLellan of the diaconate-training program; Molly Callaghan; Deacon Alexander MacGregor and Olga MacLellan. The committee, then, had two bishops, six priests, three veteran deacons, two wives of deacons and one woman religious.[45]

The committee met from September 1990 to November 1991, usually once a month. In the course of its proceedings, it clarified the model of the diaconate and assessed the training and ministry of deacons by means of a survey questionnaire. The committee's final report, issued in November 1991, listed seven main points, made three recommendations and outlined three task-force mandates.

The committee's preparatory reading material heavily influenced the direction of its inquiry and the substance of its conclusions. It was a mix of secondary literature and in-house documentary material. The secondary works included two books, two articles and *Guidelines* on the diaconate published by the U.S. Bishops Conference in 1985. The committee members were asked to read the following: James Monroe Barnett, *The Diaconate: A Full and Equal Order*, which had become standard reading in the burgeoning world of diaconate publications; Timothy J. Shugrue, *Service Ministry of the Deacon*, which presented a distinctly Catholic interpretation of the diaconate; Matthew T. Teolis, "The Permanent Diaconate: Vision versus Reality" (parts one and two); Tibor Horvath, "Theology of a New Diaconate"; and *Permanent Deacons in the United States: Guidelines for their Formation and Ministry*.

Two observations are in order. Bishop Clune was an enthusiastic fan of Shugrue's book, at one point linking it to the archdiocese's approach to "the special vocation and ministry of the deacon."[46] His strong endorsement of one book among many on the history of the diaconate and its place in the modern world effectively put it at the top of the committee's reading list. The second publication that catches our attention is Father Horvath's "Theology of a New Diaconate." This was a lengthy and groundbreaking article on the sacramental nature of the diaconate and the relationship of the bishop to the deacon. We saw in Chapter Three Father Horvath's major contribution to the work of the Canadian Conference of Catholic Bishops on the diaconate (1966–1972), and then in Chapter Four the unfortunate disregard or unintentional ignorance of his article when the Archdiocese of Toronto was considering the restoration of the diaconate beginning in 1969. More than twenty years later, the diaconate program finally appreciated the significance of Father

Horvath's contribution to the theology of the diaconate and invited him to join the committee.

The committee's selection of documentary or primary material was an entirely different process. It chose to consult documents that the diaconate program had generated at different times and for different reasons during its organizational history. The program had an archives, and wisely turned to it to study and review its own thinking on the diaconate over the years to find substance and inspiration for charting its future. Those documents were the 1977 Review, the 1978 Policy Statement (in particular the opening quotation from Father Karl Rahner), *Policy and Procedures of the Executive Board: The Diaconate* (1986) and the Clune-Somerville-Carter correspondence of 1985 and 1987. There was only a passing reference to the 1981 Deacon Search Committee in the Minutes of the committee's meetings. Its absence from the committee's deliberations is a mystery. The inclusion of the Clune-Somerville-Carter letters, however, was not. The question of policy on the model of diaconate, initiated and pursued by Cardinal Carter, had yet to be satisfactorily answered in an official way, and now was the time. This seems to have been the opinion of both Archbishop Ambrozic and Father (now Bishop) James Wingle, rector of St. Augustine's Seminary. Before the committee had met for the first time in September 1990, they had told Bishop Clune that the current terms of diaconate service might be too narrow, and they asked the committee to consider expanding them.[47]

The first order of business was to address concerns about the model of the diaconate. But before the committee could clarify the model, it had to come to an understanding of the theology of the diaconate. Enter Father Horvath. To prepare for his work on the committee, he met with deacons at the home of Deacon George Wilson on 30 August 1990. Concerning that meeting, Father Horvath later wrote to Deacon Dan Murphy that he "was pleased to see the spiritual depth and sacramental orientation of the deacons present, values which in my view are the only guarantees for the survival of the permanent diaconate restored by Vatican II."[48] But something fundamental was lacking. Even though the current diaconal training program delivered excellent pastoral and psychological training to the candidates, according to Father Horvath, the program

> should be enriched by a spiritual and theological formation aiming at a deeper appreciation of the sacramental nature of the diaconal ordination. Deacons are not laymen anymore. They participate with the bishops and with the priests in the one and the same sacrament of ordination.... a parish without a permanent deacon is not whole.[49]

When the committee met on 9 October 1990, Father Horvath strongly argued – some thought too strongly – for a theology of the diaconate that was rooted in the early tradition of the Church, a tradition, moreover, that was confirmed by the Second Vatican Council. In short, the mission of the deacon as established in the early documents on the diaconate was to be whatever the bishop wanted him to be.[50] Explaining his position to Bishop Clune, in a letter dated the following day, Father Horvath contended that the Council had corrected certain medieval misconceptions about the nature of the episcopal ordination:

> By virtue of the sacrament of ordination the deacon receives a share in the leadership of the bishop, who, as the successor of the apostles, has both the fullness of the Sacrament of Orders (*Lumen Gentium* No. 26) and the fullness of the priesthood (*Lumen Gentium* No. 41). There is a common element in the sacrament of Orders (be it episcopal, presbyterial or diaconal), [that is] the ordained priest and the ordained deacon both represent the bishop, and in the bishop and through the bishop and with the bishop they represent the Church in its hierarchy.... the deacon, in my view, is above all a leader because he is a deacon of the bishop who is the leader "in persona Christi." By virtue of his ordination, the ministry of the deacon, like that of the bishop and of the priest, is a ministry <u>of</u> Christ, because the ordained baptized is acting not in his own person but, like a "servant," in the person of his Lord.[51]

There is nothing in the Minutes of the meetings to suggest that the committee did anything but accept Father Horvath's emphasis on the deacon's sacramental ordination as central to the theology of the diaconate. Bishop Clune was particularly grateful to him "for emphasizing several times that the Permanent Diaconate is a Sacred Order and as such is a sacrament."[52] As for Father Horvath, he told Deacon Murphy and Bishop Clune that "Models of the Diaconate," written by committee member Father Dan Donovan, was excellent and brilliantly done.[53] Where Father Horvath parted ways with the committee, and what convinced him to resign from it on 12 December 1990, was its refusal to accept his amendment of one sentence of "Models of the Diaconate." The original sentence, which remained intact, read: "One way of expanding the present ministry would be to put a greater emphasis on the Deacon's role as catalyst or animator of the laity."[54] Father Horvath's version read: "One way of expanding the present practice would be to put a greater emphasis on the deacon's *sacramental ordination* as catalyst or animator of the laity, and *as a co-worker of the bishop and of the priests*."[55] The Minutes do not reveal the committee's reasoning behind its rejection of Father Horvath's amendment. Perhaps – and this is mere speculation – it was a matter of agreeing with his theology of the diaconate but treating it as an unwritten assumption that need not find its way explicitly in the text of Father Donovan's essay.

Be that as it may, Father Donovan completed "Models of the Diaconate" within several months, by December 1990. The committee accepted it with only minor changes. It was a clear and concise reaffirmation of the traditional service/diocesan model of the diaconate. It assessed the early history of the diaconate program and the program's fidelity to the model of ministry it had chosen in 1977, and it gave sufficient allowance for individual exceptions to that model and for the possibility of an expansion of it in the area of the deacon as a catalyst or animator of the laity. Not surprisingly, that possibility conformed quite neatly to the 1977 Review's understanding of the right relationship between the diaconate and the lay apostolate.[56] Not once did Father Donovan use the words "marginalized" or "disadvantaged," wisely choosing to skirt that old chestnut that had caused so much discomfort to Cardinal Carter.

Father Donovan's two-and-a-half-page elucidation is worth quoting in full:

> Since the beginning of the Permanent Diaconate program in 1972 more than a hundred deacons [actually 139] have been ordained for service within the Archdiocese of Toronto. Inevitably the initial efforts both at defining the role of the Permanent Deacon and at developing a training program for them were marked by certain tentativeness. Before long, however, a relatively distinct model of the Diaconate emerged, one that focused on the ministry of service especially to groups beyond the reach of parish activities and concerns. These included hospitals, senior citizens' and nursing homes, prisons and the like.
>
> The model thus developed seemed to do justice to the emphasis given by Church documents to the theme of service, even while it met a genuine need within the Archdiocese. The fact that the ministry base was often outside direct parish responsibility freed the Deacons from the uncertainty sometimes associated with a change in pastor. It also underlined the special relationship of the Deacon to the Archbishop in the latter's responsibility for diocesan wide needs. The liturgical role of Deacons in this model is seen primarily in relation to their ministry of service.
>
> The training program has been developed and refined in relation to the same model. The pastoral placements in the third year, for example, have been chosen to deepen the aptitudes and skills that candidates already possess and to provide them with the kind of professional competence that will enable them to fulfill their specialized ministries within institutional and other environments.
>
> Over the years the question has been raised on different occasions whether the current model of the Permanent Diaconate should be modified or replaced by one that would focus more on the parish and forms of ministry within it. By supplementing the work of pastors, Deacons could thus help to offset the shortage of priests.

Theoretically, of course, different models of the Permanent Diaconate are possible. Moreover, the final decision in the Archdiocese about needs, their relative priority, and the role that Permanent Deacons might play in meeting them, belongs with the Archbishop. Given that, it is the opinion of the Committee that any changes that might be introduced in the ministry of deacons or in the training program should be respectful of and build upon the considerable experience and success the Archdiocese has already had in developing its distinctive model.

One way of expanding the present ministry would be to put a greater emphasis on the Deacon's role as catalyst or animator of the laity. Instead of simply working in a hospital or prison, some Deacons could be made responsible for involving and coordinating the outreach of a particular parish or parishes, to such an institution. This would give a new depth of meaning to his participation in the liturgical life of that parish.

In addition those responsible for the recruitment, training, formation and supervision of Permanent Deacons should be sensitive to particular gifts or backgrounds that might enable a candidate to fulfill special needs outside of those ordinarily envisaged. Examples here would be chaplaincy in a community college, or the coordination of an outreach program to the young within an area larger than that of a single parish.

A comparable outreach to the non-churched in an area could well be another ministry that particularly qualified Deacons might undertake. In all such cases it would be essential that the Deacon through earlier or subsequent training have the education and skills required by the ministry in question.

Any efforts to relate the ministry of Deacons more closely to parishes should be careful not to undermine but [to] enhance the involvement of the laity. It should also be sensitive to difficulties that could possibly arise on the occasion of a change of pastor. Some coordination between the personnel office of the Archdiocese and those responsible for oversight of Permanent Deacons might be required in order to avoid situations of conflict and even of possible scandal.[57]

Having dealt with the issue of model of service, the committee turned its attention to the development of a questionnaire on the training and ministry of deacons in order to determine if the present diaconate program was meeting the pastoral and social needs of the archdiocese. The assignment was given to Father Dan Donovan, Sister Rita MacLellan and Deacon Dan Murphy. By March 1991, they had produced six different questionnaires for six different target groups. They were deacons, wives, children of deacons, fifty pastors with deacons and fifty pastors without deacons (randomly selected), and twenty-five supervisors of deacons in ministry.[58] The survey was conducted during the spring and summer of 1991, and the results were presented to the committee on 5 November 1991, under the title "Report of the Survey Committee on the Permanent Diaconate in the Archdiocese of Toronto," which we will refer to as the 1991 Survey Report.[59]

The 1991 Survey Report revealed many good things about the diaconate in the Archdiocese of Toronto. Deacons believed that their primary ministry was to the marginalized (there was that word again!), that their liturgical role was understood and appreciated by the clergy, laity and supervisors, that the diaconate had enhanced their family life, bringing them closer to their wives, and that they received exceptional support from their wives in addition to support from other individual deacons, the Diaconal Association and the archdiocese. Asked to list in importance five things they did in their ministry, deacons responded with hospital visitation, visitation of the sick, preaching, baptismal ministry and liturgical ministry.

Pastors with deacons were extremely positive in their responses. They thought that diaconal ministry in the parish and outside the parish was very important to the life of the contemporary Church. The presence of a deacon was a welcome addition to liturgical celebrations, and his work in institutions was a significant contribution to the Catholic presence in public places. They were doing good work as team members in the parish where they had their liturgical base and had excellent working relationships with pastors.

Supervisors were positive in their assessment of the deacon as a Catholic presence in public institutions and as a team member who worked well with his supervisor. They also ventured to say that many people appreciated the deacon as a minister.

The survey revealed that many wives had a ministry outside the home. They served in parishes and hospitals, etc., and some of them played a part in their husband's ministry. This latter group expressed a strong sense of adequacy and achievement in their ministry, which they described as a ministry to the disadvantaged.

On the topic of the training program, the survey pointed to different opinions. Deacons thought that their training had prepared them adequately for their ministry, but ministry supervisors indicated a need for a greater emphasis on the theology of pastoral care and an increase in practical experience. Both supervisors and priests with deacons thought that the minimum requirement of two years of university education or its equivalent was appropriate, and the priests saw a four-year program as adequate.

But there were areas of concern and caution. There was a perception among many deacons that the diaconate was not being integrated into the archdiocesan pastoral plan. A large majority of deacons and wives felt that the diaconate had not increased their children's involvement in the Church, and they wanted more attention paid to family life in the training program. While both deacons and wives rated continuing education and spiritual development as very important in their lives, they believed that the program offered too few opportunities in these areas. Improvements in communication and information about the diaconate among all the stakeholders in the archdiocese were needed. This was a result of the survey's surprising revelations that, among those priests who responded to the questionnaire, a large minority of them believed that the diaconate was established to compensate for the shortage of priests and that the diaconate's primary focus should not be on service to the disadvantaged. Such beliefs contradicted the model of diaconate service that the committee had worked so assiduously to protect and promote and that the diaconate community was reluctant to sacrifice. Also, a large minority of priests and supervisors were not aware of the content of the training program. This would not do either.[60]

The Diaconate Review Committee submitted its report to Bishop Clune by the end of November 1991. Drawing from "Models of the Diaconate" and the 1991 Survey Report, it made seven points:

1. Deacons are highly regarded and appreciated by priests, ministry supervisors and laity, and a substantial number of deacons and their wives continue to be enthusiastic about their vocation and ministry. (Survey data)

2. The model of diaconate developed in this Archdiocese is focused on a ministry of service, especially to groups beyond the reach of parish activities and concerns.

3. The training program is focused on recruiting and forming men for a ministry of service, especially within institutions and other environments.

4. That while the overall attitude of those interacting with the diaconate, e.g. priests and supervisors, is very positive, the level of communication about our focus and model of diaconate, and the content of the training program is inadequate. (Survey data)

5. That deacons perceive the diaconate as not being adequately integrated into the pastoral plan of the Archdiocese. (Survey data)

6. That the present ministry of the deacon might be expanded by putting greater emphasis on his role as catalyst or animator of the laity.

7. Those responsible for recruiting, training, formation and supervision should be aware of particular gifts or backgrounds that qualify the deacon to minister to extraordinary needs.[61]

Several observations are in order. Points #2 and #3 without a doubt reaffirm the service/diocesan model of diaconate ministry, as delineated in the 1977 Review and the committee's "Models of the Diaconate." Consistency on this vital matter was maintained. Points #6 and #7, meanwhile, addressed Cardinal Carter's concerns of 1985 and 1987, and Archbishop Ambrozic's in 1990, without diluting the diaconate program's long running attachment to its primary model of service to the disadvantaged who are beyond the normal reach of parochial ministry. If the model were too narrow or restrictive, any expansion of it would be an exception to policy made to meet extraordinary needs.

At the close of the day, the main emphasis, or the standard model of service, of the permanent diaconate in the Archdiocese of Toronto – in its training program and its assignment of deacons in the field – would be what it had been since 1977: a "ministry of service to the humanly disadvantaged and neglected."[62] These words appeared in the opening paragraph of an official 1992 document on the diaconate training program. Interestingly, these same words described the mission of the diaconate in St. Augustine's Seminary report to the Association of Theological Schools in 1990, prior to the work of the Diaconate Review Committee.[63] Nothing had changed and nothing would change. According to the archdiocesan quinquennial report for 1993–1997, "The main focus [of the diaconal program] is to prepare candidates for the ministry of service towards the dispossessed and disadvantaged, those who have been pushed to the fringe of civil society by such things as poverty, sickness, crime and age. The ministry of liturgy and the ministry of the word celebrate and reflect the deacon's ministry of service."[64]

The 1991 Report of the Review Committee then distilled its seven points into three recommendations: that the archdiocese take steps to correct the perception [misperception?] that the diaconate was not adequately integrated into the archdiocesan pastoral plan; that the archdiocese accept the committee's approach to the expansion of the model of service and to this end that the training program work with the personnel committee to identify and support special diaconal charisms; and that the diaconate office, in conjunction with the training program, the personnel committee and the Diaconal Association, set up task forces that would implement the concerns of the 1991 Survey Report in the areas of continuing education, communication with priests and ministry supervisors and the integration of families into the training program.[65]

Diaconate Self-Study 2001

Ten years passed before the completion of the next official review of the diaconal program. During that time, there were forty-nine diaconal ordinations (every other year starting in 1992 and ending in 2000). By the close of 2000, there were approximately 100 active deacons, with twelve more scheduled for ordination in June 2002. Ministry activities in 2000, in terms of percentages, were hospitals (46 percent), senior citizen and nursing homes (22 percent), detention and correctional institutes (16 percent) and so-called other ministries (16 percent).[66] In most cases, deacons were either deacon visitors or deacon chaplains, with several serving as deacon visitors to more than one institution. But there were also deacons who, in addition to their regular ministry, served as deacon mentors and formation mentors. Several deacons had parish ministries, and one deacon was also pontifical master of ceremonies for the archdiocese at St. Michael's Cathedral.

The number of ministries listed as "other" had been increased to include both institutional and non-institutional settings. Some examples were Mission to Seamen, Sancta Maria House, Rosalie Hall, De Sales Chaplaincy for the Deaf, Providence Centre, Loyola Arrupe Seniors Home, the Toronto Airport chapel, Holy Cross Cemetery chaplaincy, group therapy for sex offenders released from jail, and post-abortion counselling.

There were also several organizational changes to the diaconate. The Co-ordinating Board succeeded the Council of Deacons and the Executive Board increased its membership. There was an important name change, too. On the initiative of the Episcopal Board, the Co-ordinating Board and the board of governors of St. Augustine's Seminary, the diaconate training program became known as the diaconate formation program.

And, of course, the leadership of the archdiocese had passed from Cardinal Gerald Emmett Carter to Archbishop Aloysius Ambrozic, who had been involved with the diaconate since its inception in

1972. As a professor at St. Augustine's Seminary, he was initially opposed to the restoration of the diaconate in the archdiocese, because he felt that the diaconate's two-year training program, based on the adult education model, would water down the seminary's mandate.[67] However, as soon as he was convinced that the seminary's mandate would not suffer because of the diaconate training program, he became one of the diaconate's most enthusiastic supporters, sometimes its chief cheerleader, during his long and eventful career in the archdiocese: as the first vicar of deacons (briefly); as auxiliary bishop of the archdiocese (1976); as coadjutor archbishop (1986); as archbishop (1990) and as cardinal (1998). He retired on 15 December 2006, but, as archbishop emeritus, he never lost his interest in the diaconal community, which accounts for the origins of this history.

In 1991, Archbishop Ambrozic was appointed to the Congregation for the Clergy. As a member of this Roman Congregation, he participated in the writing of *Directory for the Ministry and Life of Permanent Deacons*. The Congregation for Catholic Education was responsible for the companion piece, *Basic Norms for the Formation of Permanent Deacons*. These documents were written for those episcopal conferences that had yet to produce their own norms and directory, the Canadian Conference of Catholic Bishops being one of them.[68] They were published as two titles in a single volume in 1998.[69] Archbishop Ambrozic made a significant contribution to the content and direction of the *Directory*, since he brought with him to Rome all the major documents produced by the training program.[70] Toronto's enviable track record on the diaconate of more than a quarter century of continuous service to the Church and community prompted him to hold up his archdiocese as an example of how to implement and sustain the diaconate as a viable part of archdiocesan life. Archbishop Ambrozic was confident that the archdiocese was doing things the right way when it came to the diaconate, and he considered the program's stability and longevity a substantial achievement of his episcopacy.[71]

In the autumn of 2000, Cardinal Ambrozic called for a self-study of the diaconate. Committee members were Bishop John Boissonneau, rector of St. Augustine's Seminary, who was replaced by his successor, Father Robert A. Nusca, Deacon Bert Cambre (chair), Deacon George Newman (vice-chair), Deacon Tom and Mary Lou Dea, Deacon Tom Kung, Deacon John Grieve and Sister Caroline Altpeter, IBVM (secretary). The committee's purpose was to provide the cardinal with "an evaluation of how effectively the Diaconate in the Archdiocese conformed to the formation and ministry of the deacon"[72] as described in the two 1998 Roman documents on the diaconate: *Basic Norms for the Formation of Permanent Deacons* and *Directory for the Ministry and Life of Permanent Deacons*. The objectives of the study were to evaluate the effectiveness of the formation program and the life and ministry of the deacon in the field and to recommend ways to strengthen the diaconate in both areas as it entered a new millennium.[73] The scope or focus was on the formation, life and ministry of deacons (pre- and post-ordination, and the relationship between the two) in terms of both ministry to the marginalized and liturgical ministry. The committee was directed to identify and analyze the strengths and weaknesses in both ministries and to make recommendations to Cardinal Ambrozic.[74]

The methodology of the self-study was a series of questionnaires (and comments from respondents). The questionnaires went to deacons from the two-year, three-year and four-year training programs; to all deacons for comparison; those with post-ordination experience; deacons' wives, formation and post-ordination; deacons' families; candidates in 2000–2001; formation faculty; those no longer in the program; pastors and administrators with an assigned deacon and those without an assigned deacon; parishioners; and ministry supervisors.

This self-study was different from all previous reports, reviews and self-studies in two respects. First, after twenty-eight years, diaconal ministry to the marginalized – that much maligned word resurrected by the committee – was no longer an issue. It was and would remain *the* model of diaconal service in the Archdiocese of Toronto. If it needed anything, it needed to be clarified for everyone involved in the life and work of deacons. Second, the process of self-examination this time included a third-party reviewer, Deacon Stephen Graff, from Liverpool, New York, to assess the findings and conclusions of the self-study committee before it submitted its final report to Cardinal Ambrozic. Deacon Graff inserted a running commentary throughout the document and ended it with commendations, concerns and recommendations of his own.

The committee concluded that the diaconate was strong because it was fulfilling the official norms for formation and the directives for ministry and life of deacons. Additional strength was found in ministry to the marginalized, which was focused and effective, and in liturgical ministry, which was "well enacted and well received by the parishioners."[75] The committee then made a number of recommendations, dividing them into three categories: formation, deacons in action, and ministry to the marginalized.

Formation:

1. The expectations of deacon candidates and their wives are fully clarified at the outset of the formation program.

2. The plans for the formation Program are presented to the Formation faculty and regular coordination meetings be held to ensure there is an integrated program.

3. A learning evaluation method or tool is adopted to provide feedback both to the faculty members and to the deacon candidate.

4. Practicums both in liturgical and pastoral ministry start as early as is feasible.

5. Pastors, particularly those who have deacons in training, be given an "awareness" program to advise them of the formation's goals and contents.

Deacons in Action:

1. The spiritual direction of deacons be addressed.

2. An education program on the Diaconate be developed and implemented for pastors and parish administrators.

3. The Vicar of Deacons take an active role in deacon affairs.

Ministry to the Marginalized:

1. Ministry to the marginalized be clearly defined and reviewed periodically.

2. Identified ministry to the marginalized be presented to the Director of the Formation Program to incorporate into the program.

3. An evaluation tool be developed for ministry supervisors to assess deacons in action.[76]

The committee was quite adamant about ministry to the marginalized. It recognized that there were many requests for deacons – this was a good thing, because it meant that deacons were needed – but it insisted that all requests for deacons "must be focused on the specific needs of the marginalized. It is the 'needs' of the marginalized that dictate the ministries of the Diaconate and the focus of the Formation Program."[77]

Lastly, it recommended that the director of deacons and the director of the formation program draw up an all-inclusive organizational manual for the diaconate and that Cardinal Ambrozic "sponsor an awareness program of both the formation program and diaconal ministry for the priests of the diocese to strengthen the relationship between pastors and deacons."[78]

Deacon Stephen Graff commended the diaconal program in the following areas: its good leadership and its good candidates, deacons and wives; clarity of vision; mentoring system; in-depth academic program; self-discernment and peer evaluation in the home study meetings; liturgy schedule; wives' program; ethnic and cultural diversity; and St. Augustine's Seminary. He had concerns, however, about the co-ordination between the various parts of the diaconal program, communication between mentors and faculty, academic evaluation, the absence of a propaedeutic period for aspirants to candidacy that would precede admission into the formation program, and the fact that "the placement of candidacy and the rites of lector and acolyte do not conform to the *Basic Norms for the Formation of Permanent Deacons.*"[79]

Deacon Graff made many recommendations in the areas of admissions, formation and diaconal life and ministry. For example, in relation to admissions, he strongly recommended a propaedeutic period, in accordance with paragraphs 42 and 43 of *Basic Norms*, and, as part of that preparatory period, "ministry to the marginalized in a controlled and supervised setting which then provides in turn the subject matter for group theological reflection."[80] On the matter of formation, he suggested that the office of the permanent diaconate, the director of formation, St. Augustine's Seminary and other offices and agencies of the archdiocese "engage in a process to predict, as far as possible, the future use and geographic need for permanent deacons, and to evaluate the formation course of study in light of that information."[81]

All well and good, a practical step no doubt, but in the next breath, Deacon Graff poses two questions that seem to challenge the committee's firm understanding of the model of diaconal service and even dampen his own high regard for the program's ministry to the marginalized. "Will there be a need in the future," he openly ponders, "for deacons to be engaged more deliberately in parochial ministry? Will there be a need for deacons to serve as administrators and local pastoral leaders of parishes without priests?"[82] Could this have been a polite fraternal warning to the diaconate to be on guard about changes to their model of service?

For diaconal life and ministry, Deacon Graff addressed issues concerning the promotion and expansion of continuing education, spiritual direction for the diaconal community, the crucial nature of the initial ministry assignment and the need to emphasize the ministry of the Word. For him, the Word was the "glue" that held together the other two diaconal ministries, charity and liturgy.[83]

The last word belongs to Deacon Stephen Graff. For this we return to his previously noted commendation on the diaconate program's clarity of vision. What he wrote next is high praise rarely doled out to the diaconate. "For many of us in the States, the clear connection of diaconate in Toronto with ministry to and with the marginalized and its subsequent celebration in the parish has been an inspiration and a model."[84] Indeed.

Portrait of Diaconal Ministry 2008

It has been our contention in this chapter that after many years of fine-tuning its formation program and post-ordination placements, and every so often overhauling its organizational structure, the diaconate program continued to attract the right kind of candidates and remained vigilant in its attachment to its original vision of itself as a community of the ordained called to serve all those who had been relegated to the far reaches of either the Church or society. If charity was "the ministry most characteristic of the deacon,"[85] according to *Basic Norms for the Formation of Permanent Deacons*, ministry to the marginalized was the ministry most characteristic of charity, according to the diaconate program of the Archdiocese of Toronto. Having settled upon a mandate for its mission in 1977, the diaconate successfully protected and enhanced that mandate over the years, codifying it in the 1978 Policy Statement and reaffirming it in 1981 (Deacon Search Committee), in 1991 (Deacon Review Committee) and in the 2001 *Diaconate Self-Study*. In 2004, the program prepared the first-ever policy paper devoted solely to an explanation of the model of service. Called *Diaconal Ministry of Service*, it examined the identity of the deacon, the characteristics of diaconal ministry of service and diaconal ministry in 2004, in both institutional and diocesan settings. It ended with some sobering and some hopeful thoughts about the future. *Diaconal Ministry of Service* is the closest thing to a manifesto produced by the diaconate program at any time in its history.[86]

How then did the diaconate community measure up to its own model of service? In 2008, there were 110 active deacons in the archdiocese. That year Deacon Michael Hawes and his wife, Dawn, members of the ministry and education portfolio, conducted a ministry survey on behalf of the Co-ordinating Board. Ninety-seven deacons responded. The survey excluded liturgical ministry, employment and volunteering, focusing exclusively on the ministry of service outside a parish. The results are revealing and encouraging:

- 63 deacons: single ministry, one or more locations
- 27 deacons: two ministries

- 6 deacons: three ministries
- 43 deacons: 51 nursing, senior citizen and retirement homes
- 41 deacons: 30 hospitals and health-care settings
- 9 deacons: 11 counselling ministries for addiction, bereavement, etc.
- 7 deacons: 11 shelters
- 14 deacons: 8 prisons
- 8 deacons: 8 ministries to shut-ins and home visits
- 7 deacons: 7 ministries to ex-offenders
- 7 deacons: 7 ethnic communities
- 4 deacons: 5 ministries to migrant workers, seafarers and dockworkers
- 4 deacons: 5 street ministries
- 2 deacons: 2 institutions for the mentally challenged.[87]

These numbers may not tell us everything, but they tell us enough to let us know that the diaconate, after more than thirty-five years, is flourishing in the Archdiocese of Toronto and that deacons are quietly and prayerfully busy every day of the week bringing the Gospel of Jesus Christ to countless people in need of its truth and comfort.

APPENDIXES

Appendix I: Proposed Organizational Structure for the Permanent Diaconate, 1981

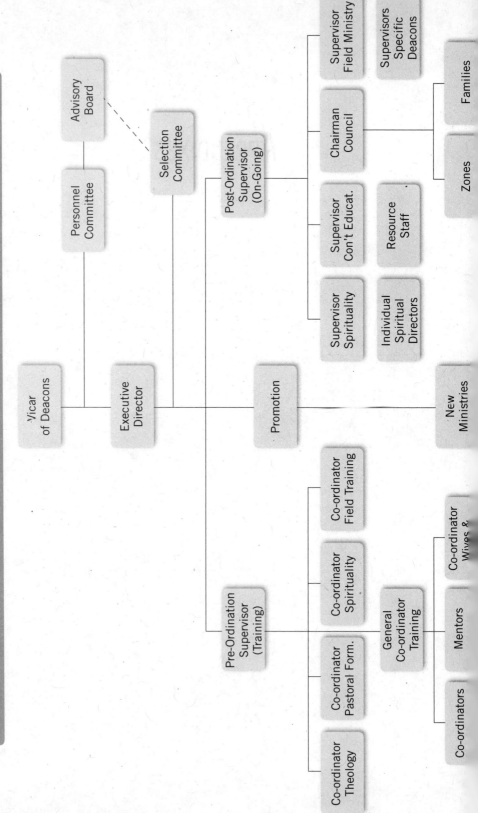

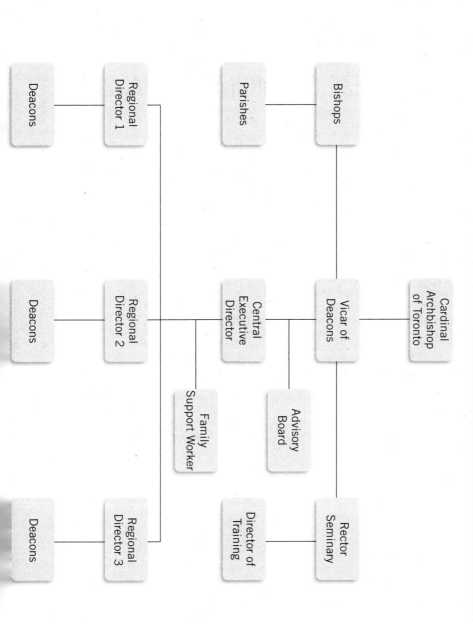

Appendix II: Proposed Organizational Structure for the Permanent Diaconate, 1983

Cardinal Archbishop of Toronto

Vicar of Deacons

Advisory Board

Bishops — Parishes

Rector Seminary — Director of Training

Central Executive Director

Family Support Worker

Regional Director 1 — Deacons

Regional Director 2 — Deacons

Regional Director 3 — Deacons

APPENDIX III

LIST OF DEACONS ORDAINED FOR THE ARCHDIOCESE OF TORONTO, 1974–2010

1974

Bannon, William
Boudreau, John
Chase, Colin
Clair, James
Côté, Jed
Cregg, James
Cresswell, Thomas
Gabourie, Walter
Kopfensteiner, Steve
Lennon, Gerald
MacGregor, Alexander
MacLellan, Stanley
Manne, Cornelius
Matthews, Patrick
Maundcote-Carter, Wilfred
McTeague, Joseph
Mooney, Orval
Murphy, Daniel
Preyra, Cecil
Rankin, William
Rogers, Lawrence
Sanderson, James
Sandford, Tony
Scandiffio, Nick
Wilson, Bernard
Yearsley, Ralph

1975

Andrews, Leonard
Cassidy, Vincent
Charbonneau, Tab
Corcoran, John
Geisel, Robert
Hall, Milton
Holy, Adolf
Jazmines, Vicente
Killoran, Leo
McFarland, Ronald
McKay, Michael
McNeil, Andrew
Mellor, James
Morley, George
O'Connor, John
Pessoa, Lino
Sabatini, Bruno
Vesey, Patrick

1976

Andrews, Desmond
Baghan, Kenneth
Cidadao, Octavio
Chomko, Kazimierz
Conlin, Michael
Cordina, John
Corrigan, Larry

Daigle, Vincent
Dixon, Samuel
Engel, Michael
Ferguson, Robert
Gaynor, Mervyn
Kosichek, Joseph
McPhee, Donald
O'Brien, Brian
O'Connor, Terrance
Robertson, Michael
Rollings Bernard
Rousseau, Jean
Seedhouse, Edward

1977

Fox, Joseph

1978

Duncan, Joseph
Hackembruch, Henri
King, George
Mason, Thomas
McCarthy, Charles
Meloche, Alphonse
Oneson, Lawrence
Partridge, Robert
Peake, Malcolm
Pillisch, Thomas
Podesta, Bruno
Scappatura, Francis
Shoreman, John
Valiquet, Louis
Vanderkooy, Leo
Wilson, George

1979

Moore, Gerry
Skelton, Derek

1980

Callaghan, William
DeSouza, Francis
Dwyer, Philip
Godsoe, Gerald
Greenaway, Clifford
Higgins, William
Verschuren, Henry

1981

Crump, John
Daly, William
Halls, James
McCance, Murray
Sutherland, Alistair

1983

Cambre, Norberto
Barker, William
Blomeley, James
Demers, Emile
MacLellan, Ronald
Manning, Roger

1984

Gittens, Peter
Pereira, Nazario

1985

Apperley, David
Birss, John
Daigle, John
Fillery, Edward
Grieve, John
Hawkshaw, William
Kim, Michael
Kinghorn, Robert
Legris, Bernard
McLean, Francis
McTeague, Frank
Miller, Stanley
Pappas, Nicola
Tustin, Gordon
Wood, Philip

1987

Bechard, Vern
Dopp, Eugene
Harris, John
MacLellan, Peter
McEvenue, St. Clair
McNally, Walter
Moulton, Albert
Newman, George
Popiel, Thaddeus
Skinner, Marven
Weiss, Gordon

1990

Belec, Paul
Di Grado, Joseph
Doucette, Alan
du Quesnay, Brian
Johnson, Gary

Klimek, Peter
Mann, Richard
Maratta, Diego
Penny, Leo
Whelton, William

1992

MacDonnell, Edward
Martineau, Paul
McKeogh, Thomas
Pignataro, Anthony
Whittaker, James

1993

Leva, Giovanni
Sparkes, Robert

1994

Baldi, Salvatore
Barringer, Stephen
Brockerville, Kevin
Dacanay, Albert
Doyle, Peter
Kung, Thomas
Lee, James Hyun
McBride, Peter
Savard, Michel

1996

Bougie, Danny
Campbell, William
Chang, Patrick
Grant, Steve
McCulloch, Wayne
Nogueira, Carlos
Quanash, William

Rosales, Roberto
Sahagun, Cesar
Savundranayagam, Joseph

1998

Almeida, Gerard
Beausoleil, Eustace
Burns, William
Caroll, Desmond
Carson, WilliamDea, Thomas
Djaja, Paul
Engel, Wolfgang
Griffin, Vance
Jeynes, Brian
McDonald, Paul
Quirke, Michel
Sylvan, Kenrick
Taylor, Hugh

2000

Allard, Philip
Ambrozaitis, Kaz
Chalmers, Bernard
Nowak, Wojciech
Rickards, Peter
Rodrigues, Inacio
Sandford, David
Stong, Alfred
Suthers, Robert

2002

Da Silva, Terence
Gana, Daniel
Kennedy, John
Lovrick, Peter
Murphy, Joseph

Ouimet, Lawrence
Popik, Milan
Schwarzbauer, John
Steyn, Gerry
Thibodeau
Tran, Vinh
Triska, Milton

2003

Harris, Bernard

2004

Blake Richard
Cannon, John
Colucci, Fred
D'Paiva, Oswald
Del Castilho, Raymond
Doyle, David
Gomes, Liionel
Hayes, Michael
Ho, Michael
Lavoie, Daniel
Mason, Brian
Masongsong, Alex
McCullogh, Don
Nimer-Boutros, Fuad
Palmer, Stephen
Pawliszko, Marian
Picotte, François
Sasco, Dominic
Schell, Miles
Sirianni, Frank
Stone, Anthony
Villardo, Ramon
Walsh, Michael
Whall, David

2006

Bertolone, Gian Luigi
Danukarjanto, Valentinus
Doucette, Bob
Fleming, Ron
Letterio, William
Munroe, Everis
Welsh, Tom

2008

Booth, Stephen
Grandy, Kevin
Jurenas, George
Langley, David
McManaman, Douglas
Radigan, William
Sirek, Jan
Teresi, Anthony
Wood, Barry

2010

Boone, Curtis
Fidalgo, Silverio
MacInnis, David
McGowan, Damien
Miranda, Michael
Morris, Alan
O'Mahoney, Michael
O'Shaughnessy, Don
Ovcjak, Rudy
Owusu-Afriyie, Joseph
Pinto, Sarfaraz
Pullano, Dominic
Rebello, Terence
Roberts, Don
Shaughnessy, James
Shaw, Larry

APPENDIX IV

IS GOD CALLING YOU TO THE DIACONATE?

"Each one of us must discern how God is calling us to serve the Church. Deacons play a vital role in evangelizing both the gathered and the scattered in our community. Their ministry is of great importance to our Archdiocese, answering the call of Jesus to love and serve."

—**His Grace, Thomas Collins,**
Archbishop of Toronto

The word "deacon" means servant. In the Archdiocese of Toronto, deacons, the vast majority of whom are married and have full-time jobs, serve the community in diverse ways: visiting the imprisoned, comforting the dying, caring for the disadvantaged and reaching out to those pushed to the fringes of society by sickness, poverty, crime or age. At your local parish, you may find deacons preparing the faithful to receive the sacraments and to carry out their vocation as baptized Christians. Deacons preach, teach, counsel and give spiritual guidance. They assist bishops and priests in liturgical celebrations. They baptize, witness marriages and preside at funerals. Whatever they do, deacons are acting on behalf of the servant Christ.

Who Can Be a Deacon?

The Diaconate Formation Program is open to men both married and single between the ages of 35 to 59 who meet the basic requirements. The applicant must have the full consent of his wife if he is married and the full support of his pastor.

Candidates accepted into the program are required to complete formation for a period of four years of part-time studies at Saint

Augustine's Seminary, meetings in the homes of other candidates and service in areas of social concern.

The Formation Program facilitates the candidate to grow into the unique character intended for him by God. Therefore, the program integrates the human, spiritual, academic and pastoral dimensions vital for a person seeking a life of commitment to Church service.

How Do Deacons Serve the Church?

A deacon is ordained to serve the people of God, assist the Bishop and work with his Priests – there are three dimensions to their service: Ministry of the Altar, Ministry of the Word and Ministry of Charity.

Ministry of the Altar

The Deacon provides fundamental and distinct sacramental assistance to the ministry of the Bishop and subordinately to that of the Priest. Founded on the Sacrament of Orders, his ministry differs in essence from any liturgical ministry entrusted to the lay faithful.

Accordingly, the Deacon:

- Assists the Bishop and Priest at the Eucharist, prays the bidding prayers and invites the faithful to exchange the sign of peace
- Distributes the Eucharist during Mass and administers Viaticum to the sick
- Proclaims the gospel
- Preaches the homily
- Administers the sacrament of Baptism
- Witnesses and blesses marriages
- Officiates at wakes, funerals and burial services
- Administers sacramentals
- Presides at prayer services, Benediction
- Prepares the faithful for reception of the sacraments and their pastoral care after receiving them.

Deacons faithfully observe the liturgical norms and rubrics of the liturgical books and have an obligation to pray, in communion with the greater Christian community, the Liturgy of the Hours every day.

Ministry of the Word

At his ordination, the Deacon hears the Bishop say, "Receive the Gospel of Christ whose herald you now are." The Deacon calls all to conversion and holiness. Sacred Scripture, Tradition and the liturgy and life of the Church are the sacred deposit that the Deacon draws on to communicate effectively the mystery of Christ. It is for the Deacon to proclaim and preach the word of God

- At the Eucharistic celebration
- In liturgical gatherings
- In Religious Education programs both in the parish and in the diocese
- At informal gatherings and meetings.

Ministry of Charity

Diocesan and parochial works of charity are among the primary duties entrusted to the Diaconate. Deacons "discharge the duties of charity and administration in the name of the Church and also serve those in our society who are in need, such as the aged, the sick, those in nursing homes, and those in prison or anyone who needs special attention to experience God's love."

How Are the Benefits of a Deacon's Service Unique?

The distinct value of the Diaconate lies in the triple aspects of its ministry: "diakonia of charity, of the liturgy and of the word." The Deacon teaches when he preaches and bears witness to the word of God. He sanctifies when he celebrates the sacrament of baptism, distributes the Holy Eucharist and the sacramentals and participates in the celebration of Holy Mass as a "minister of the blood." He is a guide as he animates the community. Over-emphasis on the Deacon's liturgical functions and on his parochial duties may lead one to see the Diaconate as a partial realization of the ordained priesthood: it should be clear that it is not.

In assisting at the altar, the Deacon represents on the one hand the people of God uniting their lives to the offering of Christ, and, on the other hand, in the name of Christ himself he "helps the Church to participate in the fruits of the sacrifice."

Deacons assist the Bishops and Priests who have a primary role in the celebration of the divine mysteries. Deacons serve God's people in the name of Christ; they are icons of Christ the servant; their focus is a service of charity in the name of the Church.

How Do Deacons Strengthen the Church Through Their Mission?

While addressing his ministry, the Deacon is aware of the missionary nature of the Church. His mission includes witness to Christ in his secular profession or occupation. Contemporary society requires a new evangelization. Deacons bring the "word" into their professional lives explicitly or by their active presence. Ordained to a ministry of service, his ministry is focussed in areas where, sent by the bishop, he can bring his talents to serve God, the Church and the community. This competence should be clarified and grounded in the form of an agreement with his Bishop or his designate.

By virtue of ordination, the Deacon is truly called to act in conformity with Christ the servant. Associated with this fundamental relationship with Christ is his relationship with the Church. The Deacon "shares Christ's love for the Church with a deep attachment because of her mission with divine institution."

In virtue of the sacrament of Holy Orders, Deacons are at the service of their brothers and sisters; they are united to one another as a sacramental community by virtue of their ordination. They exchange experiences, continue to advance their formation and encourage one another in fidelity.

Is God Calling You to the Permanent Diaconate?

We give thanks for the Permanent Diaconate in both our local and global church. If you think God may be calling you to the Permanent Diaconate, contact the Director of Deacons at the Catholic Pastoral Centre (416-934-3400 ext. 304) or find out more about us online at: www.vocationstoronto.ca.

APPENDIX V

IN GRATITUDE

This book was made possible, in part, through the gracious generosity of the many people whose names are listed below. We wish to thank them for their willingness to help bring this story to a broader audience.

Deacon Kaz & Angela Ambrozaitis
Anonymous
Deacon Sal Badali (Rose, deceased)
Mrs. Therese Bannon (Deacon William Bannon, deceased)
Mrs. Dora Barker (Deacon William Baker, deceased)
Deacon Steve & Barbara Barringer
Deacon Luigi & Albina Bertolone
Deacon Richard & Catherine Blake
Deacon Bill & Mary Callaghan
Deacon Bert & Terry Cambre
Mrs. Rosemary Chalmers (Deacon Bernard Chalmers, deceased)
Deacon Tab & Mary Charbonneau
Deacon Kazimierz Chomko
Rev. Ron Comeau
Deacon John Crump (Rita, deceased)
Deacon Terry & Wanda Da Silva
Mr. George Damiani
Deacon Paul & Jenny Djaja
Deacon Peter & Joan Doyle
Deacon Joe & Sheila Duncan
Deacon Wolfgang & Diana Engel
Deacon Cyrus Gallant
Deacon Daniel & Carmen Gana

Mrs. Maxine Geisel (Deacon Robert Giesel, deceased)
Mr. John Gennaro
Deacon Lionel & Pamela Gomes
Mrs. Catherine Grant (Deacon Steve Grant, deceased)
Deacon John & Carmel Grieve
Mrs. Maria Griffin (Deacon Vance Griffin, deceased)
Deacon Milton & Anna Hall
Deacon Bernard & Margaret Harris
Deacon John & Esther Harris
Deacon Michael & Dawn Hayes
Deacon Michael & Isabaella Ho
Deacon John and Cheryl Lee Kennedy
Mrs. Lillian Killoran (Deacon Leo Killoran, deceased)
Deacon Michael & Agnes Kim
Deacon Peter & Krystyna Klimek
Deacon Daniel & Diane Lavoie
Deacon Bernard & Shirley Legris
Mrs. Loretta Lennon (Deacon Gerald Lennon, deceased)
Deacon Alex MacGregor (Loretta, deceased)
Deacon Stan & Olga MacLellan
Deacon Corry & Shirley Manne
Deacon Diego & Diane Maratta
Deacon Tom & Margaret Mason
Mrs. Anne Mastrovita
Deacon Patrick & Kathlyn Matthews
Mr. Richard Matthews (diaconate candidate, deceased)
Deacon Chuck & Helen McCarthy
Deacon Wayne & Cheryl McCulloch
Deacon Don & Helen McCullough
Deacon Damien & Angelica McGowan
Mrs. Doris McKeogh
Mrs. Catherine McLean (Deacon Frank McLean, deceased)
Deacon Dan & Jean Murphy
Deacon Fuad & Elaine Nimer-Boutros
Deacon Michael & Anne O'Mahoney

Deacon Malcolm & Frances Peake
Mrs. Elizabeth Pillisch (Deacon Tom Pillisch, deceased)
Deacon Safaraz & Luiza Pinto
Deacon Ted & Monique Popiel
Deacon Milan & Maria Popik
Deacon Robert & Lois Probert
Deacon Bill & Sally Radigan
Mrs. Yvette Rankin (Deacon William Rankin, deceased)
Deacon Peter & Diana Rickards
Deacon Michael & Barbara Robertson
Deacon Inacio & Teresa Rodrigues
Rev. Chris Rupert S.J.
Deacon Miles & Carrie Schell
Serra International Foundation of Canada
Mrs. Sally Skinner (Deacon Marven Skinner, deceased)
Deacon Alistair and Dora Sutherland
Deacon Ken and Gemma Sylvan
Deacon Anthony & Marie Teresi
Deacon Gary & Cindy Thibodeau
Deacon Vin & Mai Tran
Deacon Gordon & Effie Tustin
Deacon Henry & Lucy Verschuren
Fr. Rudy Volk
Deacon Mike & Susan Walsh
Deacon David & Rita Whall
Deacon Bill & Claire Whelton
Deacon George Wilson (Jean, deceased)

NOTES

Chapter 1

[1] There were an incredible number of people writing about the diaconate in Europe before and after the Second World War. There was also the extraordinary work and witness of the Caritas movement in Germany. I do not wish to overlook or downplay their contribution. For a list of these writers and activists, see two works by Josef Hornef, *The New Vocation*, trans. P. Russell (Cork, Ireland: The Mercier Press, 1963), Bibliographical Notes, 145–46; and "The Genesis and Growth of the Proposal," in *Foundations for the Renewal of the Diaconate* (Washington, D.C.: United States Catholic Conference, 1993), 6–9, 12–14, 16–19. In *The New Vocation*, Hornef refers to an obscure but seminal late nineteenth-century work on the diaconate: Johann Nepomuk Seidl, *Deaconship in the Catholic Church, Its Hieratic Dignity and Historical Development* (Regensburg: 1894). In "Genesis and Growth of the Proposal," Hornef quotes from a letter, dated 20 April 1840, from J.K. Passavant, a Frankfurt physician and author, to Melchior von Diepenbrock, the future Cardinal Prince-Bishop of Breslau, and from an excerpt from Diepenbrock's reply. The subject of their correspondence was the diaconate.

[2] William J. O'Malley, "The Priests of Dachau," in *Pius XII and the Holocaust: A Reader* (Milwaukee, Wis.: Catholic League for Religious and Civil Rights, 1988), Appendix I.

[3] Otto Pies, "Block 26: Erfahrungen aus dem Priesterleben in Dachau," *Stimmen der Zeit* 141 (1947–48): 10–28. This was a Jesuit publication. Its title can be translated as *Voices of the Times*. The quotation, which is a summary of the intent of Father Pies' article, is given in Hornef, "The Genesis and Growth of the Proposal," 11. Hornef knew Father Schamoni.

[4] James Francis McDonnell, "An Examination of the Theology of the Permanent Diaconate in the Documents of the Second Vatican Council and of Three Regional Hierarchies" (master's thesis, University of St. Michael's College, 1976), 1–10.

[5] Hornef, "The Genesis and Growth of the Proposal," 9–11.

[6] Wilhelm Schamoni, *Familienväter als geweihte Diakone* (Paderborn: Schöningh, 1953); Wilhelm Schamoni, *Married Men as Ordained Deacons*, trans. Otto Eisner (London: Burns & Oates, 1955); Wilhelm Schamoni, *Ordonner Diacres des Pères de Famille* (Desclée de Brouwer, 1961). All quotations will be from the English translation. Father Schamoni opens his Preface with a reference to Seidl's *Deaconship in the Catholic Church*.

[7] Schamoni, *Married Men as Ordained Deacons*, 33–43, 55–58.

8   Ibid., *Married Men as Ordained Deacons*, 11–12.

9   Ibid., *Married Men as Ordained Deacons*, 12–13, 55–58.

10   William T. Ditewig, *The Emerging Diaconate: Servant Leaders in a Servant Church* (New York/Mahwah, N.J.: Paulist Press, 2007), 85.

11   Schamoni, *Married Men as Ordained Deacons*, 15–16.

12   Ibid., *Married Men as Ordained Deacons*, 60. On the page preceding his discussion of the Hungarian Licentiates, Father Schamoni mentions the tradition of "married clerics" in sixteenth-century India, which Father Jerome Nadal, SJ, lobbied in 1566 to introduce into Germany. Nothing came of his proposal. Father Schamoni also wrote about the failure of the Jesuits in the seventeenth century to persuade Rome to allow the ordination of mature Chinese men, including widowers, and the use of the vernacular in the liturgy, in order to avoid catastrophe similar to the one that occurred in Japan due to a lack of native priests and bishops. See 61–62.

13   Hornef, *The New Vocation*, 11. For a later summation of Hornef's ideas on the diaconate, see Josef Hornef, "The Order of Diaconate in the Roman Catholic Church," in *The Diaconate Now*, ed. Richard T. Nolan (Washington, D.C.: Corpus Books, 1968), 57–79.

14   This work was cited by Schamoni in his *Married Men as Ordained Deacons*, on page 9 as follows: Josef Hornef in *Die Besinnung*, 1949, no. 6, and 1950, no. 6; *Werkhefte für Kathl. Laienarbeit*, nos. 1 and 3.

15   Hornef was aware of the pastoral and charitable work of Protestant (Lutheran) deacons, but he also realized that they were not ordained in a sacramental way. See Hornef, *The New Vocation*, Chapter 17, in particular, 101–102.

16   McDonnell, "An Examination of the Theology of the Permanent Diaconate," 1–10.

17   Schamoni, *Married Men as Ordained Deacons*, 41.

18   William T. Ditewig, *101 Questions and Answers on Deacons* (New York/Mahwah, N.J.: Paulist Press, 2004), 63–66.

19   Hornef, *The New Vocation*, 30.

20   Ibid., *The New Vocation*, 32–34.

21   See the following works: *Guidelines of the Episcopal Committee on the Permanent Diaconate* (Ottawa: Canadian Catholic Conference, 1967), Chapters 2–3; Edward P. Echlin, *The Deacon in the Church: Past and Future* (Staten Island, N.Y.: Alba House, 1971), Chapters 1–3; James Monroe Bennett, *The Diaconate: A Full and Equal Order*, rev. ed. (Harrisburg, Penn.: Trinity Press International, 1995), Chapters 3–6; Ditewig, *The Emerging Diaconate: Servant Leaders in a Servant Church*, 62–65.

22   "Rahner, Karl," *New Catholic Encyclopedia*, vol. 18, *Supplement 1978–1988* (Washington, D.C.: Catholic University of America, 1989), 411–13.

23 Karl Rahner, "Die Theologie des Diakonates," in *Diaconia in Christo: Über Die Erneuerung Des Diakonates*, ed. Karl Rahner and Herbert Vorgrimler (Frieburg: Herder, 1962), 285–324; Ibid., "The Theology of the Restoration of the Diaconate," *Theological Investigations*, vol. 5, *Later Writings*, trans. Karl-H. Kruger (Baltimore: Helicon Press, 1966), 268–314. Other seminal works on the diaconate by Father Rahner include "The Teaching of the Second Vatican Council on the Diaconate," *Theological Investigations*, vol. 10 (New York: Herder & Herder, 1973), 222–32; and "On the Diaconate," *Theological Investigations*, vol. 12 (London: Darton, Longman & Todd, 1974), 61–76. "On the Diaconate" became required reading for candidates to the permanent diaconate in the Archdiocese of Toronto.

24 McDonnell, "An Examination of the Theology of the Permanent Diaconate," 10–14.

25 Rahner, "The Theology of the Restoration of the Diaconate," 181–82.

26 Ibid., "The Theology of the Restoration of the Diaconate," 183–84.

27 Ibid., "The Theology of the Restoration of the Diaconate," 286.

28 Ibid., "The Theology of the Restoration of the Diaconate," 287.

29 Ibid., "The Theology of the Restoration of the Diaconate," 289.

30 Ibid., "The Theology of the Restoration of the Diaconate," 273–74.

31 John Francis Fowles, "The Diaconate in the Second Vatican Council" (master's thesis, University of St. Michael's College, 1971), 2.

32 Yves Congar, *Mon Journal du Concile*, 2 vols. (Paris: Éditions du Cerf, 2002); Michel-Dominique Epagneul, "A Functional Diaconate," *Theology Digest* 7 (1959): 73–76; Paul Winninger, "The Deacon and the Lay Person," in *Foundations for the Renewal of the Diaconate*, 51–60.

33 Archives of the Roman Catholic Archdiocese of Toronto [hereafter ARCAT], Papers of Archbishop Philip Pocock [hereafter Pocock Papers], PO VA12.01, Petition; PO VA12.03, Signatures to Petition.

34 Hornef, "The Genesis and Growth of the Proposal," in *Foundations for the Renewal of the Diaconate*, 13–14; McDonnell, "An Examination of the Theology of the Permanent Diaconate," 14–16.

35 Hornef, "Genesis and Growth of the Proposal," in *Foundations for the Renewal of the Diaconate*, 19.

36 ARCAT, Pocock Papers, PO VA12.02, "The International Circle of the Diaconate."

37 Hannes Kramer, "Die liturgischen Dienste des Diakons," in *Diakonia in Christo*, 362–79; "Das religiöse Leben des Diakons," in *Diakonia in Christo*, 555–74, which was translated as "The Spiritual Life of Deacons," in *Foundations for the Renewal of the Diaconate*, 29–49.

38   ARCAT, Pocock Papers, PO VA12.10, Petition, [1].

39   Ibid., Pocock Papers, PO VA12.10, Petition, 2.

40   Ibid., Pocock Papers, PO VA12.10, Petition, 3.

41   Ibid., Pocock Papers, PO VA12.10, Petition, 5.

42   Ibid.

43   Ibid.

Chapter 2

1   *The Canons and Decrees of the Council of Trent*, trans. J. Waterworth (London: Burns and Oates, 1848), 186. This is a translation of *Consilium Tridentinum: Diariorum, Actorum, Epistularum, Tractatuum Nova Collectio*, ed. Goerresian Society, 13 vols. (Freiburg: 1901–), 9: 628.

2   "Trent, Council of," *New Catholic Encyclopedia*, vol. 14 (Washington, D.C.: Catholic University of America, 1967), 271.

3   William T. Ditewig, *The Emerging Diaconate: Servant Leaders in a Servant Church* (New York/Mahwah, N.J.: Paulist Press, 2007), 84. Ditewig writes about a "complete linkage" between the Sacrament of Order and the Sacrifice of the Mass.

4   Edward P. Echlin, *The Deacon in the Church: Past and Future* (Staten Island, N.Y.: Alba House, 1971), 99.

5   Ibid., *The Deacon in the Church: Past and Future*, 99–102 ; Ditewig, *The Emerging Diaconate*, 84–85.

6   *Concilium Tridentinum*, 9: 558. English translation in Echlin, *The Deacon in the Church*, 100.

7   *Concilium Tridentinum*, 9: 559.

8   Wilhelm Schamoni, *Married Men as Ordained Deacons*, trans. Otto Eisner (London: Burns & Oates, 1955), 15–16; Josef Hornef, "The Order of the Diaconate in the Roman Catholic Church," in *The Diaconate Now*, ed. Richard T. Nolan (Washington, D.C.: Corpus Books, 1968), 62.

9   Echlin, *The Deacon in the Church*, 102–104. The original can be found in *Consilium Tridentinum*, 9: 601.

10   *The Canons and Decrees of the Council of Trent*, 186–87. This is a translation of *Consilium Tridentinum*, 9: 627–28.

11   Ditewig, *The Emerging Diaconate*, 89–93; Echlin, *The Deacon in the Church*, 106–107.

12   Ditewig, *The Emerging Diaconate*, 102–106.

13   H. Vorgrimler, "The Hierarchical Structure of the Church: Article 29," in *Commentary on the Documents of Vatican II*, ed. K. Rahner and H. Vorgrimler, vol. 1 (New York: Herder & Herder, 1966), 226.

14 *History of Vatican II*, ed. Giuseppe Alberigo; English version ed., Joseph A. Komonchak, vol. 1 (Maryknoll, N.Y.: Orbis, 1995), 187; The original documents on the diaconate at the preparatory stage can be found in *Acta et Documenta Concilio Oecumenico Vaticano II Apparando*, series 11 (praeparatoria), vol. II, part II (Typis Polyglottis Vaticanis, 1967), 138–68.

15 Ditewig, *The Emerging Diaconate*, 106–108.

16 Ibid., *The Emerging Diaconate*, 108.

17 Ibid., *The Emerging Diaconate*, 108–109.

18 Gérard Philips, "Dogmatic Constitution on the Church: History of the Constitution," in *Commentary on the Documents of Vatican II*, 106–110.

19 Ralph M. Wiltgen, *The Rhine Flows into the Tiber: A History of Vatican II* (Rockford, Ill.: Tan Books, 1985), 96.

20 Xavier Rynne, *The Second Session: The Debates and Decrees of Vatican Council II, September 29 to December 4, 1963* (New York: Farrar, Straus & Company, 1964), 99; John Francis Fowles, "The Diaconate in the Second Vatican Council" (master's thesis, University of St. Michael's College, 1971), 49–50.

21 See footnote 1.

22 Wiltgen, *The Rhine Flows into the Tiber*, 96.

23 Philips, "Dogmatic Constitution on the Church," 110.

24 Michael Novak, *The Open Church: Vatican II, Act II* (New York: Macmillan, 1964), 121.

25 For Cardinal Spellman's intervention, see *Acta Synodalia Sacrosancti Concilii Oecumenici Vaticani II* [hereafter *AS*], vol. II, part II (Typis Polyglottis Vaticanis, 1972), 317–19. For additional material on the debate, including English translations of Cardinal Spellman's speech, and for the names of those who supported and opposed the restoration, see the following works: *Council Daybook Vatican II*, ed. Floyd Anderson (Washington, D.C.: National Catholic Welfare Conference, 1965), 163–64, 167–68, 172–74, 176, 177, 181–82, 188; Henri Fesquet, *The Drama of Vatican II: The Ecumenical Council June 1962 – December 1965*, trans. Bernard Murchland (New York: Random House, 1967), 149, 150–51, 159, 162–65, 166–67, 182; Fowles, "The Diaconate in the Second Vatican Council," 10–25; Novak, *The Open Church: Vatican II, Act II*, 121–25; Philips, "Dogmatic Constitution on the Church," 118; Rynne, *The Second Session*, 99–104, 140–48; Vorgrimler, "The Hierarchical Structure of the Church: Article 29," 226–27; Wiltgen, *The Rhine Flows into the Tiber*, 97–100.

26 Vorgrimler, "The Hierarchical Structure of the Church: Article 29," 226–27; Philips, "Dogmatic Constitution on the Church," 118. Philips gives different numbers: forty-nine Fathers (representing 150 of their colleagues) spoke against the diaconate and thirty Fathers (representing 716 of their colleagues) spoke for it. Regardless of the different sets of numbers, it was obvious that

the supporters of Paragraph 15 had a commanding lead over opponents of the restoration.

27 *Council Speeches of Vatican II*, ed. Hans Küng, Yves Congar and Daniel O'Hanlon (Glen Rock, N.Y.: Paulist Press, 1964), 103–07; the original version can be found in *AS*, vol. II, part II, 317–19. All interventions were in Latin.

28 Philips, "Dogmatic Constitution on the Church," 116.

29 Ibid.

30 Fesquet, *The Drama of Vatican II*, 326.

31 Ibid., *The Drama of Vatican II*, 328.

32 Ditewig, *The Emerging Diaconate*, 117–18; Fesquet, *The Drama of Vatican II*, 366; Philips, "Dogmatic Constitution on the Church," 130. Ditewig writes that the voting took place in October 1964. This is incorrect.

33 *Vatican Council II: The Conciliar and Post Conciliar Documents*, ed. Austin Flannery (Collegeville, Minn.: The Liturgical Press, 1975), 387. The first quotation – "not unto the priesthood but unto the ministry" – is taken from the *Constitutions of the Egyptian Church* (see footnote 74). The second quotation is from St. Polycarp's Letter to the Philippians (see footnote 75).

34 Vorgrimler, "The Hierarchical Structure of the Church: Article 29," 228.

35 *Vatican Council II: The Conciliar and Post Conciliar Documents*, 832–33.

36 Karl Rahner, "The Theology of the Restoration of the Diaconate," *Theological Investigations*, vol. 5, *Later Writings*, trans. Karl-H. Kruger (Baltimore: Helicon Press, 1966), 183–84; "The Teaching of the Second Vatican Council on the Diaconate," *Theological Investigations*, vol. 10 (New York: Herder & Herder, 1973), 231.

37 Paul VI, *Motu Proprio Sacrum Diaconatus Ordinem* [hereafter *SDO*], *Acta Apostolicae Sedis* LIX (1967): 697–704. English translation is in Canadian Catholic Conference, *Guidelines of the Episcopal Committee on the Permanent Diaconate (Guidance Manual)* (Ottawa: Canadian Catholic Conference, 1967), 52–59. All references to this document are from this translation.

38 *Guidance Manual*, 52.

39 *Early Christian Writings: The Apostolic Fathers*, trans. Maxwell Staniforth; rev. trans. Andrew Louth (London: Penguin Books, 1987), 79.

40 *SDO*, 59. See also James Monroe Barnett, *The Diaconate: A Full and Equal Order*, rev. ed. (Harrisburg, Penn.: Trinity Press International, 1995), 56, fn. 9.

41 Paul VI, *Motu Proprio Ad Pascendum, Acta Apostolicae Sedis*, LXIV (1972): 534–40. English translation is in *Vatican Council II: The Conciliar and Post Conciliar Documents*, 433–40. All references to this document are from this translation.

42 *The St. Joseph Medium Size Edition of the American Bible* (New York: Catholic Book Publishing Co., 1970).

43   Ibid.

44   *Vatican Council II: The Conciliar and Post Conciliar Documents*, 435–36.

45   Paul VI, *Motu Proprio Ministeria Quaedam, Acta Apostolicae Sedis*, LXIV (1972): 529–34. English translation is in *Vatican Council II: The Conciliar and Post Conciliar Documents*, 427–32. All references to this document are from this translation.

46   *Vatican Council II: The Conciliar and Post Conciliar Documents*, 429.

47   Ibid.

Chapter 3

1   Remi De Roo to the author, e-mail communication, 1 December 2008. Bishop De Roo did not recall that "celibacy was a problem for the Canadian bishops generally" during their discussions on opening up the permanent diaconate to married men. But he did remember that such was not the case at the Second Vatican Council. He said that it was quite a "bugbear for many Church Fathers during the debates on the diaconate." He should know, because he was there and participated in those debates.

2   Canadian Conference of Catholic Bishops (formerly known as the Canadian Catholic Conference; hereafter referred to as CCCB), Plenary Assembly, 23–27 September 1969, Agenda Item No. 12.

3   Remi De Roo to the author, e-mail communication, 1 December 2008. It must be understood that the initiative to begin any kind of formal discussion on the diaconate had to originate with Archbishop Louis Levesque, president of the CCCB, with the approval of his council.

4   CCCB, Plenary Assembly, 12–14 October 1966, Agenda Item No. 5.

5   Ibid., Ad Hoc Committee on the Diaconate in Canada, 1966 to 1969, Document Series A, No. 1, "Ratification of the Nomination of Members of the Episcopal Committee."

6   Ibid., Ad Hoc Committee on the Diaconate in Canada, 1966 to 1969, Document Series A, No. 3, letter of 27 February 1967, from Archbishop Albert Sanschagrin, OMI, to Archbishop Louis Levesque, President of the CCCB; Document Series A, No. 5, "Report of Committee on the Diaconate, May 16, 1967," 3–4; Document Series C, No. 1, *Guidelines of the Episcopal Committee on the Permanent Diaconate (Guidance Manual)* (Ottawa: Canadian Catholic Conference, 1967), "Address of His Holiness Pope Paul VI to the representatives of the episcopal conferences gathered together in Rome, February 22–24, 1967, to study the project of the legal framework (loi-cadre) on the restoration of the diaconate," 24 February 1967.

[7] Ibid., Ad Hoc Committee on the Diaconate in Canada, 1966 to 1969, Document Series A, No. 2, "Minutes of the Meeting of the Ad Hoc Committee, 27 January 1967," 4.

[8] Ibid.

[9] Ibid.

[10] Ibid., Ad Hoc Committee on the Diaconate in Canada, 1966 to 1969, Document Series A, No. 2, "Minutes of the Meeting of the Ad Hoc Committee, 27 January 1967," 8.

[11] Ibid., Ad Hoc Committee on the Diaconate in Canada, 1966 to 1969, Document Series A, No. 2, "Minutes of the Meeting of the Ad Hoc Committee, 27 January 1967, 5.

[12] Tibor Horvath, "Theology of a New Diaconate," *Revue de l'Université d'Ottawa* 38 (1968), 495–523. See also Tibor Horvath, *Thinking about Faith: Speculative Theology*, vol. 1, *Love* (Montreal & Kingston: McGill-Queen's University Press, 2006), 197–212.

[13] CCCB, Ad Hoc Committee on the Diaconate in Canada, 1966 to 1969, Document Series A, No. 4, "Report of the Committee on the Diaconate in preparation for a General Assembly Meeting, April 3, 1967," 3.

[14] Ibid., Ad Hoc Committee on the Diaconate in Canada, 1966 to 1969, Document Series B, "General Information on the Diaconate Outside Canada."

[15] Ibid., Ad Hoc Committee on the Diaconate in Canada, 1966 to 1969, Document Series A, No. 4, "Report of the Committee on the Diaconate in preparation for a General Assembly Meeting, April 3, 1967," 4–12.

[16] *Guidance Manual*, 48–49.

[17] Ibid., 49.

[18] Ibid., 1.

[19] Ibid.

[20] Among the more prominent works would be the following, given in chronological order of publishing: Edward P. Echlin, *The Deacon in the Church: Past and Future* (Staten Island, N.Y.: Alba House, 1971), 3–124; James Monroe Barnett, *The Diaconate: A Full and Equal Order*, rev. ed. (Harrisburg, Penn.: Trinity Press International, 1995), 43–125; Owen F. Cummings, *Deacons and the Church* (New York/Mahwah, N.J.: Paulist Press, 2004), 30–50; Edward J. Enright, "The History of the Diaconate," *The Deacon Reader*, ed. James Keating (New York/Mahwah, N.J.: Paulist Press, 2006), 8–23; William Ditewig, *The Emerging Diaconate: Servant Leaders in a Servant Church* (New York/Mahwah, N.J.: Paulist Press, 2007), 62–78.

21 CCCB, Ad Hoc Committee on the Diaconate in Canada, 1966 to 1969, Document Series A, No. 5, "Report of the Committee on the Diaconate, May 16, 1967," 6.

22 *Guidance Manual*, 23.

23 Tibor Horvath to the author, e-mail communication, 27 January 2008. Father Horvath wrote that "Theology of a New Diaconate" was written for the [ad hoc] committee. If so, he must have written Chapter III and "Theology of a New Diaconate" at the same time. A great deal of the former was included in the latter, but it is only in the latter that we find Father Horvath's elucidation of the "specific characteristic of the sacrament of the diaconate."

24 Horvath, "Theology of a New Diaconate," 496.

25 Ibid., "Theology of a New Diaconate," 514–15.

26 *Guidance Manual*, 1.

27 Ibid.

28 *Vatican Council II: The Conciliar and Post Conciliar Documents*, ed. Austin Flannery (Collegeville, Minn.: Liturgical Press, 1975), 436.

29 *Guidance Manual*, 48–49.

30 Ibid., 45.

31 Ibid., 43.

32 Ibid., 69.

33 Ibid., 94, 96, 98, 101.

34 Ibid., 45–46.

35 James F. McDonnell, "An Examination of the Theology of the Permanent Diaconate in the Documents of the Second Vatican Council and of Three Regional Hierarchies" (master's thesis, University of St. Michael's College, 1976), 46.

36 Ibid., "An Examination of the Theology of the Permanent Diaconate," 89, fn. 19.

37 Horvath, "Theology of a New Diaconate," 520.

38 Ibid., "Theology of a New Diaconate," 515. This passage was originally in italics and thus is here quoted in italics. There was once a tradition that for important liturgical occasions, such as a Pontifical High Mass or an ordination, a bishop would wear the vestments of a deacon, a priest and bishop, one on top of the other beginning with those of a deacon. A museum in St. Mary's Cathedral in Halifax displays the vestments of Bishop Edmund Burke, Vicar Apostolic of Nova Scotia, in this manner.

39 Ibid., "Theology of a New Diaconate," 521.

40 Ibid., "Theology of a New Diaconate," 520.

41 Tibor Horvath, interview by author, 31 January 2008.

42   Archives of the Roman Catholic Archdiocese of Toronto [hereafter ARCAT], Auxiliary Bishop Robert Clune Fonds, Permanent Diaconate, Letter of 3 October 1990, from Dan Murphy to "All Deacons & Wives."

43   Information concerning the questionnaire is taken from three sources: Archives of the Society of Jesus of Upper Canada (ASJUC), Box 221, File #2, J. Hochban, Permanent Diaconate, "Permanent Diaconate – Possibility of," [n.d.]; ARCAT, Canadian Conference of Catholic Bishops – Commissions: Episcopal 1968. Commission on Clergy and Seminaries: Committee on the Permanent Diaconate in Canada, 1967–1969, 1972, "A Progress Report from the Special Committee on the Restoration of the Diaconate" [April or May 1968]. (Although this item is filed in ARCAT under the Commission on Clergy and Seminaries, internal evidence suggests that it is the product of the CCCB Ad Hoc Committee on the Diaconate, 1966 to 1969, and that it was written by the committee in either April or May 1968, prior to its meeting on 18 June 1968.); CCCB, Ad Hoc Committee on the Diaconate in Canada, 1966 to 1969, Series C, No. 2, "Final Report of the Committee on the Diaconate," 30 August 1968, which contains "Final Report of the Cross-Canada Survey on the Restoration of the Permanent Diaconate," 18 June 1968.

44   *Guidance Manual*, 120; ARCAT, Chancery Office, C.C.C. [CCCB], Ad Hoc Committee on the Diaconate, 1966–1967, letter from James M. Hayes, to "Your Excellency," 26 September 1967.

45   *Guidance Manual*, 122–24.

46   CCCB, Ad Hoc Committee on the Diaconate in Canada, 1966 to 1969, Series C, No.2, "Final Report of the Committee on the Diaconate," 30 August 1968, which contains "Final Report of the Cross-Canada Survey on the Restoration of the Permanent Diaconate," 18 June 1968.

47   Diocese of St. Catharines, Archives. Papers of Bishop T.J. McCarthy, letter of 22 January 1969, from Everett MacNeil to T.J. McCarthy, "Recommendations."

48   Ibid., Papers of Bishop T.J. McCarthy, letter of 7 November 1969, circular letter from Edmund J. Roche, CCCB National Education Office, to Episcopal Commission on Clergy and Seminaries. The committee also produced an eight-page précis of this document.

49   Although the CCCB's ad hoc committee on the Diaconate in Canada distributed copies of the *Guidance Manual* to every bishop and to a wide range of professional Catholics in order to make its consultation process as transparent and reliable as possible, and the committee received acclaim for the *Guidance Manual* at an international meeting on the diaconate in Freiburg, Germany, in February 1968, the document remained very much an in-house production. It was not made available for general distribution. Archbishop Philip Pocock of Toronto, for one, probably did not share his copy with anyone in the chancery and apparently not with the members of his own committee on the diaco-

nate in 1970 or at any time thereafter. When I showed the archbishop's copy to several of the surviving members of the archdiocese's first committee on the diaconate, including Bishop (then Father) John O'Mara, they expressed surprise at its existence.

50 ARCAT, OC02 MM03, Senate of Priests, "Minutes of the meeting of the Senate of Priests held at the Chancery Office on Tuesday, May 12th, 1970, at 10:30 A.M," 3–4. There is mention in the "Minutes" of a sixty-seven-page document done under the auspices of the C.C.C. (CCCB), given to each member of the Senate for study. If one ignores the three Appendices to "Restoration of the Permanent Diaconate in Canada (Interim Guidelines)," one has a sixty-seven-page publication. This must have been an earlier version of the January 1971 "Interim Guidelines."

Chapter 4

1 Archives of the Society of Jesus of Upper Canada (hereafter ASJUC), Box 221, File #2, J. Hochban, Permanent Diaconate, as quoted in John Hochban, SJ, "The Diaconate" (paper presented in Sudbury, Ontario, 15–18 May 1972), 13.

2 *Vatican Council II: The Conciliar and Post Conciliar Documents*, ed. Austin Flannery (Collegeville, Minn.: The Liturgical Press, 1975), 766–98.

3 John O'Mara, interview by the author, Holy Rosary Parish, Thorold, Ontario, 11 February 2008.

4 Ibid.

5 Peter Meehan, telephone interview by the author, 13 February 2009.

6 *Catholic Register*, 24 November 1984, 4.

7 Archives of the Roman Catholic Archdiocese of Toronto [hereafter ARCAT], OC02 CG01, "Address of Rev. B.F. Courtemanche, J.C.D., to the election meeting of the Senate of Priests," [n.d.], "Constitution of the Senate of Priests," 1.

8 *Toronto Senate Reports* 10, no.4 (February 1978), [8].

9 ARCAT, Chancery Office: C.C.C. [Canadian Catholic Conference, now known as the Canadian Conference of Catholic Bishops, CCCB] Ad Hoc Committee on Diaconate 1969, letter from Frank Isber to John O'Mara, 10 March 1969.

10 Ibid., Chancery Office: C.C.C. Ad Hoc Committee on Diaconate 1969, letter from Everett MacNeil to Frank Isber, 27 February 1969. Isber's letter to MacNeil was dated 24 February 1969.

11 Ibid., Chancery Office: C.C.C. Ad Hoc Committee on Diaconate 1969, letter from John O'Mara to Frank Isber, 11 March 1969.

12 Ibid., OC02 MM03, Box 16, Senate of Priests, "Priests' Senate Action Group on Permanent Diaconate," ([26] April 1977), 2. According to Bishop John O'Mara, there were two committees at work at this time: a seminary committee and subsequently the Senate of Priests committee. The seminary committee gathered all the documentation and presented the material to Archbishop Pocock, who then turned to the Senate of Priests to examine the issue of the permanent diaconate for the archdiocese. John O'Mara, telephone interview by the author, 22 September 2009.

13 Ibid., OC02 MM03, Box 8, Senate of Priests, "Report of a meeting held to discuss the PERMANENT DIACONATE in Toronto," St. Augustine's Seminary, 4 April 1970, 1.

14 Ibid., OC02 MM03, Box 8, Senate of Priests, "Report of a meeting held to discuss the PERMANENT DIACONATE in Toronto," St. Augustine's Seminary, 4 April 1970, 2.

15 Ibid., OC02 MM03, Box 8, Senate of Priests, "Report on a second meeting to discuss the PERMANENT DIACONATE in Toronto," St. Augustine's Seminary, 2 May 1970, 1.

16 Ibid.

17 Ibid.

18 Ibid., OC02 MM03, Box 8, Senate of Priests, "Report on a second meeting to discuss the PERMANENT DIACONATE in Toronto, St. Augustine's Seminary, 2 May 1970, 2.

19 Ibid.

20 Ibid, OC02 MM03, Box 8, Senate of Priests, "The Committee on the PERMANENT DIACONATE in Toronto Archdiocese," [n.d.]. This was included in material for the meeting of the Senate of Priests, 16 June 1970.

21 Ibid., OC02 MM03, Box 8, Senate of Priests, "Minutes of the meeting of the Senate of Priests held in the Chancery Office on Tuesday, May 12th, 1970, at 10:30 A.M," 3. See also Chapter Three, fn. 50 for an explanation of the origins of this document.

22 Ibid., OC02 MM03, Box 8, Senate of Priests, "Minutes of the meeting of the Senate of Priests held at the Chancery Office on Tuesday June 16th, 1970 at 10:30 A.M.," 4. See also *Toronto Senate Reports*, 2, no. 8 (June 1970), [2].

23 Ibid., OC02 MM03, Box 8, Senate of Priests, "Minutes of the meeting of the Senate of Priests held at the Chancery Office on Tuesday June 16th, 1970 at 10:30 A.M.," 5.

24 CCCB, Ad Hoc Committee on the Diaconate in Canada, 1966 to 1969, Series C, No. 2. See Chapter Three, fn. 46.

25 ARCAT, OC02 MM03, Box 8, Senate of Priests, "Minutes of the meeting of the Senate of Priests held at the Chancery Office on Tuesday June 16th, 1970 at 10:30 A.M.," 4.

26 Ibid.

27 Ibid., OC02 MM03, Box 8, Senate of Priests, "Minutes of the meeting of the Senate of Priests held at the Chancery Office on Tuesday June 16th, 1970 at 10:30 A.M.," 5.

28 ASJUC, Box 221, File #2, J. Hochban, Permanent Diaconate, "The Diaconate" (paper presented in Sudbury, Ontario, 15–18 May 1972).

29 ARCAT, OC02 MM03, Box 8, Senate of Priests, "Minutes of the meeting of the Senate of Priests held in the Chancery on Tuesday, June 16th, 1970, 10:30 A.M.," 5.

30 Ibid., Chancery Office, C.C.C. Ad Hoc Committee on Diaconate 1970, Margaret Butts, et al., "Brief Submitted to the Bishops of Canada October 1970 Requesting the Restoration of the Order of Deaconess."

31 Ibid., Chancery Office, C.C.C. Ad Hoc Committee on Diaconate 1970, letter from Mary Schaeffer to Philip Pocock, 22 October 1970.

32 "Women Seek to Restore the Order of Deaconess," *Catholic Register*, 21 November 1970, 29.

33 ARCAT, C.C.C. Ad Hoc Committee on the Diaconate 1970, letter from Margaret M. McCarthy to Philip Pocock, 15 December 1970.

34 O'Mara interview; Alexander MacGregor, interview by the author, 5 April 2008; Paul Giroux, interview by author, 9 April 2008.

35 ARCAT, OC01 CO01, "Toronto Archdiocesan Questionnaire on the Role of Women in the Church and in Society," 1977. Sample sizes were lay people (1,170); clergy (164); pooled parishes (269); C.W.L. (90). There were four categories: women in the diaconate; women in the priesthood; divorced and remarried Catholics receiving the sacraments; and married clergy. Respondents were asked twenty-five questions. On the question of women in the diaconate, the results were for lay people: 59.15 percent said yes, and 16.67 percent said yes but depends on circumstances; and for clergy: 46.34 percent said yes, and 7.32 percent said yes but depends on circumstances.

36 Ibid., OC02 MM03, Box 8, Senate of Priests, "Outstanding Committees of Toronto Senate," September 1970, [3].

37 O'Mara interview.

38 ARCAT, OC02 MM03, Box 8, Senate of Priests, "Agenda – Meeting of the Toronto Senate of Priests, Tuesday, 19 January 1971 at 10:30 a.m. at the Chancery Office," "Notes on Permanent Diaconate from Chicago Conference in December 1970," 1.

39   Ibid., OC02 MM03, Box 8, Senate of Priests, "Agenda – Meeting of the Toronto Senate of Priests, Tuesday, 19 January 1971 at 10:30 a.m. at the Chancery Office," "Participation by the Wives in the Permanent Diaconate Program," 1.

40   Ibid., OC02 MM03, Box 8, Senate of Priests, "Permanent Diaconate Committee Meeting St. Augustine's Seminary Saturday, January 16th [1971] at 10:00 A.M. Proposed Agenda."

41   Ibid., OC02 MM03, Box 8, Senate of Priests, "Minutes of the Meeting of the Toronto Senate of Priests Held at the Chancery Office on Tuesday, January 19th, 1971 at 10:30 A.M.," 5.

42   ASJUC, Box 221, File #2, J. Hochban, Permanent Diaconate, undated letter from Paul Giroux to "John." It is unclear, however, when this document was produced. It could have been as early as June 1970 or it could have been presented to a meeting of the committee on 6 February 1971.

43   ARCAT, OC02 MM03, Box 8, Senate of Priests, "Suggested Training Schedule for Candidates for the Permanent Diaconate." In the text, I have changed the word "sessions" to "classes" in order to avoid confusion with "summer session" and "winter/spring session."

44   St. Augustine's Seminary [hereafter SAS], Office of the Permanent Diaconate, "History of the Permanent Diaconate," Brochure Information, [May 1972], 5.

45   Charles Amico, letter to the author, 15 May 2008, 3.

46   ARCAT, Diaconate Office Files, "Reading List for Sacred Scripture" (twelve books); "Dogma and Liturgy Reading List" (six books).

47   Ibid., OC02 MM03, Box 11, Senate of Priests, "Minutes of the meeting of the Senate of Priests held at the Chancery Office on Tuesday, January 30th, 1973 at 10:00 a.m.," "Diaconate and Seminary Program," 3.

48   Daniel Murphy, letter to the author, March 2009.

49   John O'Mara, telephone interview by the author, 5 March 2009, in response to a letter from the author, 2 March 2009.

50   Stan MacLellan, e-mail communication to the author, 20 January 2009.

51   O'Mara interview; Giroux interview; ARCAT, Chancery Office: Commissions/ Committees: Permanent Deacons 1981–1985, letter from Robert Clune to Gerald Emmett Carter, 30 December 1982. This letter is Bishop Clune's contribution to the Quinquennial Report of the Archdiocese of Toronto. It is divided into sections, with the second section devoted to the permanent diaconate. In his role as Vicar of Deacons, Bishop Clune wrote, "At the beginning, the emphasis was on a candidate's prior church involvement, rather than on academic qualifications."

52   Toronto Senate Reports, 6, no. 2 (October 1973), [3].

53   SAS, Office of the Permanent Diaconate, "History of the Permanent Diaconate, Brochure Information," [May 1972], 5.

54   Ibid., Office of the Permanent Diaconate, "History of the Permanent Diaconate, Brochure Information," [May 1972], 3.

55   ARCAT, OC02 MM03, Box 9, Senate of Priests, "Minutes of the meeting of the Senate of Priests held in the Chancery Office on Tuesday, 25th April 1972 at 10:00 a.m.," "Permanent Diaconate Program Report to Senate," May 1972. I cannot account for the May 1972 date of the "Report" that was presented at a meeting of the Senate of Priests held on 25 April 1972.

56   Ibid., OC02 MM03, Box 9, Senate of Priests, "Minutes of the meeting of the Senate of Priests held in the Chancery Office on Tuesday, 25th April 1972 at 10:00 a.m.," "Permanent Diaconate Program Report to Senate," May 1972, 2.

57   Ibid., Diaconate Office Files, "Orientation Day for Candidates and Families Entering Permanent Diaconate Program." There were three programs that day: one for candidates, one for wives and one for children. Candidates and wives attended the opening talk given by Archbishop Pocock, and everyone attended the closing Mass celebrated by the archbishop.

58   *Catholic Register*, 30 September 1972, 1, 10–11.

59   Giroux interview. Archbishop Pocock may have wanted only twenty-five candidates.

60   Daniel Murphy, interview by the author, 14 March 2008.

61   "Not to be served … but to Serve: The Permanent Diaconate in Toronto," (April 1974), back cover.

62   Prior to ordination to the diaconate, candidates were installed as lectors and acolytes. Archbishop Philip Pocock installed members of the first class as lectors in a ceremony at St. Augustine's Seminary chapel on 3 June 1973. See ARCAT, Diaconate Office Files, "Installation of the Ministry of Lector," 3 June 1973. There was also a ceremony of candidacy for those about to be ordained. For the Class of 1974, this took place on 11 May 1974, and also at the seminary chapel in conjunction with the institution of lector for the class of 1975. Bishop Francis V. Allen, auxiliary bishop of Toronto, was the presiding prelate. See ARCAT, Diaconate Office Files, "Permanent Diaconate Candidates," 11 May 1974.

63   Information supplied by Pierre Lafontaine, archivist, Archdiocese of Québec, e-mail communication to the author, 26 January 2009. The very first ordinations of permanent deacons in the Catholic Church took place in 1968: Cologne, Germany (April); Chile (June and November); Bogotá, Colombia, during the World Eucharistic Congress (August); Reute, Germany (1968); Bamberg, Germany (December); and Douala, Cameroon (December). Information supplied by Deacon Bert Cambre, Director of Deacons, Archdiocese of Toronto, e-mail communication to the author, 8 January 2009.

64   There was one member of the Class of 1974 who was ordained for the Ukrainian Catholic Eparchy of Toronto and Eastern Canada. He was George Sytnyk, who was thirty years old and married. He was ordained a deacon at St. Josephat's Cathedral on 30 September 1973.

65   Information supplied by Bert Cambre, Director of Deacons, Archdiocese of Toronto. See also *Catholic Register*, 1 June 1974, 8–9; 15 June 1974, 11; 6 July 1974, 5; *Toronto Star*, 2 September 1974, C2.

66   Only 24 of the 26 gave their ages in the published material. *See* Permanent Diaconate Program, *Permanent Deacon Class of '74* [Toronto: St. Augustine's Seminary, 1974]. It is unfortunate that a similar publication was not produced with each succeeding class.

67   *Toronto Senate Reports*, 9, no. 6 (May 1977), [3].

68   ARCAT, Archdiocese of Toronto, *Diocesan Quinquennial Report 1974–1977* [Toronto: 1977], 13.

69   Thomas A. Cresswell, "A Commentary," *Contact* (June 1986), *Supplement*, 1.

70   Patrick Matthews, interview by author, 26 March 2008; Tab Charbonneau, interview by author, 10 April 2008; Giroux interview; MacGregor interview.

71   MacGregor interview, for the phrase "hands and feet of Jesus"; Tibor Horvath, "Theology of a New Diaconate," *Revue de l'Université d'Ottawa* 38 (1968), 515.

72   ARCAT, OC02 MM03, Box 16, Senate of Priests, "Priests' Senate Action Group on Permanent Diaconate," ([26] April 1977), [i].

73   Ibid., OC02 MM03, Box 16, Senate of Priests, "Priests' Senate Action Group on Permanent Diaconate," ([26] April 1977), 2.

74   Tab Charbonneau, e-mail communication to the author, 26 January 2009.

75   Ibid.

76   Tab Charbonneau, letter to the author [22 April 2009].

77   Quoted in Charles Amico, letter to the author, 15 May 2008, 4.

78   ARCAT, OC02 MM03, Box 16, Senate of Priests, "Priests Senate Action Group on the Permanent Diaconate" ([26] April 1977), 3.

79   Karl Rahner, "On the Diaconate," *Theological Investigations*, vol. 12 (London: Dartman, Longman & Todd, 1974), 75.

80   ARCAT, OC02 MM03, Box 16, Senate of Priests, "Priests' Senate Action Group on Permanent Diaconate," ([26] April 1977), 7.

81   Charles Amico, letter to the author, 15 May 2008, 4.

82   Stan MacLellan, "'Sorry, Sir, but you're living in sin,'" *Contact* (February 1968), 4.

83   Charles Amico, letter to the author, 15 May 2008, 2; Charbonneau interview; "Program Re-Opening Next September; Candidates Being Sought," *Contact* (December 1976), 1; ARCAT, OC02 CD01, Box 16, Council of Deacons

of the Archdiocese of Toronto, "Minutes of the Executive Meeting, Blessed Trinity Church, January 17, 1977," 2, Item # 11; *Toronto Senate Reports* 9, no. 3 (December 1976), 22–23; Tab Charbonneau, telephone interview by the author, 22 April 2009.

84 Tab Charbonneau, telephone interview by author, 23 March 2009.

85 Stan MacLellan, "Current Candidates Unique, Says Their Leader," *Contact* (April 1977), 3.

86 ARCAT, OC02 CD01, Box 16, Council of Deacons of the Archdiocese of Toronto, "The following statements address the purpose of this Council."

87 Ibid., OC 02 MM03, Box 16, Senate of Priests, "Priests' Senate Action Group on Permanent Diaconate," ([26] April 1977), 4–6.

88 Charles Amico, letter to the author, 15 May 2008, 2.

89 ARCAT, CO02 MM03, Box 16, Senate of Priests, "Priests' Senate Action Group on Permanent Diaconate" ([27] April 1977), 8.

90 Ibid., 9.

91 *Toronto Senate Reports* 9, no. 6 (May 1977), 2–4.

92 ARCAT, OC02 MM03, Box 16, Senate of Priests, "Minutes of the Senate of Priests Meeting June 14, 1977," 4.

93 Ibid., OC02 MM03, Box 16, Senate of Priests, "Minutes of the Senate meeting of Nov. 8 1977," 1.

94 Ibid., OC02 MM03, Box 17, "Minutes of the Senate meeting of February 7, 1978," 1.

95 Stan MacLellan, "The Diaconate and the Priests' Senate Report: ALL SYSTEMS ARE GO," *Contact* (September 1977), 5.

96 Charles Amico, "Directions – An Important Message from the Program Director," *Contact* (September 1977), 2.

97 Ibid., "Directions: Words from the Program Director," *Contact* (January 1978), 2.

Chapter 5

1 St. Augustine's Seminary [hereafter SAS], Office of the Permanent Diaconate, letter from Peter Somerville to Robert B. Clune, 26 March 1985, 2.

2 Ibid., Office of the Permanent Diaconate, Deacon Stan MacLellan to members of the Policy Statement Committee, a preamble to the June 1977 Draft Statement.

3 Ibid., Office of the Permanent Diaconate, ""Policy that is Basic to the Permanent Diaconate Training Program," Draft Statement, May 1976.

4 Ibid.

5   Ibid., Office of the Permanent Diaconate, "Training Program for the Permanent Diaconate Archdiocese of Toronto" (June 1977). Although Deacon Stan MacLellan was the prime mover behind a whole new approach to a policy statement, according to the documentation, the authorship of the June 1977 draft remains unclear. It is highly likely that it was a collective effort, because everything in the program was conducted that way.

6   Ibid., Office of the Permanent Diaconate, "(Policy Statement) Training Program for the Permanent Diaconate Archdiocese of Toronto" [hereafter Policy Statement 1978], (January 1978). Copies of this document can be found in many different collections. Why the words Policy Statement were put in parentheses is unknown.

7   Ibid., Office of the Permanent Diaconate, the Executive Committee of the Permanent Diaconate Training Program, "Minutes," 6 February 1978; letter from Peter Somerville to Robert B. Clune, 26 March 1985, 2.

8   Ibid., Office of the Permanent Diaconate, "Policy Statement 1978," 3.

9   Ibid.

10   Tab Charbonneau, e-mail communication to the author, 2 September 2009.

11   Archives of the Roman Catholic Archdiocese of Toronto [hereafter ARCAT], Permanent Diaconate Office Files, [Tab Charbonneau], "N.A.P.P.D. Convention – 1980 Kansas City, Mo.," 16 April 1980, [1].

12   Ibid., Permanent Diaconate Office Files, "Proposed 'Search Committee' Permanent Diaconate Program," "Minutes," 28 April 1980.

13   In 1986, the training or formation period was extended to four years.

14   ARCAT, Permanent Diaconate Office Files, Diaconate Search Committee, "Recommendations to the Vicar of Deacons, Most Rev. R.B. Clune, on the Permanent Diaconate Archdiocese of Toronto" [hereafter "Recommendations"], October 1981, 30.

15   Contact (May 1980), [1].

16   ARCAT, Permanent Diaconate Office Files, Diaconate Search Committee, "Minutes – Meeting #1," 31 May 1980, 1.

17   Contact (October 1984), [1].

18   ARCAT, Permanent Diaconate Office Files, Deacon Search Committee, "Recommendations," 2.

19   Ibid., Permanent Diaconate Office Files, Deacon Search Committee, "Minutes – Meeting #3," 25 October 1980, 2.

20   Ibid., Permanent Diaconate Office Files, Deacon Search Committee, "Recommendations," 17.

21   Ibid.

22 Ibid., Aux. Bp. Clune Fonds: Archdiocese of Toronto: Permanent Diaconate, letter from Stan MacLellan to Robert B. Clune, 18 September 1980, 1.

23 Ibid., Permanent Diaconate Office Files, Deacon Search Committee, "Recommendations," 19.

24 Comments on the "academic equivalent" requirement came up repeatedly in interviews.

25 ARCAT, Permanent Diaconate Office Files, Deacon Search Committee, "Recommendations," 19.

26 Ibid., Permanent Diaconate Office Files, Deacon Search Committee, "Recommendations," 20.

27 Ibid., Permanent Diaconate Office Files, Deacon Search Committee, "Recommendations," 21–22.

28 Ibid., Permanent Diaconate Office Files, Deacon Search Committee, "Recommendations," 24–25.

29 Ibid., Permanent Diaconate Office Files, Deacon Search Committee, "Recommendations," 26.

30 Ibid., Permanent Diaconate Office Files, Deacon Search Committee, "Recommendations," 28–29.

31 Ibid., Permanent Diaconate Office Files, Deacon Search Committee, "Recommendations," 34.

32 Ibid., Permanent Diaconate Office Files, Deacon Search Committee, "Recommendations," 37–43.

33 Ibid., Permanent Diaconate Office Files, Deacon Search Committee, "Recommendations," 37, 38.

34 Ibid., Chancery Office: Commissions/Committees: Permanent Deacons, 1981–1985, letter from Robert B. Clune to Leonard J. Wall, 24 June 1981.

35 Ibid.

36 Ibid., Chancery Office: Commissions/Committees: Permanent Deacons, 1981–1985, letter from Robert B. Clune to Leonard J. Wall, 19 February 1982.

37 *Contact* (September–October 1981), 2.

38 ARCAT, Permanent Diaconate Office Files, Advisory Board, "Minutes," 15 November 1982, [1].

39 Charmaine Grillot, e-mail communication to the author, 25 May 2008.

40 *Contact* (December 1984), 3–5.

41 ARCAT, Chancery Office: Commissions/Committees: Permanent Deacons, 1981–1985, letter from Robert B. Clune to Gerald Emmett Carter, 30 December 1982, 2.

42 Ibid., Permanent Diaconate Office Files, Memorandum, "Advisory Board is Established," [n.d.]. From internal evidence, we can say that Bishop Clune's office issued this memorandum sometime between 15 April and 20 May 1982, the dates of the second and third meetings of the board.

43 Ibid., Permanent Diaconate Office Files, Advisory Board, Permanent Diaconate Program, "Minutes," 23 March 1982, 2.

44 Ibid.

45 Ibid., Permanent Diaconate Office Files, Advisory Board, "Minutes," 12 March 1982; 15 April 1982; 15 June 1982; 16 September 1982; 14 October 1982; 15 November 1982; 21 February 1983; 1 March 1983; 11 April 1983; 16 May 1983; "Agenda," 20 May 1982.

46 Ibid., Permanent Diaconate Office Files, Office of the Director, Permanent Diaconate Program [hereafter Office of the Director], memorandum from Tom Mason to Bishop Clune, Continuing Education, 18 July 1984 (rev. 3 January 1985).

47 Ibid., Permanent Diaconate Office Files, Advisory Board, "Minutes," 15 November 1982, [1].

48 Ibid., Permanent Diaconate Office Files, Deacon Search Committee, "Recommendations," 20.

49 Ibid., Permanent Diaconate Office Files, Deacon Search Committee, "Deacon Perceiver Instrument."

50 Ibid., Permanent Diaconate Office Files, Deacon Search Committee, "Minutes – Meeting #3," 25 October 1980, 2; Tom Mason, "Deacon Perceiver Process."

51 Ibid., Permanent Diaconate Office Files, Advisory Board, "Minutes," 15 April 1982, 2.

52 Ibid., Permanent Diaconate Office Files, Advisory Board, "Agenda," 20 May 1982, 2.

53 Ibid., Permanent Diaconate Office Files, Advisory Board, "Minutes," 16 September 1982, 2.

54 Jo-Ann Miller, "Discovering Talent Through the Perceiver Interview," New Catholic World (May/June 1986), 133.

55 George Newman, interview by the author, St. Catharines, Ontario, 19 May 2009.

56 Human Resources for Ministry Institute, SRI Institute, SRI Deacon Perceiver Interview (SRI Perceiver Academies, Inc., 1980), 3, 5, 7, 9, and 11.

57 ARCAT, Permanent Diaconate Office Files, Deacon Search Committee, "Minutes – Meeting #3," 25 October 1982, Tom Mason, "Deacon Perceiver Process," 2.

58 Ibid., Permanent Diaconate Office Files, Advisory Board, "Minutes," 15 November 1982, 2.

59 Ibid., Permanent Diaconate Office Files, Advisory Board, "Minutes," 21 February 1983, [1].

60 Ibid., Permanent Diaconate Office Files, Advisory Board, Committee on Organizational Structure, "Report on the Organizational Structure of the Permanent Diaconate in the Archdiocese of Toronto, Submitted to Most Reverend R. B. Clune, and the Advisory Board on the Diaconate Program" [hereafter "Report"], (31 March 1983), 2.

61 Ibid., Permanent Diaconate Office Files, Advisory Board, "Minutes," 21 February 1983, [1]–3; 14 March 1983, [1]–2; 11 April 1983, [1]–3.

62 Ibid., Chancery Office: Commissions/Committees: Permanent Deacons, 1981–1985, letter from A. Bruno Scorsone to Robert B. Clune, 9 May 1983.

63 Ibid., Permanent Diaconate Office Files, Advisory Board, Committee on Organizational Structure, "Report," 3.

64 Ibid., Permanent Diaconate Office Files, Advisory Board, Committee on Organizational Structure, "Report," [ii].

65 Ibid., Permanent Diaconate Office Files, Advisory Board, Committee on Organizational Structure, "Report," [iii] and [iv].

66 Deacon Stan MacLellan and Deacon John O'Connor presented a paper on the need for a director of deacons shortly after the formation of the Council of Deacons in 1976, and they discussed their proposal with then Bishop Aloysius Ambrozic, Father Charles Amico and Father Bernard Wilson. Upon inquiry, MacLellan searched for, but could not find, a copy of this paper. Therefore, we do not know what they meant by director of deacons, or if it was in any way a precursor of the Advisory Board's description of the position and functions of Executive Director or today's position of director of deacons. See *Contact* (May 1980), [1].

67 ARCAT, Permanent Diaconate Office Files, Advisory Board, letter from Robert B. Clune to Terry Delaney, 24 May 1983.

68 Ibid., Permanent Diaconate Office Files, Advisory Board, "Minutes," 16 May 1983, 2.

69 Ibid., Permanent Diaconate Office Files, Advisory Board, memorandum from G. Emmett Carter to Robert B. Clune, 15 June 1983.

70 Ibid., Permanent Diaconate Office Files, Archdiocese of Toronto, Chancery Office, letter from D.G. Keaveney to Tom Mason, 6 September 1983.

71 Ibid., Permanent Diaconate Office Files, Archdiocese of Toronto, *Policies and Procedures of the Executive Board: Permanent Deacons* ([1986]), 2.

72   Ibid., Permanent Diaconate Office Files, Archdiocese of Toronto, *Policies and Procedures of the Executive Board: Permanent Deacons* ([1986]), 1.

73   Archdiocese of Toronto, *Diaconate Policies, Procedures and Ceremonial* (rev. May 2009), 5.

74   ARCAT, Permanent Diaconate Office Files, letter from Robert B. Clune to Deacons and Deacons' Wives, 6 June 1989.

75   Ibid., Aux. Bp. Clune Fonds: Archdiocese of Toronto: Permanent Diaconate, memorandum from Dan Murphy to Briant Cullinane, 4 November 1992; letter from Briant Cullinane to Dan Murphy, 5 November 1992.

76   *Contact* (June 1985), 2.

77   ARCAT, Aux. Bp. Clune Fonds: Archdiocese of Toronto: Permanent Diaconate, Office of the Director, memorandum to All Deacons and Wives, 12 December 1990.

78   Ibid., Permanent Diaconate Office Files, Archdiocese of Toronto, *Policies and Procedures of the Executive Board: Permanent Deacons* ([1986]), 3–4.

79   Tab Charbonneau, e-mail communication to the author, 23 October 2009.

80   ARCAT, Permanent Diaconate Office Files, Office of the Director, memorandum from Dan Murphy to All Deacons and Wives, 12 December 1990.

81   Ibid., Permanent Diaconate Office Files, Office of the Director, memorandum from Tom Mason to Robert B. Clune, 18 July 1984 (rev. 3 January 1985); memorandum from Tom Mason to Dan Murphy, 3 January 1985.

82   Ibid., Permanent Diaconate Office Files, Council of Deacons, letter from J.A. Grieve to Brother Deacon and Wife, 28 January 1988; letter from J.A. Grieve to Robert B. Clune, 10 September 1987; appended to this letter is a summary of the findings of the survey "The Deacon Council: Its Purpose, Functions, Objectives and Pattern."

83   Ibid., Permanent Diaconate Office Files, Council of Deacons, "Proposed Constitution and Bylaws of the Diaconal Association of the Archdiocese of Toronto," (rev. 26 June 1989).

84   Ibid., Aux. Bp. Clune Fonds: Archdiocese of Toronto: Permanent Diaconate, memorandum from Ad Hoc Committee to the Permanent Diaconate Community, 29 May 1992.

85   George Newman, "History of the Toronto Permanent Diaconate Continued" (unpublished article, rev. August 1998), 2.

86   Dan Murphy, letter to the author, c. February 2009, in response to a letter from the author, 29 January 2009.

87   Archdiocese of Toronto, *Diaconate Policies, Procedures and Ceremonial* (rev. May 2009), 4.

88 SAS, Office of the Permanent Diaconate, letter from Anne Bezaire to Brian Clough, 28 March 1983. We note that the Diocese of London did not introduce a permanent diaconate program until 2000 and did not ordain its first permanent deacons until 2004, twenty-one years after Sister Bezaire's inquiry.

89 Ibid., Office of the Permanent Diaconate, letter from Brian Clough to Anne Bezaire, 11 April 1983.

90 Ibid., Office of the Permanent Diaconate, letter from Robert B. Clune to Brian Clough, 24 June 1983.

Chapter 6

1 Along with the rector, membership in the committee included the director, assistant director and the co-ordinators of selection, field education and continuing education. See St. Augustine's Seminary [hereafter SAS], Office of the Permanent Diaconate, "Organization Structure – Permanent Diaconate Training Program" (Proposed for discussion – 27 November 1978).

2 Archives of the Roman Catholic Archdiocese of Toronto [hereafter ARCAT], G. Emmett Cardinal Carter Fonds, CA AC18. 12e, letter from Charles Amico to William Hawkshaw, 14 June 1978.

3 Ibid., G. Emmett Cardinal Carter Fonds, CA AC18.11e, letter from B. McCosham to William Hawkshaw, 15 November 1978.

4 Ibid., G. Emmett Cardinal Carter Fonds, CA AC18.11b, letter from Robert B. Clune to Peter Somerville, 5 March 1985. Hawkshaw wrote to Bishop Clune about his RCIA work several weeks after this letter. See G. Emmett Cardinal Carter Fonds, CA AC18.11c, letter from William Hawkshaw to Robert B. Clune, 23 March 1985.

5 SAS, Office of the Permanent Diaconate, letter from Brian Clough to Robert B. Clune, 26 March 1985, 1.

6 Ibid., Office of the Permanent Diaconate, letter from Peter Somerville to Robert B. Clune, 26 March 1985, 1.

7 Ibid., Office of the Permanent Diaconate, "Policy Statement 1978," 3; quoted in letter from Peter Somerville to Robert B. Clune, 26 March 1985, 1.

8 Ibid., Office of the Permanent Diaconate, letter from Peter Somerville to Robert B. Clune, 26 March 1985, 2.

9 ARCAT, OC02 MM03, Box 16, Senate of Priests, "Priests Senate Action Group on Permanent Diaconate" ([26] April 1977), 9.

10 SAS, Office of the Permanent Diaconate, letter from Peter Somerville to Robert B. Clune, 26 March 1985, 2.

[11] Ibid., Office of the Permanent Diaconate, letter from Peter Somerville to Robert B. Clune, 26 March 1985, 3.

[12] Ibid.

[13] ARCAT, G. Emmett Cardinal Carter Fonds, CA AC18.11a, letter from Robert B. Clune to G. Emmett Carter, 17 April 1985, 2.

[14] Ibid.

[15] Ibid.

[16] SAS, Office of the Permanent Diaconate, letter from Robert B. Clune to G. Emmett Carter, 26 March 1985, 3.

[17] ARCAT, G. Emmett Cardinal Carter Fonds, CA AC18, 11d, letter from Charmaine Grillot to G. Emmett Carter, 26 November 1984; appended to this letter was a one-page document on the permanent diaconate and a one-page document on lay ministry, CA AC18.12.

[18] SAS, Office of the Permanent Diaconate, letter from G. Emmett Carter to Peter Somerville, 23 April 1985, 1.

[19] Ibid., Office of the Permanent Diaconate, letter from G. Emmett Carter to Peter Somerville, 23 April 1985, 2.

[20] Ibid.

[21] Ibid., Office of the Permanent Diaconate, letter from G. Emmett Carter to Peter Somerville, 23 April 1985, 3.

[22] Ibid., Office of the Permanent Diaconate, letter from Peter Somerville to G. Emmett Carter, 1 May 1985, 1.

[23] Ibid.

[24] Ibid.

[25] Ibid., Office of the Permanent Diaconate, letter from Peter Somerville to G. Emmett Carter, 1 May 1985, 3.

[26] Ibid., Office of the Permanent Diaconate, letter from Peter Somerville to G. Emmett Carter, 1 May 1985, 2.

[27] Ibid., Office of the Permanent Diaconate, letter from Peter Somerville to G. Emmett Carter, 1 May 2009, 3.

[28] Ibid.

[29] Ibid., Office of the Permanent Diaconate, letter from G. Emmett Carter to Peter Somerville, 7 May 1985, 1.

[30] Ibid., Office of the Permanent Diaconate, letter from G. Emmett Carter to Peter Somerville, 7 May 1985, 2.

[31] Ibid.

[32] Ibid.

33 Andrea D'Angelo, e-mail communication to the author, 26 October 2009.

34 ARCAT, Permanent Diaconate Office Files, Keith Callaghan to G. Emmett Carter, c. March 1986.

35 Ibid., Permanent Diaconate Office Files, G. Emmett Carter to Keith Callaghan, 25 March 1986.

36 SAS, Office of the Permanent Diaconate, memorandum from Permanent Diaconate Training Team to Robert B. Clune, 12 January 1987, 2–3.

37 Ibid., Office of the Permanent Diaconate, memorandum from Permanent Diaconate Training Team to Robert B. Clune, 12 January 1987, 2.

38 Ibid., Office of the Permanent Diaconate, memorandum from Permanent Diaconate Training Program to Robert B. Clune, 12 January 1987, 3.

39 Ibid.

40 Ibid., Office of the Permanent Diaconate, letter from G. Emmett Carter to Robert B. Clune, 17 February 1987, 1.

41 Ibid., Office of the Permanent Diaconate, letter from G. Emmett Carter to Robert B. Clune, 17 February 1987, 2.

42 ARCAT, Bp. Clune Fonds: Archdiocese of Toronto: Permanent Diaconate, Diaconate Review Committee, Minutes, 11 December 1990, "Ministry Date – December 1990."

43 SAS, Office of the Permanent Diaconate, letter from Robert B. Clune to Rita MacLellan, 5 July 1990; letter from Robert B. Clune to Attila Mikloshazy, 5 July 1990.

44 Ibid., Office of the Permanent Diaconate, letter from Robert B. Clune to John A. Boissonneau, 5 July 1990.

45 Alexander MacGregor Papers, letter from Dan Murphy to Committee Members, 9 August 1990.

46 ARCAT, Aux. Bp. Clune Fonds: Archdiocese of Toronto: Permanent Diaconate, letter from Robert B. Clune to Dear Father, 5 June 1989.

47 Ibid., Aux. Bp. Clune Fonds: Archdiocese of Toronto: Permanent Diaconate, Diaconate Review Committee, Minutes, 13 November 1990.

48 Ibid., Aux. Bp. Clune Fonds: Archdiocese of Toronto: Permanent Diaconate, Diaconate Review Committee, letter from Tibor Horvath to Daniel Murphy, 12 December 1990.

49 Ibid.

50 Ibid., Aux. Bp. Clune Fonds: Archdiocese of Toronto: Permanent Diaconate, Diaconate Review Committee, Minutes, 9 October 1990.

51 Ibid., Aux. Bp. Clune Fonds: Archdiocese of Toronto: Permanent Diaconate, Diaconate Review Committee, letter from Tibor Horvath to Robert B. Clune, 10 October 1990.

52 Ibid., Aux. Bp. Clune Fonds: Archdiocese of Toronto: Permanent Diaconate, Diaconate Review Committee, letter from Robert B. Clune to Tibor Horvath, 21 December 1990.

53 Ibid., Aux. Bp. Clune Fonds: Archdiocese of Toronto: Permanent Diaconate, Diaconate Review Committee, letter from Tibor Horvath to Daniel Murphy, 12 December 1990; letter from Tibor Horvath to Robert B. Clune, 12 December 1990.

54 Ibid., Aux. Bp. Clune Fonds: Archdiocese of Toronto: Permanent Diaconate, Diaconate Review Committee, Minutes, 11 December 1990, "Models of the Diaconate," 2.

55 Ibid., Aux. Bp. Clune Fonds: Archdiocese of Toronto: Permanent Diaconate, Diaconate Review Committee, letter from Tibor Horvath to Daniel Murphy, 12 December 1990.

56 Ibid., OC02 MM03, Box 16, Senate of Priests, "Priests Senate Action Group on Permanent Diaconate" ([26] April 1977), 9.

57 Ibid., Aux. Bp. Clune Fonds: Archdiocese of Toronto: Permanent Diaconate, Diaconate Review Committee, Minutes, 11 December 1990, "Models of the Diaconate," 1–3.

58 Ibid., Aux. Bp. Clune Fonds: Archdiocese of Toronto: Permanent Diaconate, Diaconate Review Committee, Minutes, 11 December 1990; Minutes, 19 March 1991.

59 Ibid., Aux. Bp. Clune Fonds: Archdiocese of Toronto: Permanent Diaconate, Diaconate Review Committee, letter from Daniel Murphy to Committee Members, 15 October 1991; attached to this letter was a copy of "Report of the Survey Committee on the Permanent Diaconate in the Archdiocese of Toronto" [hereafter 1991 Survey Report], (1991).

60 Ibid., Aux. Bp. Clune Fonds: Archdiocese of Toronto: Permanent Diaconate: Diaconate Review Committee, 1991 Survey Report, [I]–[iii].

61 Ibid., Aux. Bp. Clune Fonds: Archdiocese of Toronto: Permanent Diaconate, Diaconate Review Committee, memorandum from Daniel Murphy to Robert B. Clune, 29 November 1991; attached to the memorandum was a copy of a draft of "Report of the Review Committee on the Permanent Diaconate in the Archdiocese of Toronto" [hereafter 1991 Report of the Review Committee], [i]–[ii]. I was unable to locate a copy of the final report.

62 SAS, "The Toronto Permanent Diaconate 1992," 1.

63 Ibid., "ATS Self-Study Report: The Permanent Diaconate Training Programme at St. Augustine's Seminary" (1990), 4.

64 ARCAT, *Diocesan Quinquennial Report 1993–1997* (1997), Section V–10.

65 Ibid., Aux. Bp. Clune Fonds: Archdiocese of Toronto: Permanent Diaconate, memorandum from Daniel Murphy to Robert B. Clune, 29 November 1991; 1991 Report of the Review Committee, [iii]–[v].

66 ARCAT, Permanent Diaconate Office Files, memorandum from Daniel Murphy to Aloysius Ambrozic, 7 February 2000.

67 John O'Mara, telephone interview with the author, 22 September 2009.

68 In contrast to the CCCB, the United States Conference of Catholic Bishops has many editions of its own norms and ministry. See United States Conference of Catholic Bishops, *National Directory for the Formation, Ministry, and Life of Permanent Deacons in the United States* (Washington, D.C.: 2005).

69 Congregation for Catholic Education, *Basic Norms for the Formation of Permanent Deacons*, and Congregation for the Clergy, *Directory for the Ministry and Life of Permanent Deacons* (Vatican City: Libreria Editrice Vaticana, 1998).

70 George Newman, e-mail communication to the author, 9 November 2009. The material was substantial: four-year curriculum; topic outlines; list of books; outline of formation process including the adult learning system; job description of the mentor; mentor-based program; and admissions process (initial interview, candidate and wife requirements, deacon perceiver interview, home visit interview, reference forms).

71 Aloysius Ambrozic, interview with the author, 3 April 2007.

72 Archdiocese of Toronto, *Diaconate Self-Study* (2001), 4.

73 Ibid.

74 Ibid., *Diaconate Self-Study* (2001), 5.

75 Ibid., *Diaconate Self-Study* (2001), 3.

76 Ibid., *Diaconate Self-Study* (2001), 11–15.

77 Ibid., *Diaconate Self-Study* (2001), 16.

78 Ibid., *Diaconate Self-Study* (2001), 3.

79 Ibid., *Diaconate Self-Study* (2001), 18.

80 Ibid., *Diaconate Self-Study* (2001), 19.

81 Ibid.

82 Ibid.

83 Ibid., *Diaconate Self-Study* (2001), 20–21.

84 Ibid., *Diaconate Self-Study* (2001), 17.

85 Congregation for Catholic Education, *Basic Norms for the Formation of Permanent Deacons*, 27.

86 Archdiocese of Toronto, *Diaconal Ministry of Service: Prepared for the Toronto Coordinating Board* (draft version, March 2004).

87 Archdiocese of Toronto, Diaconate Office, *The Bulletin* (September 2008), 3.

BIBLIOGRAPHY

Archives

Archives of the Archdiocese of Toronto (ARCAT)
Archives of the Society of Jesus of Upper Canada (ASJUC)
Canadian Conference of Catholic Bishops (CCCB)
Diocese of St. Catharines Archives
St. Augustine's Seminary (SAS), Office of the Permanent Diaconate

Interviews

H.E. Cardinal Aloysius Ambrozic
Deacon Bert Cambre
Deacon Tab Charbonneau
Father Tom Cresswell
Bishop Remi De Roo
Paul Giroux
Sister Charmain Grillot, CPPS
Father Tibor Horvath, SJ
Deacon Alexander MacGregor
Deacon Stan MacLellan
Deacon Patrick Matthews
Peter Meehan
Deacon Dan Murphy
Deacon George Newman
Bishop John A. O'Mara
Deacon Leo Vanderkooy

Newspapers and Newsletters

Catholic Register (Toronto, Ontario)
Contact (Archdiocese of Toronto, Council of Deacons)
Toronto Senate Reports (Archdiocese of Toronto)

Printed Primary Sources

Acta et Documenta Concilio Oecumenico Vaticano II. Series II (Praeparatoria), Vol. II, Part II. Typis Polyglottis Vaticanis, 1967.

Acta Synodalia Sacrosancti Concillii Oecumenici Vaticani II. Vol. II, Part II. Typis Polyglottis Vaticanis, 1972.

The Canons and Decrees of the Council of Trent. Trans. J. Waterworth. London: Burns and Oates, 1848.

Council Speeches of Vatican II. Ed. Hans Kung, Yves Congar and Daniel O'Hanlon. Glen Rock, N.Y.: Paulist Press, 1964.

Paul VI. *Motu Proprio Ad Pascendum. Acta Apostolicae Sedis* LXIV (1972): 534–40.

———. *Motu Proprio Ministeria Quaedam. Acta Apostolicae Sedis* LXIV (1972): 529–34.

———. *Motu Proprio Sacrum Diaconatus Ordinem. Acta Apostolica Sedis* LIX (1967): 697–704.

Vatican Council II: The Conciliar and Post Conciliar Documents. Ed. Austin Flannery. Collegeville, Minn.: The Liturgical Press, 1975.

Secondary Sources: Theses, Books, Chapters in Books, Articles

Bennett, James Monroe. *A Full and Equal Order.* Rev. Ed. Harrisburg, Penn.: Trinity Press International, 1995.

Congar, Yves. *Mon Journal du Concile.* 2 Vols. Paris: Éditions du Cerf, 2002.

Council Daybook Vatican II. Ed. Floyd Anderson. Washington, D.C.: National Catholic Welfare Conference, 1965.

Cummings, Owen F. *Deacons and the Church.* New York/Mahwah, N.J.: Paulist Press, 2004.

Ditewig, William T. *The Emerging Diaconate: Servant Leaders in a Servant Church.* New York/Mahwah, N.J.: Paulist Press, 2007.

———. *101 Questions and Answers on Deacons.* New York/Mahwah, N.J.: 2004.

Early Christian Writings: The Apostolic Fathers. Trans. Maxwell Staniforth. Rev. Trans. Andrew Louth. London: Penguin Books, 1987.

Echlin, Edward P. *The Deacon in the Church: Past and Future.* New York: Alba House, 1971.

Enright, Edward J. "The History of the Diaconate." *The Deacon Reader.* Ed. James Keating. 8–23. New York/Mahwah, N.J.: Paulist Press, 2006.

Epagneul, Michel-Dominique. "A functional diaconate." *Theology Digest* 7 (1959): 73–76.

Fesquet, Henri. *The Drama of Vatican II:The Ecumenical Council June 1962— December 1965.* Trans. Bernard Murchland. New York: Random House, 1967.

Fowles, John Francis. "The Diaconate in the Second Vatican Council." Master's Thesis, University of St. Michael's College, 1971.

Guidelines of the Episcopal Committee on the Permanent Diaconate (Guidance Manual). Ottawa: Canadian Catholic Conference, 1967.

History of Vatican II. Ed. Giuseppe Albergio; English version ed. Joseph A. Komonchak. Vol 1. Maryknoll, N.Y.: Orbis, 1995.

Hornef, Josef. "Genesis and Growth of the Proposal." *Foundations for the Renewal of the Diaconate.* 5–27. Washington, D.C.: United States Catholic Conference, 1993.

———. *The New Vocation.* Trans. P. Russell. Cork, Ireland: The Mercier Press, 1963.

———. "The Order of Diaconate in the Roman Catholic Church." *The Diaconate Now.* 57–79. Ed. Richard T. Nolan. Washington, D.C./ Cleveland: Corpus Books, 1968.

Horvath, Tibor. "Theology of a New Diaconate." *Revue de l'Université d'Ottawa* 38 (1968): 495–523.

———. *Thinking About Faith: Speculative Theology.* Vol. 1. Love. 197–212. Montreal & Kingston: McGill-Queen's University Press, 2006.

Kramer, Hannes. "The Spiritual Life of Deacons." *Foundations for the Renewal of the Diaconate.* 29–49. Washington, D.C.: United States Catholic Conference, 1993.

McDonnell, James Francis. "An Examination of the Theology of the Permanent Diaconate in the Documents of the Second Vatican Council and of Three Regional Hierarchies." Master's Thesis, University of St. Michael's College, 1976.

Novak, Michael. *The Open Church:Vatican II,Act II.* New York: Macmillan, 1964.

O'Malley, William J. "The Priests of Dachau," Appendix I. *Pius XII and the Holocaust: A Reader.* Milwaukee, Wis.: Catholic League for Religious and Civil Rights, 1988.

Philips, Gérard. "Dogmatic Constitution on the Church: History of the Constitution." *Commentary on the Documents of Vatican II.* Ed. R. Rahner and H.Vorgrimler.Vol. 1. 106–10. NewYork: Herder and Herder, 1966.

Pies, Otto, "Block 26: Erfahrungen aus dem Priesterleben in Dachau." *Stimmen der Zeit* 141 (1947–48): 10–28.

"Rahner, Karl." *New Catholic Encyclopedia.*Vol. 18. Supplement 1978–1988, 411–13. Washington, D.C.: Catholic University of America, 1989.

Rahner, Karl. "On the Diaconate." *Theological Investigations.*Vol. 12. 61–76. London: Darton, Longman & Todd, 1974.

———. "The Teaching of the Second Vatican Council on the Diaconate." *Theological Investigations.* Vol. 10. 222–32. New York: Herder & Herder, 1973.

———. "The Theology of the Restoration of the Diaconate." *Theological Investigations.*Vol. 5. 268–314. *Later Writings.*Trans. Karl-H. Kruger. Baltimore: Helicon Press, 1966.

Rynne, Xavier. *The Second Session: The Debates and Decrees of Vatican II, September 29 to December 4, 1963.* New York: Farrar, Straus & Company, 1964.

Schamoni, William. *Married Men as Ordained Deacons.* Trans. Otto Eisner. London: Burns & Oates, 1955.

Seidl, Johann Nepomuk. *Deaconship in the Catholic Church, its Hieratic Dignity and Historical Development.* Regensburg: 1894.

The St. Joseph Medium Size Edition of the American Bible. New York: Catholic Book Publishing Co., 1970.

"Trent, Council of." *New Catholic Encyclopedia.*Vol 14: 271–78.Washington, D.C.: Catholic University of America, 1967.

Vorgrimler, H. "The Hierarchical Structure of the Church: Article 29." *Commentary on the Documents of Vatican II.* Ed. K. Rahner and H. Vorgrimler.Vol. 1. New York: Herder & Herder, 1966.

Wiltgen, Ralph M. *The Rhine Flows into the Tiber: A History of Vatican II.* Rockford, Ill.: Tan Books, 1985.

Winninger, Paul. "The Deacon and the Lay Person." *Foundations for the Renewal of the Diaconate.* 51–60. Washington, D.C.: United States Catholic Conference, 1993.

INDEX

A

Ad Gentes Divinitus (Decree on the Missionary Activity of the Church) #16, 41, 48, 63–64

Ad Pascendum, 41, 66–67, 79, 129, 130

Advisory Board 1981–1983, 151–65; membership, 151; organizational structure of the diaconate, 155–58; purpose, 151; recommendations, 156–57

Agagianian, Gregorio, 50

Against Heresies (Irenaeus), 65, 77

Agde, Council of, 78

Altpeter, Caroline, 195

Ambrozic, Aloysius, 14, 15, 113, 182, 193–94, 197

Amico, Charles, 113, 114, 122, 123, 126, 128, 131, 133, 151, 168

Andrews, Philomena, 150

Apostolicam Actuositatem (Decree on the Apostolate of Lay People), 93

Apostolic Constitutions, 77

Apostolic Tradition (Hippolytus), 66, 77

Aquinas, Thomas, 43

Archdiocese of Detroit, 89

Archdiocese of Montréal, 107

Association of Theological Schools, 192

Audet, Lionel, 73

Augustine, 66

B

Bannon, William, 117

Barnett, Monroe, 183

Basic Norms for the Formation of Permanent Deacons, 194, 195, 197, 199

Bekkum, Willem van, 39

Beriault, Marshal, 168

Bezaire, Anne, 135, 162–63

Black, Bernard, 104

Boissonneau, John, 182, 194

Boudreau, John, 117

Brisbois, Ed, 98

Butts, Margaret, 105

C

Callaghan, Keith, 177–78

Callaghan, Molly, 151, 182

Cambre, Bert, 159, 195

Canadian Catholic Conference. *See* Canadian Conference of Catholic Bishops

Canadian Conference of Catholic Bishops (CCCB), 69–90; Ad Hoc Committee on the Diaconate in Canada, 72–87; Episcopal Commission on Clergy and Seminaries, 87–90; "Final Report of the Committee on the Diaconate," 103; "Final Report of the Cross-Canada Survey on the Restoration of the Permanent Diaconate," 103; *Guidance*

Manual, 69–70, 73, 74, 75, 76–87, 89, 97, 99, 104; "The Restoration of the Permanent Diaconate in Canada," 88–89; survey on *Guidance Manual*, 85–87

Carter, Gerald Emmett, 15, 17, 144, 193; Advisory Board 1981–1983 recommendations, 157–58, 160; correspondence with Robert B. Clune and Peter Somerville concerning William Hawkshaw, 167–81; dislike of the word "marginalized," 164–65, 173, 186; proposed change to Policy Statement on the Training Program, 173–74; the right of the Ordinary to establish the needs of the archdiocese, 139, 140, 173

Catholic Family Movement, 115

Catholic Women's League, 107

celibacy, 25, 34, 35, 37, 52, 58, 60

"Cell Block 26," 20, 22

"Cell Block 26: Experiences of Priestly Life in Dachau" (Pies), 26

Charbonneau, Mary, 138

Charbonneau, Tab, 123, 126, 127, 138, 142, 149, 150, 151, 153, 159, 182

Charismatic prayer groups, 115

Chase, Colin, 112, 114, 116, 117, 122, 123, 126, 131, 137, 151, 153–54

Christus Dominus (Decree on the Pastoral Office of Bishop in the Church) #27, 96

Cicognani, Amleto, 50

Clair, James, 117

Class of 1974, profile, 117–21

Clement VIII, 77

Clement of Alexandria, 78

Clough, Brian, 135, 151, 162, 163–64, 165

Clune, Robert B., 15, 119; Advisory Board 1981–1983, 151, 155, 160; correspondence with Peter Somerville and Gerald Emmett Carter concerning William Hawkshaw, 167–81; Deacon Search Committee 1980–1981, 139, 140, 141, 144, 149; Diaconate Review Committee 1990–1991, 182, 183, 185; reaction to Gerald Emmett Carter's dislike of the word "marginalized," 165

Clune-Somerville-Carter correspondence 1985 and 1987, 167–81, 184

Code of Canon Law (1917), 47

Codex Canonum Ecclesiasticorum, 78

Collins, Thomas, 15

Confalonieri, Carlo, 87

Congar, Yves, 34

Congregation for the Clergy, 194

Constitution on the Sacred Liturgy. *See Sacrosanctum Concilium*

Contact (newsletter), 132, 133

Cooper, Noel, 98, 101–2

Co-ordinating Board, 161–62

Corriveau, Raymond, 113, 122

Côté, Jed, 117

essential characteristics, 75–76; ministries, 181–82, 193; models, 130, 134–35, 140, 169, 170, 175, 176, 177–81, 186–89, 195; norms, 65; organizational structure, 147–48, 155–58; petition, 34, 36–38; practical needs, 57; reasons for restoration, 51; Review 1977, 122–33; scriptural sources, 24, 29, 37, 55, 65, 66; service, 21, 28–29, 35, 62–63, 66–67, 74, 85, 115, 124–25, 125–26, 137, 140, 175, 180, 186–89, 199; special characteristics, 62–63; specific characteristic. *See specific characteristic of the diaconate*

Diaconate, The: A Full and Equal Order (Barnett), 183

"diaconate circles," 14

"Diaconate Circle Working Paper," 25

Diaconate Review Committee 1990–1991, 181–93; membership, 182; "Models of the Diaconate," 186–89; questionnaire on training and ministry, 189; reading material, 183; recommendations, 192–93; seven points, 191–92; Survey Report 1991, 189–91

Diaconate Self-Study 2001, 193–98; membership, 194–95; methodology, 195; recommendations, 196–98

Diaconia in Christo, 31, 34, 36

Diakonia. See service

Diakonia (newsletter), 100

Didache #15, 77

Didascalia Apostolorum, 66, 77

diocesan ministry, 22

Diocese of Sault Ste. Marie, 107

Directory for the Ministry and Life of Permanent Deacons, 194, 195

Ditewig, William, 24

Dogmatic Constitution on Divine Revelation. *See Dei Verbum*

Dogmatic Constitution on the Church. *See Lumen Gentium*

Donovan, Dan, 182, 186–89

D'Souza, Eugene, 39

Dwyer, Phil, 161

Dwyer, Theresa, 161

E

"Early Christian Office of Deaconess as a Sacramental Order, The," 100

Ecclesia Sanctae, 96

Echlin, Edward, 43, 45

Elvira, Council of, 78

English, John, 113

Epagneul, Michel-Dominique, 34

Executive Board, 158–59

Executive Director, 156, 157

F

Ferguson, Bob, 150

First Apology (Justin Martyr), 77

First Vatican Council, 40

Firth, Wilfred B., 122

Flood, Marie Walter, 105, 106

Frani, Franjo, 59

G

Gabourie, Walter, 117

M

MacGregor, Alexander, 117, 126, 153, 182
MacKay, Sadie, 150
MacLean, Don, 182
MacLellan, Olga, 182
MacLellan, Rita, 150, 182, 187
MacLellan, Stan, 114, 117, 132, 136–37, 142, 144, 149, 150, 151, 159, 169
MacNeil, Everett, 87, 96–97
Majeu, Sabina, 105
Malone, Mary, 105
Manne, Corry, 117
marginalized: ministry to, 134–35, 137, 164, 166, 169, 186, 189, 195, 196
marriage preparation, 115
Married Men as Ordained Deacons (Schamoni), 23–24, 26, 29, 45
Masella, Benedetto, 49, 50
Mason, Tom, 142, 150, 152, 153, 158, 160, 169
Matthews, Mary, 155
Matthews, Patrick, 117, 122
Maundcote-Carter, Wilfred, 112, 117, 122
McCarthy, Margaret M., 106
McCarthy, T.J., 87
McDonald, Mike, 98
McDonnell, James F., 82
McGregor, James C., 94
McNeil, Andrew, 127
McTeague, Joseph, 117
Mikloshazy, Attila, 113, 182
Ministeria Quaedam, 41, 67, 129
minor orders, 67

"Models of the Diaconate" (Donovan), 186–89, 191
Molinari, Joseph, 151
Mooney, Orval, 117
Morley, George, 127, 142
Moss, John, 113, 122
Moulton, Joan, 161
Murphy, Daniel, 117, 122, 150, 151, 159, 160, 161, 184, 189
Murphy, Jean, 150

N

National Association of Permanent Diaconate Directors (NAPDD), 138, 152
National Education Office (CCCB), 88–90
National Polish Seminary (Archdiocese of Detroit), 89
Newman, Cam, 161
Newman, George, 161, 195
New Vocation, The (Hornef), 25, 27–30
Nicea, Council of, 78
Novak, Michael, 53
Nusca, Robert A., 195

O

O'Brien, Brian, 142
O'Connor, John, 127, 142, 151
O'Malley, Leonard, 182
O'Mara, John, 92, 94, 96, 97, 98, 107–8, 109, 114, 115, 122
On Baptism (Tertullian), 77
O'Neill, Harold, 122, 126
Oneson, Helen, 150

S

Sacrament of Order, 17, 28, 43, 67, 79, 83, 84, 94

Sacrosanctum Concilium (Constitution on the Sacred Liturgy) #35, 41

Sacrum Diaconatus Ordinem, 41 64–66, 68, 70, 74, 77, 129, 137

Sanderson, James, 117

Sandford, Anthony, 117

Sanschagrin, Albert, 69, 70, 71, 72, 73

Scandiffio, Nicholas, 117

Schaeffen, Mary, 105–6

Schamoni, Wilhelm, 20, 22–25, 27, 33, 34, 45, 64

Schwalm, Clement, 103

Scorsone, Bruno, 151

Scripture sources for diaconate, 24, 29, 37, 55, 65, 66, 77, 124

Second Vatican Council, 40–42, 47–62; debate and voting on the diaconate, 49–50, 51, 52, 53–60

Selection Research, Inc. (SRI), 145, 152

Senate of Priests (Archdiocese of Toronto), 15, 92, 119, 170; origins, 95–96; work on permanent diaconate, 96–117

service, 21, 28–29, 35, 62–63, 66–67, 74, 85, 115, 124–25, 125–26; *Diaconal Ministry of Service*, 199; "Models of the Diaconate," 186–89; primary ministry, 137, 140, 175, 180

Service Ministry of the Deacon (Shugrue), 183

The Shepherd of Hermes, 77

Shugrue, Timothy J., 183

Simpson, Barrett, 151, 159

Somerville, Peter: correspondence with Robert B. Clune and Gerald Emmett Carter concerning William Hawkshaw, 167–81

Spear, Linda, 105

specific characteristic of the diaconate, 74, 75, 80–85, 100, 121, 124

Spellman, Francis, 54

St. Augustine's Seminary, 95, 98, 107, 112, 116, 135, 182, 192, 193, 197

St. John's University (Collegeville, Minnesota), 89

St. Vincent de Paul Society, 115

Stephen (Acts of the Apostles), 65

Suenens, Leon, 54–58

Survey Report 1991, 189–91

T

Teolis, Matthew T., 183

Tertullian, 66, 77

Theological Investigations, 30

"Theological Notes on Council Texts Concerning the Diaconate" (Tillard), 75–76

"Theology of a New Diaconate" (Horvath), 74, 82–85, 100, 183

"Theology of the Restoration of the Diaconate, The" (Rahner), 31–34

Thottumkal, Thomas, 113

Tillard, J.M., 73, 75, 80–82

Trent, Council of, 24–25, 42–47, 53